The Founding Fathers:

What Did They Really Say?

Mat Clark

Copyright 2019

"It is the duty of every good citizen to use all the opportunities which occur to him for preserving documents relating to the history of our country."

Thomas Jefferson letter to Hugh P. Taylor, 1823

"Every child in America should be acquainted with his own country. He should read books that furnish him with ideas that will be useful to him in life and practice. As soon as he opens his lips, he should rehearse the history of his own country."

Noah Webster, 1788

T he Founding Fathers are a very misunderstood group of men

from a period of time that no person living today could ever relate to. The period of time in which the founding of the United States of America took place was a time of turmoil and the testing of loyalties, friendships and family ties.

Normally these types of ties bind people together forever but in the case of the Founders those ties were tested; some ties were strengthened and some ties were stretched to the point that those very strong ties were broken.

The Founding Fathers did not found this nation on the Christian religion; they founded this nation on Christian principles.

Among those principles is the right to live freely without government infringement on our God-given rights.

The Founders grew weary of their king trampling on those rights; they no longer viewed King George III as a monarch who represented God and in their eyes a king who no longer represented the authority of God was not a king of men.

The most important things that we can remember about the Founders were that they knew who they were and their strength was their unfaltering principles. There was a knowledge and acceptance on their part that if they failed to deliver liberty and freedom from the clutches of King George III that they would all either die a terrible death or be forced into exile somewhere in the world. To go into self-exile and remain unrecognized would have been nearly impossible if the Crown were to hunt for them because England controlled most of the civilized world and becoming anonymous would have been a tricky feat.

It is because the Founders knew who they were and they had unfaltering principles which gave them the strength and resolve to endure the darkest days of the Revolutionary War and to see their fight for independence through to success. There are so many myths and misinformation spread throughout the world today about the Founders and who they really were and what formed their beliefs.

Some people claim that the Founders were Deists who did not truly embrace the belief of the Christian God in the Holy Bible nor that the Founders saw the hand of God in the founding of the United States.

Some people claim that several of the Founders absolutely did not believe in God.

These allegations are completely false.

These groups of people have spread their misinformation in an attempt to revise history and remove the truth from public knowledge, this book intends to reverse the misinformation replace it with the facts.

This book will use legitimate documentation held in various archives to share those facts. Founding documents, speeches, letters, Presidential proclamations and other documents of fact will be used to tell the truth.

Those who disagree that this nation was founded UPON the principle teachings of Jesus and that the Founders proclaimed the United States as a nation gifted to people by God are welcome to continue believing as they choose to believe…but through this book the truth will be told.

This book is the fulfillment of my wish to share the words of the Founders concerning the founding of this nation, its intent and design to anyone who wishes to know the truth about the United States of America.

This book is not an all-inclusive book of facts but rather a starter book for people in search of the truth of the founding of this nation.

This book is dedicated to the sacrifices and in the memory of the Founding Fathers and what they really said.

The falsehoods and lies perpetrated by those whose goal is to pervert the real truth about the founding of this nation will not be allowed to go unchallenged. The historical documentation presented in this book and in its accurate context will prove that this nation was founded upon the Christian principles of the Founders and the intended influence of those principles upon this nation.

Here is the truth.

Part One

Our Founding Documents

Declaration of the Causes and Necessity of Taking Up Arms

Declaration on Taking Arms; July 6, 1775

THURSDAY, JULY 6, 1775

(First Draft)

The large advances strides of late taken by the legislature of Great Britain towards establishing in over these colonies their absolute rule, and the hardiness of their present attempt to effect by force of arms what by law or right they could never effect, render it necessary for us also to shift change the ground of opposition and to close with their last appeal from reason to arms. And as it behaves those who are called to this great decision to be assured that their cause is approved before supreme reason, so is it of great avail that it's justice be made known to the world whose prayers cannot be wanting intercessions affections will ever be favorable to a people take part with those encountering oppression. Our forefathers, inhabitants of the island of Gr. Britain harassed having there vainly long endeavored to bear up against the evils of misrule, left their native land to seek on these shores a residence for civil and religious freedom. At the expense of their blood, with to the less ruin of their fortunes, with the relinquishment of everything a quiet and comfortable in life, they effected settlements in the inhospitable wilds of America; they there established civil societies under with various forms of constitution, but possessing all, what is inherent in all, the full and perfect powers of legislation. To continue their connection with the friends whom they had left and but loved they arranged themselves by charters of compact under the same one common king who became the thro' whom union was ensured to the multiplied who thus became the control link uniting of union between the several parts of the empire. Some occasional assumptions of power by the part. of Gr. Brit. however foreign and unknown to unacknowledged by the constitution we had formed of our governments were finally acquiesced in thro' the warmth of affection. Proceeding thus in the fullness of mutual harmony and confidence both parts of the empire increased in population and in wealth with a rapidity unknown in the history of man. The various soils political institutions of America, it's various climes soils and climates opening sure certain resource to the unfortunate and to the enterprising of all every country where and ensured to them the acquisition and free possession of property. Great Britain too acquired a lustre and a weight in the political system among the powers of the world earth which it is thought her internal resources could never have given her. To the communication of the wealth and the power of the several parts of the whole every part of the empire we may surely ascribe in some measure surely ascribe the illustrious character she sustained thro' her last European war and its successful event. At the close of that war however Gr. Britain having subdued all her foes she took up the unfortunate idea of subduing her friends also. Her parliament then for the first time asserted a right of unbounded legislation for over the colonies of America: by an several acts passed in the years of the 5th 6th and the 7th and the 8th years of the resign of his present majesty several duties were imposed for the purpose of raising a revenue on the American colonists, the power of the courts of Admiralty were extended beyond their ancient limits and the inestimable right [of being tried in all cases civil] trial by twelve peers of our vicinage was taken away in cases affecting both life and property. By part an act passed in the 12th year of the present reign an American colonist chat, the offences charged in that act may be transported beyond sea for trial [of such offense] by the very persons, against whose pretended sovereignty [the supposed offense] is supposed to be committed and pursuing with eagerness the newly assumed thought have in the space of 10 years during, which they have exercise yt right have made given such decisive severe specimens of the spirit in which this new legislation Would be exercised conducted towards the establishment of absolute government over us as leaves no room to doubt the consequence of our further acquiescence under it by two three two other acts passed in the 14th year of his present majesty they have assumed a right of altering the form of our governments altogether, and of thereby talking away every security for the possession of life or of property.

By several acts of parliament passed in the reign of his present majesty within ~~scope that period~~ *space of time they have imposed upon us duties for the purpose of raising a revenue attempted to take from us our money without our consent, they have taken away the* ~~interdicted all commerce~~ *first of one of our principal trading towns thereby annihilating its property, in the hands of the holders, and more lately they have cut off our the commercial intercourse with all of several of these of whole colonies with all foreign countries whatsoever; they have extended the jurisdiction of the courts of admiralty beyond their ancient limits thereby depriving us of the inestimable right of trial by jury in cases affecting both life and property and subjecting both to the* ~~decision~~ *arbitrary decision of a single and dependent judge; they have declared that American subjects* ~~committing~~ *charged with certain pretended offences shall be transported beyond sea for trial to be tried before the very persons against whose pretended* ~~sovereignty~~ *offense is supposed to be committed; they have attempted fundamentally to alter the form of government in one of these colonies, a form established by acts of its own legislature, and further secured to them by charters of* ~~compact with and~~ *grants from on the part of the crown; they have erected a tyranny in a neighbouring province, acquired by the joint arms of Great Britain and America, a tyranny dangerous to the very existence of all these colonies. But why should we enumerate their injuries in the detail? By one act they have suspended the powers of one American legislature and by another they have declared they may legislate for us themselves in all cases whatsoever. These two acts alone form a basis broad enough whereon to erect a despotism of unlimited extent, when it is considered that the persons by whom these acts are passed are not* ~~with us~~ *subject to their agents and what is to* ~~prevent~~ *secure us against the demolition of our present and establishment of new and despotic forms of government?* ~~this dreaded evil ?~~ *The persons who* ~~assuming these powers~~ *of doing this are not chosen by* ~~ourselves~~ *us, are not subject to* ~~us our~~ *control from us are themselves* ~~freed~~ *exempted by their situation from the operation of these laws they thus pass, and remove from themselves as much burthen as they impose on us.* ~~lighten their own burthens in proportion as they increase ours. These are temptations might put to trial the severest characters of ancient virtue: with what new armor then shall a British parliament then encounters the rude assault?~~ *To ward these deadly injuries from the tender plant of liberty which we have brought over and with*

10

so much affection we have planted and have fostered on these our own shores we have pursued every lawful and every respectful measure. We have supplicated our king at various times in terms almost disgraceful to freedom; we have reasoned, we have remonstrated with parliament in the most mild and decent language; we have even proceeded to break off our commercial intercourse with them altogether as to the last peaceable admonition of our determination to be free by breaking of altogether our commercial intercourse with them break off our commercial intercourse with them our fellow subjects as the last peaceable admonition that our attachment to no nation on earth should supplant our attachment to liberty: and here we had well hoped was the ultimate step of the controversy. But subsequent events have shown how vain was even this last remain of confidence in the moderation of the British ministry. During the course of the last year they their troops in a hostile manner invested the town of Boston in the province of Massachusetts bay, and from that time have held the same beleaguered by sea and land. On the 19th day of April last in the present year they made an unprovoked attack assault on the inhabitants of the said province at the town of Lexington, killed, murdered eight of them on the spot and wounded many others. From thence they proceeded in the same warlike manner all the array of war to the town of Concord where they attacked set upon another party of the inhabitants of the said same province killing many of them also burning their houses and laying waste their property and continuing these depredations repressed by the arms of the people assembled to oppose this hostile unprovoked cruel invasion aggression on their lives and properties. Hostilities being thus commenced on the part of the British Ministerial troops they army have been since without respite by them pursued the same by them without regard to faith or to fame. The inhabitants of the said town of Boston having entered into treaty with a certain Thomas Gage said to be commander in chief of those adverse troops and who has been a principal actor in the siege of the town of Boston, proffered to the inhabitants of the said town a liberty to depart from the same on principal and instigator of these enormities violence enormities, it was stipulated that the said inhabitants having first deposited their arms and military their own magistrates their arms and military stores should have free liberty to depart out of the same from out of the town taking with them their other goods and other effects. Their arms and military stores were they accordingly delivered in to their magistrates, and claimed the stipulated license of departing with their effects. But in open violation of plighted faith and honour, in defiance of these that the sacred laws of nations obligations of treaty which even the savage nations observe, their arms and warlike stores deposited with their own magistrates to be kept preserved as their property were immediately seized by a body of armed men under orders from the said Thomas Gage, the greater part of the inhabitants were detained in the town and the few permitted to depart were compelled to leave their most valuable goods effects behind. We leave to the world there to its own reflections on this atrocious perfidy. The same Thos. Gage on the 18th day of June That we might no longer be in doubt the ultimate purpose object aim of these Ministerial maneuvers, the same Thos. Gage by proclaim bearing date the 12th day of June by after reciting the most abandon grossest falsehoods and calumnies against the good people of America these colonies proceeds to declare them all, either by name or description, to be rebels and traitors, to supersede by his own authority the exercise of the common law of the land of the said province and to proclaim and order instead thereof the use and exercise of the law martial throughout the said province. This bloody edict issued, he has proceeded to commit further ravages and murders in the same province burning the town of Charlestown, and attacking and killing great numbers of the people residing or assembled therein; and is now going on in an avowed course of murder and devastation, taking every occasion to destroying the lives and properties of the inhabitants of the said province whenever he find occasion to get them within his power.

*To oppose their arms we also have taken up arms. We should be wanting to ourselves, we should be wanting perfidious to our posterity, we should be unworthy that free ancestry from which both they and we are derived our one common birth, whom we derive our birth descent, were we to suffer ourselves to be butchered and our properties to be laid waste should we submit with folded arms to military butchery and depredation to gratify the lordly ambition of any nation on earth and or sate avarice of a British ministry. We do then most solemnly before in the presence of before **God** and the world declare, that, regardless of every consequence at the risk of every distress, that the arms we have been compelled to assume we will wage with bitter* *perseverance, exerting to their utmost energies all those powers with which our **Creator** hath invested given us to guard preserve that sacred Liberty which **He** committed to us in sacred deposit, and to protect from every hostile hand our lives and our properties. But that this our declaration and our determined resolution may give disquietude to not disquiet the minds of our good fellow subjects in any part of the empire, we do further declare add assure them that we mean not in any wise to affect that union with them in which we have so long and so happily lived and which we wish so much to see again restored: that necessity must be hard indeed which could may force upon us this desperate measure, or induce us to avail ourselves of any aid which their enemies of Great Britain might proffer. We took up arms to defend in defense of our persons and properties under actual violation: when that violence shall be removed, when hostilities shall cease on the ministerial the ministerial party therefore shall cease be suspended hostilities on the part ministerial of the aggressors, hostilities they shall be suspended cease on our part also; when the moment they withdraw their armies we will disband ours. next to a vigorous exertion of our own internal force, we throw ourselves for towards we did not embody men a soldiery to commit aggression on them; we did not raise armies for march to or to glory, glory or for conquest; we did not invade their island, proffering carrying death or slavery to its inhabitants Towards the achievement of this happy event we call for and confide on in the good offices of our fellow subjects beyond the Atlantic. Of their friendly dispositions we confide we hope with justice reason cannot yet cease to hope and assure them they are aware as they must be that they have nothing more to expect from the same common enemy than the humble favour of being last devoured.*

Declaration on Taking Arms

(Second Draft)

A Declaration by

We the representatives of the United colonies of America now sitting in General Congress, to all nations send greeting of setting forth the causes and necessity of their taking up arms:

The large strides of late taken by the legislature of Great Britain towards establishing over these colonies their absolute rule, and the hardiness of the present attempt to effect by force of arms what by law or right they could never effect, render it necessary for us also to change the ground of opposition, and to close with their last appeal from reason to arms. And as it behooves those, who are called to this great decision, to be assured that their cause is approved before supreme reason; so is it of great avail that it's justice be made known to the world, whose affections will ever take part with those encountering oppression. Our forefathers, inhabitants of the island of Great Britain, having long endeavored to bear up against the evils of misrule, left their native land to seek on these shores a residence for civil and religious freedom. At the expense of their blood, with to the ruin of their fortunes, with the relinquishment of everything quiet and comfortable in life, they effected settlements in the inhospitable wilds of America; they and their established civil societies with various forms of constitution. But possessing all, what in inherent in all, the full and perfect powers of legislation To continue their connection with the friends whom they had left, they arranged themselves by charters of compact under one the same common king, who thus completed their powers of full and perfect legislation and became the link of union between the several parts of the empire.

Some occasional assumptions of power by the parliament of Great Britain, however unacknowledged by the constitution of our governments, were finally acquiesced in thro' warmth of affection. Proceeding thus in the fullness of mutual harmony and confidence, both parts of the empire increased in population and in wealth with a rapidity unknown in the history of man. The political institutions of America, its various soils and climates opened a certain resource to the unfortunate and to the enterprising of every country, and ensured to them the acquisition and free possession of property.

Great Britain too acquired a lustre and a weight among the powers of the earth which her internal resources could never have given her. To a communication of the wealth and the power of the whole every part of the empire we may surely ascribe in some measure the illustrious character she sustained through her last European war, and its successful event. At the close of that war however having subdued all her foes it pleased our sovereign to make a change in his counsels. The new ministry finding all the foes of Britain subdued she took up the unfortunate idea of subduing her friends also her parliament then for the first time asserted a right assumed a power of unbounded legislation over the colonies of America; and in the space course of ten years during which they have proceeded to exercise this right, have given such decisive specimen of the spirit of this new legislation, as leaves no room to doubt the consequence of acquiescence under it.

By several acts of parliament passed within that space of time they have attempted to take from us undertaken to give and grant our money without our consent: a right of which we have ever had the exclusive exercise; they have interdicted all commerce to one of our principal towns, thereby annihilating it's property in the hands of the holders; they have cut off the commercial intercourse of whole colonies with foreign countries; they have extended the jurisdiction of courts of admiralty beyond their ancient limits; thereby they have deprived us of the inestimable right privilege of trial by a jury of the vicinage in cases affecting both life and property; they have declared that American Subjects charged with certain offenses shall be transported beyond sea to be tried before the very persons against whose pretended sovereignty the offense is supposed to be committed; they have attempted fundamentally to alter the form of government in one of these colonies, a form established secured by charters on the part of the crown and confirmed by acts of its own legislature; and further secured by charters on the part of the crown; they have erected in a neighboring province, acquired by the joint arms of Great Britain and America, a tyranny dangerous to the very existence of all these colonies. But why should we enumerate their injuries in the detail? By one act they have suspended the powers of one American legislature, and by another have declared they may legislate for us themselves in all cases whatsoever. These two acts alone form a basis broad enough whereon to erect a despotism of unlimited extent. And what is to secure us against this dreaded evil? The persons assuming these powers are not chosen by us, are not subject to our controul or influence, are exempted by their situation from the operation of these laws, and lighten their own burthens in proportion as they increase ours.

These temptations might put to trial the severest characters of ancient virtue: with what new armor then shall a British parliament encounter the rude assault? to ward these deadly injuries from the tender plant of liberty which we have brought over, and with so much affection fostered on these our own shores, we have pursued every temperate, every respectful measure. We have supplicated our king at various times, in terms almost disgraceful to freedom; we have reasoned, we have remonstrated with parliament in the most mild and decent language; we have even proceeded to break off our commercial intercourse with our fellow subjects, as the last peaceable admonition that our attachment to no nation on earth should supplant our attachment to liberty. And here we had well hoped was the ultimate step of the controversy. But subsequent events have shown how vain was even this last remaining of confidence in the moderation of the British ministry. During the course of the last year their troops in a hostile manner invested the town of Boston in the province of Massachusetts Bay, and from that time have held the same beleaguered by sea and land. On the 19th day of April in the present year they made an unprovoked attack assault on the inhabitants of the said province at the town of Lexington, murdered eight of them on the spot and wounded many others. From thence they proceeded in Me all the array of war to the town of Concord, where they set upon another party of the inhabitants of the same province, killing many of them also, burning houses, and laying waste property, until repressed by the arms of a the people suddenly assembled to oppose this cruel aggression. Hostilities thus commenced on the part of the ministerial army have been since by them pursued without regard to faith or to fame. The inhabitants of the town of Boston in order to procure their enlargement having entered into treaty with a certain Thomas Gage General Gage their Governor principal instigator of these enormities it was stipulated that the said inhabitants, having first deposited their arms with their own magistrates their arms and military stores should have free liberty to depart from out of the said town taking with them their other good and effects.

Their arms and military stores they accordingly delivered in, and claimed the stipulated license of departing with their effects. But in open violation of plighted faith and honour, in defiance of the sacred obligations of treaty which even savage nations observe, their arms and warlike stores, deposited with their own magistrates to be preserved as their property, were immediately seized by a body of armed men under orders from the said Thomas Gage General, the greater part of the inhabitants were detained in the town, and the few permitted to depart were compelled to leave their most valuable effects behind. We leave the world to their own reflections on this atrocious perfidy. That we might no longer doubt the ultimate aim of these ministerial maneuvers the same Thomas General Gage, by proclamation bearing date the 12th day of June, after reciting the grossest falsehoods and calumnies against the good people of these colonies, proceeds to declare them all, either by name or description, to be rebels and traitors, to supersede by his own authority the exercise of the common law of the said province, and to proclaim and order instead thereof the use and exercise of the law martial. This bloody edict issued, he has proceeded to commit further ravages and murders in the same province, burning the town of Charlestown, attacking and killing great numbers of the people residing or assembled therein; and is now going on in an avowed course of murder and devastation, taking every occasion to destroy the lives and properties of the inhabitants of the said province.

*To oppose his arms, we also have taken arms. We should be wanting to ourselves, we should be perfidious to posterity, we should be unworthy that free ancestry from whom which we derive our descent, should we submit with folded arms to military butchery and depredation to gratify the lordly ambition, or sate the avarice of a British ministry. We do then most solemnly, before **God** and the world declare that, regardless of every consequence, at the risk of every distress, the arms we have been compelled to assume we will* *wage use with perseverance, exerting to their utmost energies all those powers which our **Creator** hath given us, to guard preserve that liberty which he committed to us in sacred deposit and to protect from every hostile hand our lives and our properties. But that this our declaration may not disquiet the minds of our good fellow subjects in any parts of the empire, we do further assure them that we mean not in any wise to affect that union with them in which we have so long and so happily lived, and which we wish so much to see again restored That necessity must be hard indeed which may force upon us this desperate measure, or induce us to avail ourselves of any aid which their enemies might proffer. We did not embody a soldiery to commit aggression on them; we did not raise armies for glory or for conquest; we did not invade their island carrying death or slavery to its inhabitants. We took arms in defence of our persons and properties under actual violation, we have taken up arms we took up arms; when that violence shall be removed, when hostilities shall cease on the part of the aggressors, hostilities shall cease on our part also. The moment they withdraw their arms we will disband ours. For the achievement of this happy event, we call for and confide in the good offices of our fellow subjects beyond the Atlantic. Of their friendly dispositions we do not yet cease to hope; aware, as they must be, that they have nothing more to expect from the same common enemy, than the humble favour of being last devoured. And we devoutly implore the assistance of **Almighty God** to conduct us happily thro' this great conflict, to dispose the minds of his majesty, his ministers, and parliament to reasonable terms reconciliation with us on reasonable terms, and to deliver us from the evils of a civil war.*

(JOHN DICKINSON'S DRAFT)

A Declaration by the Representatives of the United Colonies of North America now sitting met in General Congress at Philadelphia, setting forth the Causes and Necessity of their taking up Arms

*If it was possible for Beings who entered feel a proper Reverence for endued with Reason to believe that the **Divine Author** of their Existence Men, who exercise their Reason in contemplating the works of **Creation**, to believe, that the **Divine Author** of our Existence, intended a Part of the human Race to hold an absolute property in and an unbounded Power over others, marked out by **His** infinite Mercy Goodness and Wisdom, as the legal Objects of a Domination never rightfully to be resistible, however severe and oppressive, the Inhabitants of these Colonies would might with at least with propriety at least require from the Parliament of Great Britain some Evidence, that this dreadful Authority was vested in that Body Authority over them has been granted to that Body. But since Reflecti Considerations drawn a due Reverence a Reverence for our great **Creator**, Sentiments Principles of Humanity and the Dictates of Reason have convinced the wise and good and the Dictates of Common Sense, have must convince all those who will reflect upon the Subject, that Government was instituted to promote the Welfare of Mankind, and ought to be administered for the Attainment of that End, since these generous and noble Principles have on no Part of the Earth been so well asserted vindicated and enforced as in Great Britain, the Legislature of that Kingdom hurried on by an inordinate passion for Power, of Ambition for a Power which their own most admired Writers and their very Constitution, demonstrate to be unjust; and which they know to be inconsistent with their own political Constitution the Legislature of Great Britain stimulated by an inordinate Passion for a Power not only generally pronounced held to be unjust, but unjustifiable, but which they know to be peculiarly reprobated by the very Constitution of that Kingdom, and desperate of Success in a Mode of Contest in any Mode of Contest, where any a Regard should be had to Truth, or Justice, or Reason, have at last appealed length Law or Right, have at length attempted to effect their cruel and impolitic Purpose by Violence, and have thereby rendered it necessary for us to change close with their last*

Appeal from Reason to Arms. Yet however blinded they that Assembly may be by their intemperate Rage, yet we esteem ourselves bound by Obligations of Respect to the rest of the World, to make known the Justice of our Cause.

Our Forefathers, inhabitants of the Island of G. B. left their native Land, to seek in the distant and inhospitable Wilds of America on these Shores, a Residence for civil and religious Liberty Freedom. To describe the Dangers' Difficulties and Distresses, the Expense of Blood and Fortune, Treasure they were obliged to encounter in executing their generous Resolutions, would require Volumes. It may suffice to observe, that, at the Expense of their Blood, to the Ruin of their Fortunes, and every Prospect of Advantage in their native Country without the least Charge to the Country from which they removed, with by unceasing Labor and an unconquerable Spirit, they effected Settlements in the distant and inhospitable Wilds of America, then filled with numerous and warlike Nations of Barbarians. Societies or Governments, vested with perfect legislatures within them, were formed under Charters from the Crown, and such an harmonious Intercourse and Union was established between the Colonies and the Kingdom from which they derived their Origin. The mutual benefits of this Union that some occasional Assumptions of The mutual Benefits of this Union became in a short Time so extraordinary as to excite the Astonishment of other Nations. Every British Writer of Eminence, who has treated of the Subject Politics for near a Century past, has uniformly asserted that the amazing Increase of the Wealth, Strength and Navigation of that Kingdom the Realm, arose from this Source; and the Minister who so gloriously presided ably wisely and successfully directed the Councils, Affairs, Measures of Great Britain during in the last War, publicly declared, that these Colonies had enabled her to triumph over her Enemies.

At Towards the Conclusion of that War, it pleased our Sovereign to make a Change in his Counsels. From that fatal Moment, the Affairs of the British Empire began to slide fall into Confusion, that since has been continually increasing and now has produced the most alarming Effects and gradually declining sliding from that splendid Summit of glorious Prosperity to which they had been carried advanced by the Virtues and Abilities of one Man, are at Length distracted by the present most alarming Convulsions, that now shake it to its lowest deepest Foundations. The new Ministry finding the brave, brave Foes of Britain subdued, took up the unfortunate Idea of defeated bravely tho frequently defeated, yet bravely still contending, took up the unfortunate Ideas of granting them a hasty Peace and these to them, and then of subduing her faithful Friends.

They judged those devoted Colonies were judged to present to then

These devoted Colonies were judged to be in such a State as to present a Prospect Victories without Bloodshed, and all the easy Emoluments of statutable Plunder. The uninterrupted Tenor of their peaceable and respectful Behaviour from the Beginning of Colonization, their dutiful, zealous and useful services during the War, that has been mentioned, tho so recently and amply acknowledged in the most honorable Manner by his Majesty, by the late King, and by Parliament could not avail to save them from the meditated Innovations. Parliament influenced to adopt the pernicious Project, and to facilitate its execution by assuming a new Power over them, have in the Course of eleven Years, given such decisive Specimens of the Spirit and Consequences attending this Power, as to leave no Doubt concerning the Effects of Acquiescence under it. Statutes have been passed for taking our Money from us without our own Consent, tho every Colony on this Continent has from its Beginning always we have ever exercised an exclusive Right to dispose of our own Property; for extending the Jurisdiction of Courts of Admiralty and Vice admiralty beyond their ancient Limits; for depriving us of the accustomed and inestimable Privilege of Trial by Jury in Cases affecting both Life and Property; for interdicting all Commerce to one of our principle Towns; for exempting the Murderers of Colonists from legal Punishment for suspending the Powers of Legislature of one of the Colonies; for interdicting all Commerce of another; and for altering fundamentally the Form of Government in one of the Colonies, a Form secured established by Charter and confirmed secured by Acts of its own Legislature solemnly and assented to confirmed by the Crown; her erecting in neighbouring for exempting the "Murderers" of colonists from legal Punishment; for erecting in a neighbouring Province, conquered acquired by the joint Arms of Great

Britain and America, a Tyranny Despotism dangerous to the our very existence of the Colonies and for quartering Officers and Soldiers upon the Colonists in time of profound Peace. It has also been declared resolved in Parliament that Colonists charged with committing certain Offenses, shall by Virtue of a Statute made before any of be transported to England to be tried.

But why should we enumerate our Injuries in Detail? By one Act of Parl Statute it is declared, that Parliament can "of right make Laws to bind us IN ALL CASES WHATSOEVER." What is to defend us against such so enormous a Power so enormous, so unlimited a Power? The persons assuming them Not one of a single Man of those who assume it, is chosen by us; or is subject to our Control or Influence; but on the contrary is they are all of them exempt from the Operations of such Laws, and actually lighten their own Burdens, in exact proportion to those the Burdens they impose on us. These Temptations might put scarce are too great to be offered To Characters of the severest

Administration, sensible that we should regard these oppressive Measures as Freemen ought to do, sent over Fleets and Armies to enforce them. The Indignation of the colonies was roused by their Virtue Americans was roused, it is true: but it was the Indignation of a virtuous, peaceable, loyal, subjects and affectionate People. A Congress of Delegates from the United Colonies was assembled at Philadelphia on the fifth Day of last September. We felt saw the Weapons leveled at our Brea Bosoms, but we perceived them at the same Time held in grasped by a Parent's Hands. We cast ourselves upon our Knees prostrate at the Foot of the Throne our Sovereign. Tho for ten years we had fatigued the besieged the Throne Ears of Authority with Petitions, Supplications, yet the ineffectually besieged the Throne as Supplicants, yet we resolved again to over an humble and dutiful Petition to the King, and agreed also to send an Address to our Fellow Subjects in Great Britain, informing them of our agreement at a certain Days to break off all our Commercial Intercourse with our Fellow Subjects in Great Britain as the last peaceable them as a peaceable Admonition, that our Attachment to no Nation upon the Earth should supplant our Attachment to Liberty. This, we flattered ourselves, was the ultimate Step of the Controversy: But subsequent Events have shewn, how vain was this last Hope of Moderation in the Ministry our Enemies.

*Our Petition was treated with Contempt. Without the least Mention of its our Application several threatening Expressions against the Colonies were inserted in his Majesty's Speech to both the two Houses of Parliament; and afterwards the Petition was huddled into the House of Commons the last amongst a neglected Bundle of American Papers. The Lords and Commons in their Address to his Majesty, in the Month of February, said, that "a Rebellion at that Time actually existed within the Province of Massachusetts Bay; and that those concerned in it, had been countenanced and encouraged by unlawful Combinations and Engagements entered into by his Majesty's Subjects in several of the other Colonies; and therefore they besought his Majesty, that he would take the most effectual Measures to enforce due Obedience to the Laws and **Authority of the Supreme Legislature.**" Soon after the commercial Intercourse of whole Colonies with foreign Countries was cut off by an Act of Parliament; and by another, several of them were entirely prohibited from the Fisheries in the neighbouring Seas near their coasts, on which they always depended for their Sustenance; and large Reinforcements of Ships and Troops were immediately sent over to General Gage.*

With such a headlong heedless Rage fury were these outrageous Proceedings hurried on, that all the Prayers Fruitless were all the Entreaties, Arguments and Eloquence of the a very considerable an illustrious Band of the most distinguished Peers and Commoners, who nobly confess and strenuously asserted the Justice of our Cause, to stay or even to mitigate the heedless Fury of with which these accumulated and unexampled Outrages were rapidly hurried on. Equally fruitless was the interference of that the august City of London, supplicating of Bristol, and many other respectable Towns in our Favor. A Plan of Reconciliation digested by the patriotic Cares of that great and good man before-mentioned, and which might easily have been improved to produce every Effect his generous Heart desired, was contemptuously rejected, to give way to an insidious Ministerial Maneuver, calculated to divide us, to establish a perpetual Auction of Taxation, where Colony should bid against Colony, all of them uninformed what Ransom would redeem their Lives, and thus to extort from us at the Point of the Bayonet Sums the unknown Sums that should be sufficient to gratify, if possible to gratify, ministerial Rapacity, with the miserable Indulgence left to us of raising in our own Modes the prescribed Tribute.

When the Intelligence of these Proceedings arrived on this Continent, we perceived it appeared evident, that our Destruction was determined upon, and that we had no Alternative or choice to make but of. Our choice must be either an "unconditional Submission," as one of the Ministry expressed himself, or of Resistance.

Soon after the Intelligence of these Proceedings arrived on this Continent, where General Gage, who in the Course of the last Year, had taken Possession of the Town of Boston, in the Province of Massachusetts Bay, and still occupied it as a Garrison, Plans, on the 19th Day of last April last, sent out of from that Place a large Detachment of his Army, who made an unprovoked Assault on the Inhabitants of the said Province, at the Town of Lexington, as appears by the Affidavits of a great Number of Persons, some of whom were Officers and Soldiers of that Detachment, murdered Eight of the Inhabitants, and wounded many others. From thence the Troops proceeded in warlike array to the Town of Concord, where they set upon another party of the Inhabitants of the same Province, killing several and wounding others more, until compelled to retreat by the People suddenly assembled to repel this cruel Aggression. Hostilities thus commenced by the British Troops, have been since prosecuted by them without Regard to Faith or Reputation. The Inhabitants of Boston being confined within that Town by the General their Governor and having in order to procure their Dismission entered into a Treaty with him, it was stipulated between the that the said Inhabitants having deposited their arms with their own Magistrates, should have free Liberty to depart, out of the said Town, taking with them their other Effects. They accordingly delivered up their Arms, but in open violation of Honor, in Defiance of the Obligations of a Treaties, which even savage Nations esteem sacred, General Gage the Governor ordered the Arms deposited as aforesaid that they might be preserved for their Owners, to be seized by a Body of armed

24

men, soldiers, detained the greater Part of the Inhabitants in the Town, and compelled the few who were permitted to retire, to leave their most valuable Effects behind. By this perfidy, wives are separated from their Husbands, children from their Parents, the aged and sick from their Relatives and Friends who wish to attend and relieve take care of them; and those who have been used to live with Elegance in Plenty and even Elegance, are reduced to deplorable Distress.

The General further emulating the his ministerial Masters, by a Proclamation bearing Date on the 12th Day of June, after venting the grossest Falsehoods and Calumnies against the good People of these Colonies, proceeds to "declare them all either by Name or Description to be Rebels and Traitors, to supersede the Course of the Common Law, and instead thereof to publish and order the Use and Exercise of the Law Martial." His Troops have butchered our Countrymen; have burnt Charlestown, besides a considerable Number of Houses in other Places; our Ships and Vessels are seized; and the necessary supplies of Provisions are stopped intercepted; and he is now Destruction and Devastation around him as far as he can, all the complicated Cal and he is exerting the utmost Power to spread Destruction and Devastation around him. We have received certain Intelligence that Governor General Carleton, the Governor of Canada, by Orders from the Ministry is instigating the People of that Province and the Indians to fall upon us; and that Schemes have been form'd to excite domestic Enemies against us. In brief, a Part of the Colonies now feels, and all of them are sure of feeling, as far as the Vengeance of Administration can inflict them, all the complicated Calamities of Fire, Sword and Famine. By our The Suggestions of Duty and affection can no longer lull us into a lethargic Notion, too lately relinquished, that Armies and fleets are only designed to intimidate us. We are reduced to the Alternative of abusing an unconditional Submission to the Tyrannic Vengeance of irritated who know we despise them and that they deserve to be thus despised are therefore implacable Tyranny of irritated ministers, or Resistance by Force. The latter is our Choice.

We know, that by an infamous Surrender of the Freedom and Happiness of ourselves and our Posterity, we might obtain that wretched Honor, Justly

Humanity forbid us basely to surrender that Freedom Liberty and Happiness which we received from our gallant Ancestors, and which it is our duty to transmit undiminished to our Posterity. Called upon by the law of self-preservation implanted in our nature by our all-wise **Creator***, with prepared Hands We have counted the Cost of this Contest, and being perfectly convinced, it is infinitely find nothing so dreadful and resolved Hearts we will in our Computation, as Infamy and voluntary Slavery united, Honor, Justice and Humanity forbid us tamely to surrender that Freedom which we received from our gallant Ancestors, and which our innocent Posterity have a Right to receive from us. We cannot endure the Infamy and Guilt of resigning succeeding Generations to that Wretchedness which inevitably awaits them, if we basely entail hereditary Bondage upon them.*

Our Cause is just.

Our Union is perfect.

Our hearts are resolved.

Our Hands are prepared.

Our preparations are nearly completed.

Our internal Resources within our own Country are many great; and our Assurance of foreign Assistance is certain.

We gratefully acknowledge as a singular instance of the **Divine** *Goodness Favor and consider it as a singular mark of* **His** *Favor towards us, in not permitting us to be that* **His** *Providence would not permit us to be called into the severe Controversy, until our we were grown up to our present Strength, was had been previously exercised in warlike Operations, to which some Years ago we were almost entire Strangers, and that we were possessed of the Means for defending ourselves, of which till lately we were in Want. With Hearts fortified by these animating Reflections, We do most solemnly before* **God** *and the World declare, that, exerting the utmost Energies of those Powers, which our beneficent* **Creator** *hath graciously bestowed upon us, the arms we have been thus compelled by our Enemies to assume for our just Defence, we will* *in Defiance of every Hazard with unabating Firmness and perseverance, in Defiance of every Hazard, now we will employ for the preservation of our Liberties, deeming it infinitely preferable being with one Mind resolved to dye free men rather than to live Slaves.*

Least this Declaration should disquiet the Minds of our Friends and fellow subjects in any part of the World Empire, we assure them, that we mean not in any Manner to dissolve that Union with them in which we have has so long and so happily lived subsisted between us, and which we so ardently much sincerely wish to see restored. The Necessity must be hard indeed has not yet driven us into that desperate Measure, or to excite their other Nations to war against them. We have not raised armies from with ambitious Designs of separating from Great Britain and establishing independent States. We have fight not invaded that Island proffering to its Inhabitants Death or Slavery for Glory or for Conquest. We exhibit to Mankind the remarkable Spectacle of a People charged till attacked without any Imputation or even Suspicion of Offence by unprovoked Enemies, who proffer to them the not milder Forms Conditions than Death or Slavery boast of their Freedom Privileges and Civilization, and yet proffer no milder Conditions than Death or Slav Servitude or Death.

In our Native Land, in Defence of Liberties the Liberty Freedom that is our Birthright, and which we ever enjoyed till the late Violations of it,-for the Protection of our Property acquired, solely by the honest Industry of our Forefathers and ourselves, against we have taken up arms, solely to oppose and repel the violence actually offered to us Violence actually offered, we have taken up Arms. We shall lay them down when Hostilities shall cease on the Part of the Aggressors, and all Danger of their being renewed, shall be removed, and not before.

*With an humble Confidence in the divine Mercies of the supreme and impartial **Judge and Ruler of the Universe**, we most devoutly implore **Almighty God His divine Goodness** to conduct us happily thro' this great Conflict, to dispose our Adversaries to Reconciliation on Reasonable Terns, and thereby to relieve the Empire from the Evils Calamities of Civil War.*

FINAL FORM

A declaration by the Representatives of the United Colonies of North America, now met in General Congress at Philadelphia, setting forth the causes and necessity of their taking up arms.

*If it was possible for men, who exercise their reason, to believe, that the **Divine Author** of our existence intended a part of the human race to hold an absolute property in, and an unbounded power over others, marked out by **His** infinite goodness and wisdom, as the objects of a legal domination never rightfully resistible, however severe and oppressive, the Inhabitants of these Colonies might at least require from the Parliament of Great Britain some evidence, that this dreadful authority over them, has been granted to that body. But a reverence for our great **Creator**, principles of humanity, and the dictates of common sense, must convince all those who reflect upon the subject, that government was instituted to promote the welfare of mankind, and ought to be administered for the attainment of that end. The legislature of Great Britain, however, stimulated by an inordinate passion for a power, not only unjustifiable, but which they know to be peculiarly reprobated by the very constitution of that kingdom, and desperate of success in any mode of contest, where regard should be had to truth, law, or right, have at length, deserting those, attempted to effect their cruel and impolitic purpose of enslaving these Colonies by violence, and have thereby rendered it necessary for us to close with their last appeal from Reason to Arms.-Yet, however blinded that assembly may be, by their intemperate rage for unlimited domination, so to slight justice and the opinion of mankind, we esteem ourselves bound, by obligations of respect to the rest of the world, to make known the justice of our cause.*

Our forefathers, inhabitants of the island of Great Britain, left their native land, to seek on these shores a residence for civil and religious freedom. At the expense of their blood, at the hazard of their fortunes, without the least charge to the country from which they removed, by unceasing labor, and an unconquerable spirit, they effected settlements in the distant and inhospitable wilds of America, then filled with numerous and warlike nations of barbarians. Societies or governments, vested with perfect legislatures, were formed under charters from the crown, and an harmonious intercourse was established between the colonies and the kingdom from which they derived their origin. The mutual benefits of this union became in a short time so extraordinary, as to excite astonishment. It is universally confessed, that the amazing increase of the wealth, strength, and navigation of the realm, arose from this source; and the minister, who so wisely and successfully directed the measures of Great Britain in the late war, publicly declared, that these colonies enabled her to triumph over her enemies.-Towards the conclusion of that war, it pleased our sovereign to make a change in his counsels.

From that fatal moment, the affairs of the British empire began to fall into confusion, and gradually sliding from the summit of glorious prosperity, to which they had been advanced by the virtues and abilities of one man, are at length distracted by the convulsions, that now shake it to its deepest foundations. The new ministry finding the brave foes of Britain, though frequently defeated, yet still contending, took up the unfortunate idea of granting them a hasty peace, and of then subduing her faithful friends.

These devoted colonies were judged to be in such a state, as to present victories without bloodshed, and all the easy emoluments of statuteable plunder.

The uninterrupted tenor of their peaceable and respectful behaviour from the beginning of colonization, their dutiful, zealous, and useful services during the war, though so recently and amply acknowledged in the most honorable manner by his majesty, by the late king, and by Parliament, could not save them from the meditated innovations.-Parliament was influenced to adopt the pernicious project, and assuming a new power over them, have, in the course of eleven years, given such decisive specimens of the spirit and consequences attending this power, as to leave no doubt concerning the effects of acquiescence under it. They have undertaken to give and grant our money without our consent, though we have ever exercised an exclusive right to dispose of our own property; statutes have been passed for extending the jurisdiction of courts of Admiralty and Vice-Admiralty beyond their ancient limits; for depriving us of the accustomed and inestimable privilege of trial by jury, in cases affecting both life and property; for suspending the legislature of one of the colonies; for interdicting all commerce to the capital of another; and for altering fundamentally the form of government established by charter, and secured by acts of its own legislature solemnly confirmed by the crown; for exempting the " murderers " of colonists from legal trial, and in effect, from punishment; for erecting in a neighboring province, acquired by the joint arms of Great Britain and America, a despotism dangerous to our very existence; and for quartering soldiers upon the colonists in time of profound peace. It has also been resolved in parliament, that colonists charged with committing certain offences, shall be transported to England to be tried.

But why should we enumerate our injuries in detail? By one statute it is declared, that parliament can "of right make laws to bind us IN ALL CASES WHATSOEVER" What is to defend us against so enormous, so unlimited a power? Not a single man of those who assume it, is chosen by us; or is subject to our control or influence; but, on the contrary, they are all of them exempt from the operation of such laws, and an American revenue, if not diverted from the ostensible purposes for which it is raised, would actually lighten their own burdens in proportion as they increase ours. We saw the misery to which such despotism would reduce us. We for ten years incessantly and ineffectually besieged the Throne as supplicants; we reasoned, we remonstrated with parliament, in the most mild and decent language. But Administration, sensible that we should regard these oppressive measures as freemen ought to do, sent over fleets and armies to enforce them. The indignation of the Americans was roused, it is true; hut it was the indignation of a virtuous, loyal, and affectionate people. A Congress of Delegates from the United Colonies was assembled at Philadelphia, on the fifth day of last September. We resolved again to offer an humble and dutiful petition to the King, and also addressed our fellow-subjects of Great Britain. We have pursued every temperate, every respectful measure: we have even proceeded to break off our commercial intercourse with our fellow-subjects, as the last peaceable admonition, that our attachment to no nation upon earth should supplant our attachment to liberty.- This, we flattered ourselves, was the ultimate step of the controversy: But subsequent events have strewn, how vain was this hope of finding moderation in our enemies.

Several threatening expressions against the colonies were inserted in his Majesty's speech; our petition, though we were told it was a decent one, and that his Majesty had been pleased to receive it graciously, and to promise laying it before his Parliament, was huddled into both houses amongst a bundle of American papers, and there neglected. The Lords and Commons in their address, in the month of February, said, that "a rebellion at that time actually existed within the province of Massachusetts bay; and that those concerned in it, had been countenanced and encouraged by unlawful combinations and engagements, entered into by his Majesty's subjects in several of the other colonies; and therefore they besought his Majesty, that he would take the most effectual measures to enforce due obedience to the laws and authority of the supreme legislature."-Soon after, the commercial intercourse of whole colonies, with foreign countries, and with each other, was cut off by an act of Parliament; by another, several of them were entirely prohibited from the fisheries in the seas near their coasts, on which they always depended for their sustenance; and large re-enforcements of ships and troops were immediately sent over to General Gage.

Fruitless were all the entreaties, arguments, and eloquence of an illustrious band of the most distinguished Peers, and Commoners, who nobly and strenuously asserted the justice of our cause, to stay, or even to mitigate the heedless fury with which these accumulated and unexampled outrages were hurried on.-Equally fruitless was the interference of the city of London, of Bristol, and many other respectable towns in our favour. Parliament adopted an insidious maneuver calculated to divide us, to establish a perpetual auction of taxations where colony should bid against colony, all of them uninformed what ransom would redeem their lives; and thus to extort from us, at the point of the bayonet, the unknown sums that should be sufficient to gratify, if possible to gratify, ministerial rapacity, with the miserable indulgence left to us of raising, in our own mode, the prescribed tribute. What terms more rigid and humiliating could have been dictated by remorseless victors to conquered enemies? In our circumstances to accept them, would be to deserve them.

Soon after the intelligence of these proceedings arrived on this continent, General Gage, who in the course of the last year had taken possession of the town of Boston, in the province of Massachusetts Bay, and still occupied it as a garrison, on the 19th day of April, sent out from that place a large detachment of his army, who made an unprovoked assault on the inhabitants of the said province, at the town of Lexington, as appears by the affidavits of a great number of persons, some of whom were officers and soldiers of that detachment, murdered eight of the inhabitants, and wounded many others. From thence the troops proceeded in warlike array to the town of Concord, where they set upon another party of the inhabitants of the same province, killing several and wounding more, until compelled to retreat by the country people suddenly assembled to repel this cruel aggression. Hostilities, thus commenced by the British troops, have been since prosecuted by them without regard to faith or reputation.-The inhabitants of Boston being confined within that town by the General their Governor, and having, in order to procure their dismission, entered into a treaty with him, it was stipulated that the said inhabitants having deposited their arms with their own magistrates, should have liberty to depart, taking with them their other ejects. They accordingly delivered up their arms, but in open violation of honor, in defiance of the obligation of treaties, which even savage nations esteemed sacred, the Governor ordered the arms deposited as aforesaid, that they might be preserved for their owners, to be seized by a body of soldiers; detained the greatest part of the inhabitants in the town, and compelled the few who were permitted to retire, to leave their most valuable effects behind.

By this perfidy wives are separated from their husbands, children from their parents, the aged and the sick from their relations and friends, who wish to attend and comfort them; and those who have been used to live in plenty and even elegance, are reduced to deplorable distress.

The General, further emulating his ministerial masters, by a proclamation bearing date on the 12th day of June, after venting the grossest falsehoods and calumnies against the good people of these colonies, proceeds to "declare them all, either by name or description, to be rebels and traitors, to supersede the course of the common law, and instead thereof to publish and order the use and exercise of the law martial."-His troops have butchered our countrymen, have wantonly burns Charles-town, besides a considerable number of houses in other places; our ships and vessels are seized; the necessary supplies of provisions are intercepted, and he is exerting his utmost power to spread destruction and devastation around him.

We have received certain intelligence that General Carleton, the Governor of Canada, is instigating the people of that province and the Indians to fall upon us; and we have but too much reason to apprehend, that schemes have been formed to excite domestic enemies against us. In brief, a part of these colonies now feels, and all of them are sure of feeling, as far as the vengeance of administration can inflict them, the complicated calamities of fire, sword, and famine.- We are reduced to the alternative of choosing an unconditional submission to the tyranny of irritated ministers, or resistance by force.- The latter is our choice.-We have counted the cost of this contest, and find nothing so dreadful as voluntary slavery.-Honor, justice, and humanity, forbid us tamely to surrender that freedom which we received from our gallant ancestors, and which our innocent posterity have a right to receive from us. We cannot endure the infamy and guilt of resigning succeeding generations to that wretchedness which inevitably awaits them, if we basely entail hereditary bondage upon them.

Our cause is just.

Our union is perfect.

Our internal resources are great, and, if necessary, foreign assistance is undoubtedly attainable.

We gratefully acknowledge, as signal instances of the **Divine** favour towards us, that **His** Providence would not permit us to be called into this severe controversy, until we were grown up to our present strength, had been previously exercised in warlike operation, and possessed of the means of defending ourselves.- With hearts fortified with these animating reflections, we most solemnly, before **God** and the world, declare, that, exerting the utmost energy of those powers, which our beneficent **Creator** hath graciously bestowed upon us, the arms we have been compelled by our enemies to assume, we will, in defiance of every hazard, with unabating firmness and *perseverance, employ for the preservation of our liberties; being with our [one] mind resolved to dye Free-men rather than live Slaves.*

Lest this declaration should disquiet the minds of our friends and fellow-subjects in any part of the empire, we assure them that we mean not to dissolve that Union which has so long and so happily subsisted between us, and which we sincerely wish to see restored.- Necessity has not yet driven us into that desperate measure, or induced us to excite any other nation to war against them.-We have not raised armies with ambitious designs of separating from Great Britain, and establishing independent states. We fight not for glory or for conquest. We exhibit to mankind the remarkable spectacle of a people attacked by unprovoked enemies, without any imputation or even suspicion of offence. They boast of their privileges and civilization, and yet proffer no milder conditions than servitude or death.

In our own native land, in defence of the freedom that is our birth-right, and which we ever enjoyed till the late violation of it-for the protection of our property, acquired solely by the honest industry of our fore-fathers and ourselves, against violence actually offered, we have taken up arms. We shall lay them down when hostilities shall cease on the part of the aggressors, and all danger of their being renewed shall be removed, and not before.

*With an humble confidence in the mercies of the supreme and impartial **Judge and Ruler of the universe'** we most devoutly implore **His** divine goodness to protect us happily through this great conflict, to dispose our adversaries to reconciliation on reasonable terms, and thereby to relieve the empire from the calamities of civil war.*

By order of Congress,

JOHN HANCOCK,

President

Attested,

CHARLES THOMSON,

Secretary I

Philadelphia, July 6th, 1775

On motion, Resolved, That a letter be prepared to the Lord Mayor, Aldermen, and Livery of the city of London, expressing the thanks of this Congress, for their virtuous and spirited opposition to the oppressive and ruinous system of colony administration adopted by the British ministry.

Richard Henry Lee of Virginia drafted a proposed declaration of independence from England on June 7, 1776 to the Second Continental Congress. That document is known as the Lee Resolution.

That resolution read:

"Resolved, That these United Colonies are, and of right to be, free and independent States, that they are absolved from all allegiance to the British Crown, and that all political connection between them and the State of Great Britain is, and ought to be, totally dissolved. That it is expedient forthwith to take the most effectual measures for forming foreign Alliances. That a plan of confederation be prepared and transmitted to the respective Colonies for their consideration and approbation."

The "Committee of Five" was formed on June 11, 1776 by the Congress to draft an official declaration which would be sent to England. This committee consisted of Thomas Jefferson of Virginia, Roger Sherman of Connecticut, Robert R. Livingston of New York, Benjamin Franklin of Pennsylvania and John Adams of Massachusetts.

The Committee of Five first presented the declaration to Congress on June 28, 1776.

The Declaration of Independence

Thomas Jefferson's first rough draft:

A Declaration of the Representatives of the UNITED STATES OF AMERICA, in General Congress assembled.

*When in the course of human events it becomes necessary for a people to advance from that subordination in which they have hitherto remained, & to assume among the powers of the earth the equal & independent station to which the **laws of nature & of nature's God** entitle them, a decent respect to the opinions of mankind requires that they should declare the causes which impel them to the change.*

We hold these truths to be sacred & undeniable; that all men are created equal & independent, that from that equal creation they derive rights inherent & inalienable, among which are the preservation of life, & liberty, & the pursuit of happiness; that to secure these ends, governments are instituted among men, deriving their just powers from the consent of the governed; that whenever any form of government shall become destructive of these ends, it is the right of the people to alter or to abolish it, & to institute new government, laying it's foundation on such principles & organizing it's powers in such form, as to them shall seem most likely to effect their safety & happiness. Prudence indeed will dictate that governments long established should not be changed for light & transient causes: and accordingly all experience hath shewn that mankind are more disposed to suffer while evils are sufferable, than to right themselves by abolishing the forms to which they are accustomed. but when a long train of abuses & usurpations, begun at a distinguished period, & pursuing invariably the same object, evinces a design to subject them to arbitrary power, it is their right, it is their duty, to throw off such government & to provide new guards for their future security. Such has been the patient sufferance of these colonies; & such is now the necessity which constrains them to expunge their former systems of government. the history of his present majesty is a history of unremitting injuries and usurpations, among which no one fact stands single or solitary to contradict the uniform tenor of the rest, all of which have in direct object the establishment of an absolute tyranny over these states. to prove this, let facts be submitted to a candid world, for the truth of which we pledge a faith yet unsullied by falsehood.

He has refused his assent to laws the most wholesome and necessary for the public good:

He has forbidden his governors to pass laws of immediate & pressing importance, unless suspended in their operation till his assent should be obtained; and when so suspended, he has neglected utterly to attend to them.

He has refused to pass other laws for the accommodation of large districts of people unless those people would relinquish the right of representation, a right inestimable to them, formidable to tyrants alone:

He has dissolved Representative houses repeatedly & continually, for opposing with manly firmness his invasions on the rights of the people:

He has refused for a long space of time to cause others to be elected, whereby the legislative powers, incapable of annihilation, have returned to the people at large for their exercise, the state remaining in the mean-time exposed to all the dangers of invasion from without, & convulsions within:

He has endeavored to prevent the population of these states; for that purpose obstructing the laws for naturalization of foreigners; refusing to pass others to encourage their migrations hither; & raising the conditions of new appropriations of lands:

He has suffered the administration of justice totally to cease in some of these colonies, refusing his assent to laws for establishing judiciary powers:

He has made our judges dependent on his will alone, for the tenure of their offices, and amount of their salaries:

He has erected a multitude of new offices by a self-assumed power, & sent hither swarms of officers to harass our people & eat out their substance:

He has kept among us in times of peace standing armies & ships of war:

He has affected to render the military, independent of & superior to the civil power:

He has combined with others to subject us to a jurisdiction foreign to our constitutions and unacknowledged by our laws; giving his assent to their pretended acts of legislation, for quartering large bodies of armed troops among us;

For protecting them by a mock-trial from punishment for any murders they should commit on the inhabitants of these states;

For cutting off our trade with all parts of the world;

For imposing taxes on us without our consent;

For depriving us of the benefits of trial by jury;

For transporting us beyond seas to be tried for pretended offences: for taking away our charters, & altering fundamentally the forms of our governments;

For suspending our own legislatures & declaring themselves invested with power to legislate for us in all cases whatsoever:

He has abdicated government here, withdrawing his governors, & declaring us out of his allegiance & protection:

He has plundered our seas, ravaged our coasts, burnt our towns & destroyed the lives of our people:

He is at this time transporting large armies of foreign mercenaries to complete the works of death, desolation & tyranny, already begun with circumstances of cruelty & perfidy unworthy the head of a civilized nation:

He has endeavored to bring on the inhabitants of our frontiers the merciless Indian savages, whose known rule of warfare is an undistinguished destruction of all ages, sexes, & conditions of existence:

He has incited treasonable insurrections in our fellow-subjects, with the allurements of forfeiture & confiscation of our property:

He has waged cruel war against human nature itself, violating its most sacred rights of life & liberty in the persons of a distant people who never offended him, captivating & carrying them into slavery in another hemisphere, or to incur miserable death in their transportation thither. This piratical warfare, the opprobrium of infidel powers, is the warfare of the **CHRISTIAN** *king of Great Britain. determined to keep open a market where MEN should be bought & sold, he has prostituted his negative for suppressing every legislative attempt to prohibit or to restrain this execrable commerce: and that this assemblage of horrors might want no fact of distinguished die, he is now exciting those very people to rise in arms among us, and to purchase that liberty of which he has deprived them, & murdering the people upon whom he also obtruded them; thus paying off former crimes committed against the liberties of one people, with crimes which he urges them to commit against the lives of another.*

In every stage of these oppressions we have petitioned for redress in the most humble terms; our repeated petitions have been answered by repeated injury. A prince whose character is thus marked by every act which may define a tyrant, is unfit to be the ruler of a people who mean to be free. Future ages will scarce believe that the hardiness of one man, adventured within the short compass of 12 years only, on so many acts of tyranny without a mask, over a people fostered & fixed in principles of liberty.

Nor have we been wanting in attentions to our British brethren. We have warned them from time to time of attempts by their legislature to extend a jurisdiction over these our states. we have reminded them of the circumstances of our emigration & settlement here, no one of which could warrant so strange a pretension: that these were effected at the expense of our own blood & treasure, unassisted by the wealth or the strength of Great Britain: that in constituting indeed our several forms of government, we had adopted one common king, thereby laying a foundation for perpetual league & amity with them: but that submission to their parliament was no part of our constitution, nor ever in idea, if history may be credited: and we appealed to their native justice & magnanimity, as well as to the ties of our common kindred to disavow these usurpations which were likely to interrupt our correspondence & connection. They too have been deaf to the voice of justice & of consanguinity, & when occasions have been given them, by the regular course of their laws, of removing from their councils the disturbers of our harmony; they have by their free election re-established them in power. At this very time too they are permitting their chief magistrate to send over not only soldiers of our common blood, but Scotch & foreign mercenaries to invade & deluge us in blood. These facts have given the last stab to agonizing affection, and manly spirit bids us to renounce for-ever these unfeeling brethren. We must endeavor to forget our former love for them, and to hold them as we hold the rest of mankind, enemies in war, in peace friends. We might have been a free & great people together; but a communication of grandeur & of freedom it seems is below their dignity. Be it so, since they will have it: the road to glory & happiness is open to us too; we will climb it in a separate state, and acquiesce in the necessity which pronounces our everlasting Adieu!

We therefore the representatives of the United States of America in General Congress assembled do, in the name & by authority of the good people of these states, reject and renounce a11 allegiance & subjection to the kings of Great Britain & all others who may hereafter claim by, though, or under them; we utterly dissolve & break off a11 political connection which may have heretofore subsisted between us & the people or parliament of Great Britain; and finally we do assert and declare these a colonies to be free and independent states, and that as free & independent states they shall hereafter have power to levy war, conclude peace, contract alliances, establish commerce, & to do all other acts and things which independent states may of right do. And for the support of this declaration we mutually pledge to each other our lives, our fortunes, & our sacred honour.

A little known fact is that Thomas Jefferson did not want to write this world-changing document.

Thomas Jefferson wanted John Adams to be the author of our declaration of independence from England.

On August 6, 1822, John Adams wrote in a letter to Timothy Pickering, a friend of Adams and a politician from Massachusetts the following: *"Jefferson proposed to me to make the draft. "I said, 'I will not,' 'You should do it.' 'Oh! no.' 'Why will you not? You ought to do it.' 'I will not.' 'Why?' 'Reasons enough.' 'What can be your reasons?' 'Reason first, you are a Virginian, and a Virginian ought to appear at the head of this business. Reason second, I am obnoxious, suspected, and unpopular. You are very much otherwise. Reason third, you can write ten times better than I can.' 'Well,' said Jefferson, 'if you are decided, I will do as well as I can.' 'Very well. When you have drawn it up, we will have a meeting.'"*

In early July Congress debated and revised Jefferson's version of the declaration.

On July 2, 1776 Congress declared independence by adopting the Lee Resolution.

The Declaration of Independence

(The adopted version)

The Declaration of Independence: A Transcription

IN CONGRESS, July 4, 1776

The unanimous Declaration of the thirteen united States of America,

*When in the Course of human events, it becomes necessary for one people to dissolve the political bands which have connected them with another, and to assume among the powers of the earth, the separate and equal station to which the **Laws of Nature and of Nature's God** entitle them, a decent respect to the opinions of mankind requires that they should declare the causes which impel them to the separation.*

*We hold these truths to be self-evident, that all men are created equal, that they are endowed by their **Creator** with certain unalienable Rights, that among these are Life, Liberty and the pursuit of Happiness.--That to secure these rights, Governments are instituted among Men, deriving their just powers from the consent of the governed, --That whenever any Form of Government becomes destructive of these ends, it is the Right of the People to alter or to abolish it, and to institute new Government, laying its foundation on such principles and organizing its powers in such form, as to them shall seem most likely to effect their Safety and Happiness. Prudence, indeed, will dictate that Governments long established should not be changed for light and transient causes; and accordingly all experience hath shewn, that mankind are more disposed to suffer, while evils are sufferable, than to right themselves by abolishing the forms to which they are accustomed. But when a long train of abuses and usurpations, pursuing invariably the same Object evinces a design to reduce them under absolute Despotism, it is their right, it is their duty, to throw off such Government, and to provide new Guards for their future security.--Such has been the patient sufferance of these Colonies; and such is now the necessity which constrains them to alter their former Systems of Government. The history of the present King of Great Britain is a history of* repeated injuries and usurpations, all having in direct object the establishment of an absolute Tyranny over these States. To prove this, let Facts be submitted to a candid world.

He has refused his Assent to Laws, the most wholesome and necessary for the public good.

He has forbidden his Governors to pass Laws of immediate and pressing importance, unless suspended in their operation till his Assent should be obtained; and when so suspended, he has utterly neglected to attend to them.

He has refused to pass other Laws for the accommodation of large districts of people, unless those people would relinquish the right of Representation in the Legislature, a right inestimable to them and formidable to tyrants only.

He has called together legislative bodies at places unusual, uncomfortable, and distant from the depository of their public Records, for the sole purpose of fatiguing them into compliance with his measures.

He has dissolved Representative Houses repeatedly, for opposing with manly firmness his invasions on the rights of the people.

He has refused for a long time, after such dissolutions, to cause others to be elected; whereby the Legislative powers, incapable of Annihilation, have returned to the People at large for their exercise; the State remaining in the mean-time exposed to all the dangers of invasion from without, and convulsions within.

He has endeavoured to prevent the population of these States; for that purpose obstructing the Laws for Naturalization of Foreigners; refusing to pass others to encourage their migrations hither, and raising the conditions of new Appropriations of Lands.

He has obstructed the Administration of Justice, by refusing his Assent to Laws for establishing Judiciary powers.

He has made Judges dependent on his Will alone, for the tenure of their offices, and the amount and payment of their salaries.

He has erected a multitude of New Offices, and sent hither swarms of Officers to harass our people, and eat out their substance.

He has kept among us, in times of peace, Standing Armies without the Consent of our legislatures.

He has affected to render the Military independent of and superior to the Civil power.

He has combined with others to subject us to a jurisdiction foreign to our constitution, and unacknowledged by our laws; giving his Assent to their Acts of pretended Legislation:

For Quartering large bodies of armed troops among us:

For protecting them, by a mock Trial, from punishment for any Murders which they should commit on the Inhabitants of these States:

For cutting off our Trade with all parts of the world:

For imposing Taxes on us without our Consent:

For depriving us in many cases, of the benefits of Trial by Jury:

For transporting us beyond Seas to be tried for pretended offences

For abolishing the free System of English Laws in a neighbouring Province, establishing therein an Arbitrary government, and enlarging its Boundaries so as to render it at once an example and fit instrument for introducing the same absolute rule into these Colonies:

For taking away our Charters, abolishing our most valuable Laws, and altering fundamentally the Forms of our Governments:

For suspending our own Legislatures and declaring themselves invested with power to legislate for us in all cases whatsoever.

He has abdicated Government here, by declaring us out of his Protection and waging War against us.

He has plundered our seas, ravaged our Coasts, burnt our towns, and destroyed the lives of our people.

He is at this time transporting large Armies of foreign Mercenaries to compleat the works of death, desolation and tyranny, already begun with circumstances of Cruelty & perfidy scarcely paralleled in the most barbarous ages, and totally unworthy the Head of a civilized nation.

He has constrained our fellow Citizens taken Captive on the high Seas to bear Arms against their Country, to become the executioners of their friends and Brethren, or to fall themselves by their Hands.

He has excited domestic insurrections amongst us, and has endeavoured to bring on the inhabitants of our frontiers, the merciless Indian Savages, whose known rule of warfare, is an undistinguished destruction of all ages, sexes and conditions.

In every stage of these Oppressions We have Petitioned for Redress in the most humble terms: Our repeated Petitions have been answered only by repeated injury. A Prince, whose character is thus marked by every act which may define a Tyrant, is unfit to be the ruler of a free people.

Nor have We been wanting in attentions to our British brethren. We have warned them from time to time of attempts by their legislature to extend an unwarrantable jurisdiction over us. We have reminded them of the circumstances of our emigration and settlement here. We have appealed to their native justice and magnanimity, and we have conjured them by the ties of our common kindred to disavow these usurpations, which would inevitably interrupt our connections and correspondence. They too have been deaf to the voice of justice and of consanguinity. We must, therefore, acquiesce in the necessity, which denounces our Separation, and hold them, as we hold the rest of mankind, Enemies in War, in Peace Friends.

We, therefore, the Representatives of the united States of America, in General Congress, Assembled, appealing to the Supreme Judge of the world for the rectitude of our intentions, do, in the Name, and by Authority of the good People of these Colonies, solemnly publish and declare, That these United

Colonies are, and of Right ought to be Free and Independent States; that they are Absolved from all Allegiance to the British Crown, and that all political connection between them and the State of Great Britain, is and ought to be totally dissolved; and that as Free and Independent States, they have full Power to levy War, conclude Peace, contract Alliances, establish Commerce, and to do all other Acts and Things which Independent States may of right do. And for the support of this Declaration, with a firm reliance on the protection of divine Providence, we mutually pledge to each other our Lives, our Fortunes and our sacred Honor.

New Hampshire

Josiah Bartlett

William Whipple

Matthew Thornton

Massachusetts

John Hancock

Samuel Adams,

John Adams

Robert Treat Paine

Elbridge Gerry

Rhode Island

Stephen Hopkins

William Ellery

Connecticut

Roger Sherman

Samuel Huntington

William Williams

Oliver Wolcott

New York

William Floyd

Philip Livingston

Francis Lewis

Lewis Morris

New Jersey

Richard Stockton

John Witherspoon

Francis Hopkinson

John Hart

Abraham Clark

Pennsylvania

Robert Morris

Benjamin Rush

Benjamin Franklin

John Morton

George Clymer

James Smith

George Taylor

James Wilson

George Ross

Delaware

Caesar Rodney

George Read

Thomas McKean

Maryland

Samuel Chase

William Paca

Thomas Stone

Charles Carroll of Carrollton

Virginia

George Wythe

Richard Henry Lee

Thomas Jefferson

Benjamin Harrison

Thomas Nelson, Jr.

Francis Lightfoot Lee

Carter Braxton

North Carolina

William Hooper

Joseph Hewes

John Penn

South Carolina

Edward Rutledge

Thomas Heyward, Jr.

Thomas Lynch, Jr.

Arthur Middleton

Georgia

Button Gwinnett

Lyman Hall

George Walton

On July 4, 1776 Congress adopted the Declaration of Independence and ordered it to be printed.

On July 19, 1776 Congress ordered the Declaration of Independence to be officially inscribed and signed by members of Congress.

August 2, 1776 the Declaration of Independence was signed but not by every delegate. The following signed on a later date: *Elbridge Gerry, Oliver Wolcott, Lewis Morris, Thomas McKean, and Matthew Thornton.*

The Founders expressed their belief that our rights and freedoms come from the Creator of all things, God. These natural rights are given to us so that we can use free will to make our own life decisions and choices.

As Patrick Henry stated, *"The great pillars of all government and of social life [are] virtue, morality, and religion. This is the armor, my friend, and this alone, that renders us invincible."* **Patrick Henry letter to Archibald Blair on January 8, 1799**

Religious belief was not to govern this nation but our nation is built upon the principles of Christianity.

*"Well aware that the opinions and belief of men depend not on their own will, but follow involuntarily the evidence proposed to their minds; that **Almighty God** hath created the mind free, and manifested **His** supreme will that free it shall remain by making it altogether insusceptible of restraint; that all attempts to influence it by temporal punishments, or burthens, or by civil incapacitations, tend only to beget habits of hypocrisy and meanness, and are a departure from the plan of the **holy author** of our religion..."* **Thomas Jefferson, "A Bill for Establishing Religious Freedom", Section 1, June 18, 1779**

*"But let them [members of the parliament of Great Britain] not think to exclude us from going to other markets, to dispose of those commodities which they cannot use, nor to supply those wants which they cannot supply. Still less let it be proposed that our properties within our own territories shall be taxed or regulated by any power on earth but our own. The **God** who gave us*

life gave us liberty at the same time: the hand of force may destroy, but cannot disjoin them." **"A Summary View of the Rights of British America"**

"For in a warm climate, no man will labour for himself who can make another labour for him. This is so true, that of the proprietors of slaves a very small proportion indeed are ever seen to labor. And can the liberties of a nation be thought secure when we have removed their only firm basis, a conviction in the minds of the people that these liberties are the gift of **God**? *That they are not to be violated but with* **His** *wrath? Indeed I tremble for my country when I reflect that* **God** *is just: that his justice cannot sleep forever."* **Notes on the State of Virginia, Query XVIII**

"We hold these truths to be self-evident: that all men are created equal, that they are endowed by their **Creator** *with certain inalienable rights, among these are life, liberty, and the pursuit of happiness, that to secure these rights governments are instituted among men. We...solemnly publish and declare that these colonies are and of right ought to be free and independent states...And for the support of this declaration, with a firm reliance on the protection of* **divine providence**, *we mutually pledge our lives, our fortunes, and our sacred honor."* **The Declaration of Independence**

"The general Principles, on which the Fathers Achieved Independence, were the only Principles in which, that beautiful Assembly of young Gentlemen could Unite, and these Principles only could be intended by them in their Address, or by me in my Answer. And what were these general Principles? I answer, the general Principles of **Christianity**, *in which all those Sects were United: And the general Principles of English and American Liberty, in which all those young Men United, and which had United all Parties in America, in Majorities Sufficient to assert and maintain her Independence."*

"Now I will avow that I then believed, and now believe, that those general **Principles of Christianity** *are as eternal and immutable, as the* **Existence and Attributes of God**: *and that those Principles of Liberty, are as unalterable as human Nature and our terrestrial, mundane System."* **John Adams letter to Thomas Jefferson, June 28, 1813**

"God grant, that not only the Love of Liberty, but a thorough Knowledge of the Rights of Man, may pervade all the Nations of the Earth, so that a Philosopher may set his Foot anywhere on its Surface, and say, "This is my Country." **Benjamin Franklin letter to David Hartley, December 4, 1789**

United States Articles of Confederation

America's First Constitution

Adopted by Congress on November 15, 1777

To all to whom these Presents shall come, we the undersigned Delegates of the States affixed to our Names send greeting.

The Articles of Confederation and perpetual Union between the states of New Hampshire, Massachusetts-bay Rhode Island and Providence Plantations, Connecticut, New York, New Jersey, Pennsylvania, Delaware, Maryland, Virginia, North Carolina, South Carolina and Georgia.

Article I

The Stile of this Confederacy shall be "The United States of America".

Article II

Each state retains its sovereignty, freedom, and independence, and every power, jurisdiction, and right, which is not by this Confederation expressly delegated to the United States, in Congress assembled.

Article III

*The said States hereby severally enter into a firm league of friendship with each other, for their common defense, the security of their liberties, and their mutual and general welfare, binding themselves to assist each other, against all force offered to, or attacks made upon them, or any of them, **on account of religion**, sovereignty, trade, or any other pretense whatever.*

Article IV

The better to secure and perpetuate mutual friendship and intercourse among the people of the different States in this Union, the free inhabitants of each of these States, paupers, vagabonds, and fugitives from justice excepted, shall be entitled to all privileges and immunities of free citizens in the several States; and the people of each State shall free ingress and regress to and from any other State, and shall enjoy therein all the privileges of trade and commerce, subject to the same duties, impositions, and restrictions as the inhabitants thereof respectively, provided that such restrictions shall not extend so far as to prevent the removal of property imported into any State, to any other State, of which the owner is an inhabitant; provided also that no imposition, duties or restriction shall be laid by any State, on the property of the United States, or either of them.

If any person guilty of, or charged with, treason, felony, or other high misdemeanor in any State, shall flee from justice, and be found in any of the United States, he shall, upon demand of the Governor or executive power of the State from which he fled, be delivered up and removed to the State having jurisdiction of his offense.

Full faith and credit shall be given in each of these States to the records, acts, and judicial proceedings of the courts and magistrates of every other State.

Article V

For the most convenient management of the general interests of the United States, delegates shall be annually appointed in such manner as the legislatures of each State shall direct, to meet in Congress on the first Monday in November, in every year, with a power reserved to each State to recall its delegates, or any of them, at any time within the year, and to send others in their stead for the remainder of the year.

No State shall be represented in Congress by less than two, nor more than seven members; and no person shall be capable of being a delegate for more than three years in any term of six years; nor shall any person, being a delegate, be capable of holding any office under the United States, for which he, or another for his benefit, receives any salary, fees or emolument of any kind.

Each State shall maintain its own delegates in a meeting of the States, and while they act as members of the committee of the States.

In determining questions in the United States in Congress assembled, each State shall have one vote.

Freedom of speech and debate in Congress shall not be impeached or questioned in any court or place out of Congress, and the members of Congress shall be protected in their persons from arrests or imprisonments, during the time of their going to and from, and attendance on Congress, except for treason, felony, or breach of the peace.

Article VI

No State, without the consent of the United States in Congress assembled, shall send any embassy to, or receive any embassy from, or enter into any conference, agreement, alliance or treaty with any King, Prince or State; nor shall any person holding any office of profit or trust under the United States, or any of them, accept any present, emolument, office or title of any kind whatever from any King, Prince or foreign State; nor shall the United States in Congress assembled, or any of them, grant any title of nobility.

No two or more States shall enter into any treaty, confederation or alliance whatever between them, without the consent of the United States in Congress assembled, specifying accurately the purposes for which the same is to be entered into, and how long it shall continue.

No State shall lay any imposts or duties, which may interfere with any stipulations in treaties, entered into by the United States in Congress assembled, with any King, Prince or State, in pursuance of any treaties already proposed by Congress, to the courts of France and Spain.

No vessel of war shall be kept up in time of peace by any State, except such number only, as shall be deemed necessary by the United States in Congress assembled, for the defense of such State, or its trade; nor shall anybody of forces be kept up by any State in time of peace, except such number only, as in the judgement of the United States in Congress assembled, shall be deemed requisite to garrison the forts necessary for the defense of such State; but every State shall always keep up a well-regulated and disciplined militia, sufficiently armed and accoutered, and shall provide and constantly have ready for use, in public stores, a due number of filed pieces and tents, and a proper quantity of arms, ammunition and camp equipage.

No State shall engage in any war without the consent of the United States in Congress assembled, unless such State be actually invaded by enemies, or shall have received certain advice of a resolution being formed by some nation of Indians to invade such State, and the danger is so imminent as not to admit of a delay till the United States in Congress assembled can be consulted; nor shall any State grant commissions to any ships or vessels of war, nor letters of marque or reprisal, except it be after a declaration of war by the United States in Congress assembled, and then only against the Kingdom or State and the subjects thereof, against which war has been so declared, and under such regulations as shall be established by the United States in Congress assembled, unless such State be infested by pirates, in which case vessels of war may be fitted out for that occasion, and kept so long as the danger shall continue, or until the United States in Congress assembled shall determine otherwise.

Article VII

When land forces are raised by any State for the common defense, all officers of or under the rank of colonel, shall be appointed by the legislature of each State respectively, by whom such forces shall be raised, or in such manner as such State shall direct, and all vacancies shall be filled up by the State which first made the appointment.

Article VIII

All charges of war, and all other expenses that shall be incurred for the common defense or general welfare, and allowed by the United States in Congress assembled, shall be defrayed out of a common treasury, which shall be supplied by the several States in proportion to the value of all land within each State, granted or surveyed for any person, as such land and the buildings and improvements thereon shall be estimated according to such mode as the United States in Congress assembled, shall from time to time direct and appoint.

The taxes for paying that proportion shall be laid and levied by the authority and direction of the legislatures of the several States within the time agreed upon by the United States in Congress assembled.

Article IX

The United States in Congress assembled, shall have the sole and exclusive right and power of determining on peace and war, except in the cases mentioned in the sixth article – of sending and receiving ambassadors – entering into treaties and alliances, provided that no treaty of commerce shall be made whereby the legislative power of the respective States shall be restrained from imposing such imposts and duties on foreigners, as their own people are subjected to, or from prohibiting the exportation or importation of any species of goods or commodities whatsoever – of establishing rules for deciding in all cases, what captures on land or water shall be legal, and in what manner prizes taken by land or naval forces in the service of the United States shall be divided or appropriated – of granting letters of marque and reprisal in times of peace – appointing courts for the trial of piracies and felonies committed on the high seas and establishing courts for receiving and determining finally appeals in all cases of captures, provided that no member of Congress shall be appointed a judge of any of the said courts.

The United States in Congress assembled shall also be the last resort on appeal in all disputes and differences now subsisting or that hereafter may arise between two or more States concerning boundary, jurisdiction or any other causes whatever; which authority shall always be exercised in the manner following. Whenever the legislative or executive authority or lawful agent of any State in controversy with another shall present a petition to Congress stating the matter in question and praying for a hearing, notice thereof shall be given by order of Congress to the legislative or executive *authority of the other State in controversy, and a day assigned for the appearance of the parties by their lawful agents, who shall then be directed to appoint by joint consent, commissioners or judges to constitute a court for hearing and determining the matter in question: but if they cannot agree, Congress shall name three persons out of each of the United States, and from the list of such persons each party shall alternately strike out one, the petitioners beginning, until the number shall be reduced to thirteen; and from that number not less than seven, nor more than nine names as Congress shall direct, shall in the presence of Congress be drawn out by lot, and the persons whose names shall be so drawn or any five of them, shall be commissioners or judges, to hear and finally determine the controversy, so always as a major part of the judges who shall hear the cause shall agree in the determination: and if either party shall neglect to attend at the day appointed, without showing reasons, which Congress shall judge sufficient, or being present shall refuse to strike, the Congress shall proceed to nominate three persons out of each State, and the secretary of Congress shall strike in behalf of such party absent or refusing; and the judgement and sentence of the court to be appointed, in the manner before prescribed, shall be final and conclusive; and if any of the parties shall refuse to submit to the authority of such court, or to appear or defend their claim or cause, the court shall nevertheless proceed to pronounce sentence, or judgement, which shall in like manner be final and decisive, the judgement or sentence and other proceedings being in either case transmitted to Congress, and lodged among the acts of Congress for the security of the parties concerned: provided that every commissioner, before he sits in judgement, shall take an oath to be administered by one of the judges of the supreme or superior court of the State, where the cause shall be tried, 'well and truly to hear and determine the matter in question, according to the best of his judgement, without favor, affection or hope of reward': provided also, that no State shall be deprived of territory for the benefit of the United States.*

All controversies concerning the private right of soil claimed under different grants of two or more States, whose jurisdictions as they may respect such lands, and the States which passed such grants are adjusted, the said grants or either of them being at the same time claimed to have originated antecedent to such settlement of jurisdiction, shall on the petition of either party to the

Congress of the United States, be finally determined as near as may be in the same manner as is before prescribed for deciding disputes respecting territorial jurisdiction between different States.

The United States in Congress assembled shall also have the sole and exclusive right and power of regulating the alloy and value of coin struck by their own authority, or by that of the respective States – fixing the standards of weights and measures throughout the United States – regulating the trade and managing all affairs with the Indians, not members of any of the States, provided that the legislative right of any State within its own limits be not infringed or violated – establishing or regulating post offices from one State to another, throughout all the United States, and exacting such postage on the papers passing through the same as may be requisite to defray the expenses of the said office – appointing all officers of the land forces, in the service of the United States, excepting regimental officers – appointing all the officers of the naval forces, and commissioning all officers whatever in the service of the United States – making rules for the government and regulation of the said land and naval forces, and directing their operations.

The United States in Congress assembled shall have authority to appoint a committee, to sit in the recess of Congress, to be denominated 'A Committee of the States', and to consist of one delegate from each State; and to appoint such other committees and civil officers as may be necessary for managing the general affairs of the United States under their direction – to appoint one of their members to preside, provided that no person be allowed to serve in the office of president more than one year in any term of three years; to ascertain the necessary sums of money to be raised for the service of the United States, and to appropriate and apply the same for defraying the public expenses – to borrow money, or emit bills on the credit of the United States, transmitting every half-year to the respective States an account of the sums of money so borrowed or emitted – to build and equip a navy – to agree upon the number of land forces, and to make requisitions from each State for its quota, in proportion to the number of white inhabitants in such State; which requisition shall be binding, and thereupon the legislature of each State shall appoint the regimental officers, raise the men and cloath, arm and equip them in a solid-like manner, at the expense of the United States; and the officers and men so cloathed, armed and equipped shall march to the place appointed, and within the time agreed on by the United States in Congress assembled. But if the United States in Congress assembled shall, on consideration of circumstances judge proper that any State should not raise men, or should raise a smaller number of men than the quota thereof, such extra number shall be raised, officered, cloathed, armed and equipped in the same manner as the quota of each State, unless the legislature of such State shall judge that such extra number cannot be safely spread out in the same, in which case they shall raise, officer, cloath, arm and equip as many of such extra number as they judge can be safely spared. And the officers and men so cloathed, armed, and equipped, shall march to the place appointed, and within the time agreed on by the United States in Congress assembled.

The United States in Congress assembled shall never engage in a war, nor grant letters of marque or reprisal in time of peace, nor enter into any treaties or alliances, nor coin money, nor regulate the value thereof, nor ascertain the sums and expenses necessary for the defense and welfare of the United States, or any of them, nor emit bills, nor borrow money on the credit of the United States, nor appropriate money, nor agree upon the number of vessels of war, to be built or purchased, or the number of land or sea forces to be raised, nor appoint a commander in chief of the army or navy, unless nine States assent to the same: nor shall a question on any other point, except for adjourning from day to day be determined, unless by the votes of the majority of the United States in Congress assembled.

The Congress of the United States shall have power to adjourn to any time within the year, and to any place within the United States, so that no period of adjournment be for a longer duration than the space of six months, and shall publish the journal of their proceedings monthly, except such parts thereof relating to treaties, alliances or military operations, as in their judgement require secrecy; and the yeas and nays of the delegates of each State on any question shall be entered on the journal, when it is desired by any delegates of a State, or any of them, at his or their request shall be furnished with a transcript of the said journal, except such parts as are above excepted, to lay before the legislatures of the several States.

Article X

The Committee of the States, or any nine of them, shall be authorized to execute, in the recess of Congress, such of the powers of Congress as the United States in Congress assembled, by the consent of the nine States, shall from time to time think expedient to vest them with; provided that no power be delegated to the said Committee, for the exercise of which, by the Articles of Confederation, the voice of nine States in the Congress of the United States assembled be requisite.

Article XI

Canada acceding to this confederation, and adjoining in the measures of the United States, shall be admitted into, and entitled to all the advantages of this Union; but no other colony shall be admitted into the same, unless such admission be agreed to by nine States.

Article XII

All bills of credit emitted, monies borrowed, and debts contracted by, or under the authority of Congress, before the assembling of the United States, in pursuance of the present confederation, shall be deemed and considered as a charge against the United States, for payment and satisfaction whereof the said United States, and the public faith are hereby solemnly pledged.

Article XIII

Every State shall abide by the determination of the United States in Congress assembled, on all questions which by this confederation are submitted to them. And the Articles of this Confederation shall be inviolably observed by every State, and the Union shall be perpetual; nor shall any alteration at any time hereafter be made in any of them; unless such alteration be agreed to in a Congress of the United States, and be afterwards confirmed by the legislatures of every State.

*And Whereas it hath pleased the **Great Governor of the World** to incline the hearts of the legislatures we respectively represent in Congress, to approve of, and to authorize us to ratify the said Articles of Confederation and perpetual Union. Know Ye that we the undersigned delegates, by virtue of the power and authority to us given for that purpose, do by these presents, in the name and in behalf of our respective constituents, fully and entirely ratify and confirm each and every of the said Articles of Confederation and perpetual Union, and all and singular the matters and things therein contained: And we do further solemnly plight and engage the faith of our respective constituents, that they shall abide by the determinations of the United States in Congress assembled, on all questions, which by the said Confederation are submitted to them. And that the Articles thereof shall be inviolably observed by the States we respectively represent, and that the Union shall be perpetual.*

*In Witness whereof we have hereunto set our hands in Congress. Done at Philadelphia in the State of Pennsylvania the ninth day of July in the **Year of our Lord** One Thousand Seven Hundred and Seventy-Eight, and in the Third Year of the independence of America.*

Agreed to by Congress

15 November 1777

In force after ratification by Maryland, 1 March 1781

President of the Continental Congress (Signers of the Articles of Confederation) Henry Laurens

New Hampshire

Josiah Bartlett

John Wentworth Jr.

Massachusetts

John Hancock

Samuel Adams

Elbridge Gerry

Francis Dana

James Lovell

Samuel Holten

Rhode Island

William Ellery

Henry Marchant

John Collins

Connecticut

Roger Sherman

Samuel Huntington

Oliver Wolcott

Titus Hosmer

Andrew Adams

New York

James Duane

Francis Lewis

William Duer

Gouverneur Morris

New Jersey

John Witherspoon

Nathaniel Scudder

Pennsylvania

Robert Morris

Daniel Roberdeau

Jonathan Bayard Smith

William Clingan

Joseph Reed

Delaware

Thomas McKean

John Dickinson

Nicholas Van Dyke

Maryland

John Hanson

Daniel Carroll

Virginia

Richard Henry Lee

John Banister

Thomas Adams

John Harvie

Francis Lightfoot Lee

North Carolina

John Penn

Cornelius Harnett

John Williams

South Carolina

William Henry Drayton

John Mathews

Richard Hutson

Thomas Heyward Jr.

Georgia

John Walton

Edward Telfair

Edward Langworthy

The Definitive Treaty of Peace 1783

In the Name of the most Holy & undivided Trinity

*It having pleased the Divine Providence to dispose the Hearts of the most Serene and most Potent Prince George the Third, **by the Grace of God**, King of Great Britain, France, and Ireland, Defender of the Faith, Duke of Brunswick and Lunebourg, Arch- Treasurer and Prince Elector of the Holy Roman Empire etc.. and of the United States of America, to forget all past Misunderstandings and Differences that have unhappily interrupted the good Correspondence and Friendship which they mutually wish to restore; and to establish such a beneficial and satisfactory Intercourse between the two countries upon the ground of reciprocal Advantages and mutual Convenience as may promote and secure to both perpetual Peace and Harmony; and having for this desirable End already laid the Foundation of Peace & Reconciliation by the Provisional Articles signed at Paris on the 30th of November 1782, by the Commissioners empowered on each Part, which Articles were agreed to be inserted in and constitute the Treaty of Peace proposed to be concluded between the Crown of Great Britain and the said United States, but which Treaty was not to be concluded until Terms of Peace should be agreed upon between Great Britain & France, and his Britannic Majesty should be ready to conclude such Treaty accordingly: and the treaty between Great Britain & France having since been concluded, his Britannic Majesty & the United States of America, in Order to carry into full Effect the Provisional Articles above mentioned, according to the Tenor thereof, have constituted & appointed, that is to say his Britannic Majesty on his Part, David Hartley, Esqr., Member of the Parliament of Great Britain, and the said United States on their Part, - stop point - John Adams, Esqr., late a Commissioner of the United States of America at the Court of Versailles, late Delegate in Congress from the State of Massachusetts, and Chief Justice of the said State, and Minister Plenipotentiary of the said United States to their High Mightiness's the States General of the United Netherlands; - stop point - Benjamin*

Franklin, Esqr., late Delegate in Congress from the State of Pennsylvania, President of the Convention of the said State, and Minister Plenipotentiary from the United States of America at the Court of Versailles; John Jay, Esqr., late President of Congress and Chief Justice of the state of New York, and Minister Plenipotentiary from the said United States at the Court of Madrid; to be Plenipotentiaries for the concluding and signing the Present Definitive Treaty; who after having reciprocally communicated their respective full Powers have agreed upon and confirmed the following Articles.

Article 1st

His Britannic Majesty acknowledges the said United States, viz., New Hampshire, Massachusetts Bay, Rhode Island and Providence Plantations, Connecticut, New York, New Jersey, Pennsylvania, Delaware, Maryland, Virginia, North Carolina, South Carolina and Georgia, to be free sovereign and Independent States; that he treats with them as such, and for himself his Heirs & Successors, relinquishes all claims to the Government, Propriety, and Territorial Rights of the same and every Part thereof.

Article 2d

And that all Disputes which might arise in future on the subject of the Boundaries of the said United States may be prevented, it is hereby agreed and declared, that the following are and shall be their Boundaries, viz.; from the Northwest Angle of Nova Scotia, viz., that Angle which is formed by a Line drawn due North from the Source of St. Croix River to the Highlands; along the said Highlands which divide those Rivers that empty themselves into the river St. Lawrence, from those which fall into the Atlantic Ocean, to the northwestern-most Head of Connecticut River; Thence down along the middle of that River to the forty-fifth Degree of North Latitude; From thence by a Line due West on said Latitude until it strikes the River Iroquois or Cataraquy; Thence along the middle of said River into Lake Ontario; through the Middle of said Lake until it strikes the Communication by Water between that Lake & Lake Erie; Thence along the middle of said Communication into Lake Erie, through the middle of said Lake until it arrives at the Water Communication between that lake & Lake Huron; Thence along the middle of said Water Communication into the Lake Huron, thence through the middle of said Lake to the Water Communication between that Lake and Lake Superior; thence through Lake Superior Northward of the Isles Royal & Phelipeaux to the Long Lake; Thence through the middle of said Long Lake and the Water Communication between it & the Lake of the Woods, to the said Lake of the Woods; Thence through the said Lake to the most Northwestern Point thereof, and from thence on a due West Course to the river Mississippi; Thence by a Line to be drawn along the Middle of the said river Mississippi until it shall intersect the Northernmost Part of the thirty-first Degree of North Latitude, South, by a Line to be drawn due East from the Determination of the Line last mentioned in the Latitude of thirty-one Degrees of the Equator to the middle of the River Apalachicola or Catahouche; Thence along the middle thereof to its junction with the Flint River; Thence straight to the Head of Saint Mary's River, and thence down along the middle of Saint Mary's River to the Atlantic Ocean. East, by a Line to be drawn along the Middle of the river Saint Croix, from its Mouth in the Bay of Fundy to its Source, and from its Source directly North to the aforesaid Highlands, which divide the Rivers that fall into the Atlantic Ocean from those which fall into the river Saint Lawrence; comprehending all Islands within twenty Leagues of any Part of the Shores of the United States, and lying between Lines to be drawn due East from the Points where the aforesaid Boundaries between Nova Scotia on the one Part and East Florida on the other shall, respectively, touch the Bay of Fundy and the Atlantic Ocean, excepting such Islands as now are or heretofore have been within the limits of the said Province of Nova Scotia.

Article 3d

It is agreed that the People of the United States shall continue to enjoy unmolested the Right to take Fish of every kind on the Grand Bank and on all the other Banks of Newfoundland, also in the Gulf of Saint Lawrence and at all other Places in the Sea, where the Inhabitants of both Countries used at any time heretofore to fish. And also that the Inhabitants of the United States shall have Liberty to take Fish of every Kind on such Part of the Coast of Newfoundland as British Fishermen shall use, (but not to dry or cure the same on that Island) And also on the Coasts, Bays & Creeks of all other of his Britannic Majesty's Dominions in America; and that the American Fishermen shall have Liberty to dry and cure Fish in any of the unsettled Bays, Harbors, and Creeks of Nova Scotia, Magdalen Islands, and Labrador, so long as the same shall remain unsettled, but so soon as the same or either of them shall be settled, it shall not be lawful for the said Fishermen to dry or cure Fish at such Settlement without a previous Agreement for that purpose with the Inhabitants, Proprietors, or Possessors of the Ground.

Article 4th

It is agreed that Creditors on either Side shall meet with no lawful Impediment to the Recovery of the full Value in Sterling Money of all bona fide Debts heretofore contracted.

Article 5th

It is agreed that Congress shall earnestly recommend it to the Legislatures of the respective States to provide for the Restitution of all Estates, Rights, and Properties, which have been confiscated belonging to real British Subjects; and also of the Estates, Rights, and Properties of Persons resident in Districts in the Possession on his Majesty's Arms and who have not borne Arms against the said United States. And that Persons of any other Description shall have free Liberty to go to any Part or Parts of any of the thirteen United States and therein to remain twelve Months unmolested in their Endeavors to obtain the Restitution of such of their Estates – Rights & Properties as may have been confiscated. And that Congress shall also earnestly recommend to the several States a Reconsideration and Revision of all Acts or Laws regarding the Premises, so as to render the said Laws or Acts perfectly consistent not only with Justice and Equity but with that Spirit of Conciliation which on the Return of the Blessings of Peace should universally prevail. And that Congress shall also earnestly recommend to the several States that the Estates, Rights, and Properties of such last mentioned Persons shall be restored to them, they refunding to any Persons who may be now in Possession the Bona fide Price (where any has been given) which such Persons may have paid on purchasing any of the said Lands, Rights, or Properties since the Confiscation.

And it is agreed that all Persons who have any Interest in confiscated Lands, either by Debts, Marriage Settlements, or otherwise, shall meet with no lawful Impediment in the Prosecution of their just Rights.

Article 6th

That there shall be no future Confiscations made nor any Prosecutions commenced against any Person or Persons for, or by Reason of the Part, which he or they may have taken in the present War, and that no Person shall on that Account suffer any future Loss or Damage, either in his Person, Liberty, or Property; and that those who may be in Confinement on such Charges at the Time of the Ratification of the Treaty in America shall be immediately set at Liberty, and the Prosecutions so commenced be discontinued.

Article 7th

There shall be a firm and perpetual Peace between his Britannic Majesty and the said States, and between the Subjects of the one and the Citizens of the other, wherefore all Hostilities both by Sea and Land shall from henceforth cease: All prisoners on both Sides shall be set at Liberty, and his Britannic Majesty shall with all convenient speed, and without causing any Destruction, or carrying away any Negroes or other Property of the American inhabitants, withdraw all his Armies, Garrisons & Fleets from the said United States, and from every Post, Place and Harbour within the same; leaving in all Fortifications, the American Artillery that may be therein: And shall also Order & cause all Archives, Records, Deeds & Papers belonging to any of the said States, or their Citizens, which in the Course of the War may have fallen into the hands of his Officers, to be forthwith restored and delivered to the proper States and Persons to whom they belong.

Article 8th

The Navigation of the river Mississippi, from its source to the Ocean, shall forever remain free and open to the Subjects of Great Britain and the Citizens of the United States.

Article 9th

In case it should so happen that any Place or Territory belonging to great Britain or to the United States should have been conquered by the Arms of either from the other before the Arrival of the said Provisional Articles in America, it is agreed that the same shall be restored without Difficulty and without requiring any Compensation.

Article 10th

The solemn Ratifications of the present Treaty expedited in good & due Form shall be exchanged between the contracting Parties in the Space of Six Months or sooner if possible to be computed from the Day of the Signature of the present Treaty. In witness whereof we the undersigned their Ministers Plenipotentiary have in their Name and in Virtue of our Full Powers, signed with our Hands the present Definitive Treaty, and caused the Seals of our Arms to be affixed thereto.

Done at Paris, this third day of September, **in the year of our Lord,** one thousand seven hundred and eighty-three.

D HARTLEY

JOHN ADAMS

B FRANKLIN

JOHN JAY

The Constitution of the United States of America

Preamble

We the People of the United States, in Order to form a more perfect Union, establish Justice, insure domestic Tranquility, provide for the common defence, promote the general Welfare, and secure the Blessings of Liberty to ourselves and our Posterity, do ordain and establish this Constitution for the United States of America.

Article I

Section 1

All legislative Powers herein granted shall be vested in a Congress of the United States, which shall consist of a Senate and House of Representatives.

Section 2

The House of Representatives shall be composed of Members chosen every second Year by the People of the several States, and the Electors in each State shall have the Qualifications requisite for Electors of the most numerous Branch of the State Legislature.

No Person shall be a Representative who shall not have attained to the Age of twenty five Years, and been seven Years a Citizen of the United States, and who shall not, when elected, be an Inhabitant of that State in which he shall be chosen.

Representatives and direct Taxes shall be apportioned among the several States which may be included within this Union, according to their respective Numbers, which shall be determined by adding to the whole Number of free Persons, including those bound to Service for a Term of Years, and excluding Indians not taxed, three fifths of all other Persons. The actual Enumeration shall be made within three Years after the first Meeting of the Congress of the

United States, and within every subsequent Term of ten Years, in such Manner as they shall by Law direct. The Number of Representatives shall not exceed one for every thirty Thousand, but each State shall have at Least one Representative; and until such enumeration shall be made, the State of New Hampshire shall be entitled to choose three, Massachusetts eight, Rhode-Island and Providence Plantations one, Connecticut five, New-York six, New Jersey four, Pennsylvania eight, Delaware one, Maryland six, Virginia ten, North Carolina five, South Carolina five, and Georgia three.

When vacancies happen in the Representation from any State, the Executive Authority thereof shall issue Writs of Election to fill such Vacancies.

The House of Representatives shall choose their Speaker and other Officers; and shall have the sole Power of Impeachment.

Section 3

The Senate of the United States shall be composed of two Senators from each State, chosen by the Legislature thereof, for six Years; and each Senator shall have one Vote.

Immediately after they shall be assembled in Consequence of the first Election, they shall be divided as equally as may be into three Classes. The Seats of the Senators of the first Class shall be vacated at the Expiration of the second Year, of the second Class at the Expiration of the fourth Year, and of the third Class at the Expiration of the sixth Year, so that one third may be chosen every second Year; and if Vacancies happen by Resignation, or otherwise, during the Recess of the Legislature of any State, the Executive thereof may make temporary Appointments until the next Meeting of the Legislature, which shall then fill such Vacancies.

No Person shall be a Senator who shall not have attained to the Age of thirty Years, and been nine Years a Citizen of the United States, and who shall not, when elected, be an Inhabitant of that State for which he shall be chosen.

The Vice President of the United States shall be President of the Senate, but shall have no Vote, unless they be equally divided.

The Senate shall choose their other Officers, and also a President pro tempore, in the Absence of the Vice President, or when he shall exercise the Office of President of the United States.

The Senate shall have the sole Power to try all Impeachments. When sitting for that Purpose, they shall be on Oath or Affirmation. When the President of the United States is tried, the Chief Justice shall preside: And no Person shall be convicted without the Concurrence of two thirds of the Members present.

Judgment in Cases of Impeachment shall not extend further than to removal from Office, and disqualification to hold and enjoy any Office of honor, Trust or Profit under the United States: but the Party convicted shall nevertheless be liable and subject to Indictment, Trial, Judgment and Punishment, according to Law.

Section 4

The Times, Places and Manner of holding Elections for Senators and Representatives, shall be prescribed in each State by the Legislature thereof; but the Congress may at any time by Law make or alter such Regulations, except as to the Places of choosing Senators.

The Congress shall assemble at least once in every Year, and such Meeting shall be on the first Monday in December, unless they shall by Law appoint a different Day.

Section 5

Each House shall be the Judge of the Elections, Returns and Qualifications of its own Members, and a Majority of each shall constitute a Quorum to do Business; but a smaller Number may adjourn from day to day, and may be authorized to compel the Attendance of absent Members, in such Manner, and under such Penalties as each House may provide.

Each House may determine the Rules of its Proceedings, punish its Members for disorderly Behaviour, and, with the Concurrence of two thirds, expel a Member.

Each House shall keep a Journal of its Proceedings, and from time to time publish the same, excepting such Parts as may in their Judgment require Secrecy; and the Yeas and Nays of the Members of either House on any question shall, at the Desire of one fifth of those Present, be entered on the Journal.

Neither House, during the Session of Congress, shall, without the Consent of the other, adjourn for more than three days, nor to any other Place than that in which the two Houses shall be sitting.

Section 6

The Senators and Representatives shall receive a Compensation for their Services, to be ascertained by Law, and paid out of the Treasury of the United States. They shall in all Cases, except Treason, Felony and Breach of the Peace, be privileged from Arrest during their Attendance at the Session of their respective Houses, and in going to and returning from the same; and for any Speech or Debate in either House, they shall not be questioned in any other Place.

No Senator or Representative shall, during the Time for which he was elected, be appointed to any civil Office under the Authority of the United States, which shall have been created, or the Emoluments whereof shall have been increased during such time; and no Person holding any Office under the United States, shall be a Member of either House during his Continuance in Office.

Section 7

All Bills for raising Revenue shall originate in the House of Representatives; but the Senate may propose or concur with Amendments as on other Bills.

Every Bill which shall have passed the House of Representatives and the Senate, shall, before it become a Law, be presented to the President of the United States; If he approve he shall sign it, but if not he shall return it, with his Objections to that House in which it shall have originated, who shall enter the Objections at large on their Journal, and proceed to reconsider it. If after such Reconsideration two thirds of that House shall agree to pass the Bill, it shall be sent, together with the Objections, to the other House, by which it shall likewise be reconsidered, and if approved by two thirds of that House, it shall become a Law. But in all such Cases the Votes of both Houses shall be determined by yeas and Nays, and the Names of the Persons voting for and against the Bill shall be entered on the Journal of each House respectively. If any Bill shall not be returned by the President within ten Days (Sundays excepted) after it shall have been presented to him, the Same shall be a Law, in like Manner as if he had signed it, unless the Congress by their Adjournment prevent its Return, in which Case it shall not be a Law.

Every Order, Resolution, or Vote to which the Concurrence of the Senate and House of Representatives may be necessary (except on a question of Adjournment) shall be presented to the President of the United States; and before the Same shall take Effect, shall be approved by him, or being disapproved by him, shall be repassed by two thirds of the Senate and House of Representatives, according to the Rules and Limitations prescribed in the Case of a Bill.

Section 8

The Congress shall have Power To lay and collect Taxes, Duties, Imposts and Excises, to pay the Debts and provide for the common Defence and general Welfare of the United States; but all Duties, Imposts and Excises shall be uniform throughout the United States;

To borrow Money on the credit of the United States;

To regulate Commerce with foreign Nations, and among the several States, and with the Indian Tribes;

To establish an uniform Rule of Naturalization, and uniform Laws on the subject of Bankruptcies throughout the United States;

To coin Money, regulate the Value thereof, and of foreign Coin, and fix the Standard of Weights and Measures;

To provide for the Punishment of counterfeiting the Securities and current Coin of the United States;

To establish Post Offices and post Roads;

To promote the Progress of Science and useful Arts, by securing for limited Times to Authors and Inventors the exclusive Right to their respective Writings and Discoveries;

To constitute Tribunals inferior to the Supreme Court;

To define and punish Piracies and Felonies committed on the high Seas, and Offences against the Law of Nations;

To declare War, grant Letters of Marque and Reprisal, and make Rules concerning Captures on Land and Water;

To raise and support Armies, but no Appropriation of Money to that Use shall be for a longer Term than two Years;

To provide and maintain a Navy;

To make Rules for the Government and Regulation of the land and naval Forces;

To provide for calling forth the Militia to execute the Laws of the Union, suppress Insurrections and repel Invasions;

To provide for organizing, arming, and disciplining, the Militia, and for governing such Part of them as may be employed in the Service of the United States, reserving to the States respectively, the Appointment of the Officers, and the Authority of training the Militia according to the discipline prescribed by Congress;

To exercise exclusive Legislation in all Cases whatsoever, over such District (not exceeding ten Miles square) as may, by Cession of particular States, and the Acceptance of Congress, become the Seat of the Government of the United States, and to exercise like Authority over all Places purchased by the Consent of the Legislature of the State in which the Same shall be, for the Erection of Forts, Magazines, Arsenals, dock-Yards, and other needful Buildings; – And

To make all Laws which shall be necessary and proper for carrying into Execution the foregoing Powers, and all other Powers vested by this Constitution in the Government of the United States, or in any Department or Officer thereof.

Section 9

The Migration or Importation of such Persons as any of the States now existing shall think proper to admit, shall not be prohibited by the Congress prior to the Year one thousand eight hundred and eight, but a Tax or duty may be imposed on such Importation, not exceeding ten dollars for each Person.

The Privilege of the Writ of Habeas Corpus shall not be suspended, unless when in Cases of Rebellion or Invasion the public Safety may require it.

No Bill of Attainder or ex post facto Law shall be passed.

No Capitation, or other direct, Tax shall be laid, unless in Proportion to the Census or enumeration herein before directed to be taken.

No Tax or Duty shall be laid on Articles exported from any State.

No Preference shall be given by any Regulation of Commerce or Revenue to the Ports of one State over those of another: nor shall Vessels bound to, or from, one State, be obliged to enter, clear, or pay Duties in another.

No Money shall be drawn from the Treasury, but in Consequence of Appropriations made by Law; and a regular Statement and Account of the Receipts and Expenditures of all public Money shall be published from time to time.

No Title of Nobility shall be granted by the United States: And no Person holding any Office of Profit or Trust under them, shall, without the Consent of the Congress, accept of any present, Emolument, Office, or Title, of any kind whatever, from any King, Prince, or foreign State.

Section 10

No State shall enter into any Treaty, Alliance, or Confederation; grant Letters of Marque and Reprisal; coin Money; emit Bills of Credit; make any Thing but gold and silver Coin a Tender in Payment of Debts; pass any Bill of Attainder, ex post facto Law, or Law impairing the Obligation of Contracts, or grant any Title of Nobility.

No State shall, without the Consent of the Congress, lay any Imposts or Duties on Imports or Exports, except what may be absolutely necessary for executing it's inspection Laws: and the net Produce of all Duties and Imposts, laid by any State on Imports or Exports, shall be for the Use of the Treasury of the United States; and all such Laws shall be subject to the Revision and Control of the Congress.

No State shall, without the Consent of Congress, lay any Duty of Tonnage, keep Troops, or Ships of War in time of Peace, enter into any Agreement or Compact with another State, or with a foreign Power, or engage in War, unless actually invaded, or in such imminent Danger as will not admit of delay.

Article II

Section 1

The executive Power shall be vested in a President of the United States of America. He shall hold his Office during the Term of four Years, and, together with the Vice President, chosen for the same Term, be elected, as follows

Each State shall appoint, in such Manner as the Legislature thereof may direct, a Number of Electors, equal to the whole Number of Senators and Representatives to which the State may be entitled in the Congress: but no Senator or Representative, or Person holding an Office of Trust or Profit under the United States, shall be appointed an Elector.

The Electors shall meet in their respective States, and vote by Ballot for two Persons, of whom one at least shall not be an Inhabitant of the same State with themselves. And they shall make a List of all the Persons voted for, and of the Number of Votes for each; which List they shall sign and certify, and transmit sealed to the Seat of the Government of the United States, directed to the President of the Senate. The President of the Senate shall, in the Presence of the Senate and House of Representatives, open all the Certificates, and the Votes shall then be counted. The Person having the greatest Number of Votes shall be the President, if such Number be a Majority of the whole Number of Electors appointed; and if there be more than one who have such Majority, and have an equal Number of Votes, then the House of Representatives shall immediately choose by Ballot one of them for President; and if no Person have a Majority, then from the five highest on the List the said House shall in like Manner choose the President. But in choosing the President, the Votes shall be taken by States, the Representation from each State having one Vote; A quorum for this Purpose shall consist of a Member or Members from two thirds of the States, and a Majority of all the States shall be necessary to a Choice. In every Case, after the Choice of the President, the Person having the greatest Number of Votes of the Electors shall be the Vice President. But if there should remain two or more who have equal Votes, the Senate shall choose from them by Ballot the Vice President.

The Congress may determine the Time of choosing the Electors, and the Day on which they shall give their Votes; which Day shall be the same throughout the United States.

No Person except a natural born Citizen, or a Citizen of the United States, at the time of the Adoption of this Constitution, shall be eligible to the Office of President; neither shall any Person be eligible to that Office who shall not have attained to the Age of thirty five Years, and been fourteen Years a Resident within the United States.

In Case of the Removal of the President from Office, or of his Death, Resignation, or Inability to discharge the Powers and Duties of the said Office, the Same shall devolve on the Vice President, and the Congress may by Law provide for the Case of Removal, Death, Resignation or Inability, both of the President and Vice President, declaring what Officer shall then act as President, and such Officer shall act accordingly, until the Disability be removed, or a President shall be elected.

The President shall, at stated Times, receive for his Services, a Compensation, which shall neither be increased nor diminished during the Period for which he shall have been elected, and he shall not receive within that Period any other Emolument from the United States, or any of them.

Before he enter on the Execution of his Office, he shall take the following Oath or Affirmation: – "I do solemnly swear (or affirm) that I will faithfully execute the Office of President of the United States, and will to the best of my Ability, preserve, protect and defend the Constitution of the United States."

Section 2

The President shall be Commander in Chief of the Army and Navy of the United States, and of the Militia of the several States, when called into the actual Service of the United States; he may require the Opinion, in writing, of the principal Officer in each of the executive Departments, upon any Subject relating to the Duties of their respective Offices, and he shall have Power to grant Reprieves and Pardons for Offences against the United States, except in Cases of Impeachment.

He shall have Power, by and with the Advice and Consent of the Senate, to make Treaties, provided two thirds of the Senators present concur; and he shall nominate, and by and with the Advice and Consent of the Senate, shall appoint Ambassadors, other public Ministers and Consuls, Judges of the supreme Court, and all other Officers of the United States, whose Appointments are not herein otherwise provided for, and which shall be established by Law: but the Congress may by Law vest the Appointment of such inferior Officers, as they think proper, in the President alone, in the Courts of Law, or in the Heads of Departments.

The President shall have Power to fill up all Vacancies that may happen during the Recess of the Senate, by granting Commissions which shall expire at the End of their next Session.

Section 3

He shall from time to time give to the Congress Information of the State of the Union, and recommend to their Consideration such Measures as he shall judge necessary and expedient; he may, on extraordinary Occasions, convene both Houses, or either of them, and in Case of Disagreement between them, with Respect to the Time of Adjournment, he may adjourn them to such Time as he shall think proper; he shall receive Ambassadors and other public Ministers; he shall take Care that the Laws be faithfully executed, and shall Commission all the Officers of the United States.

Section 4

The President, Vice President and all civil Officers of the United States, shall be removed from Office on Impeachment for, and Conviction of, Treason, Bribery, or other high Crimes and Misdemeanors.

Article III

Section 1

The judicial Power of the United States shall be vested in one Supreme Court and in such inferior Courts as the Congress may from time to time ordain and establish. The Judges, both of the supreme and inferior Courts, shall hold their Offices during good Behaviour, and shall, at stated Times, receive for their Services, a Compensation, which shall not be diminished during their Continuance in Office.

Section 2

The judicial Power shall extend to all Cases, in Law and Equity, arising under this Constitution, the Laws of the United States, and Treaties made, or which shall be made, under their Authority; – to all Cases affecting Ambassadors, other public Ministers and Consuls; – to all Cases of admiralty and maritime Jurisdiction; – to Controversies to which the United States shall be a Party; – to Controversies between two or more States; – between a State and Citizens of another State, – between Citizens of different States, – between Citizens of the same State claiming Lands under Grants of different States, and between a State, or the Citizens thereof, and foreign States, Citizens or Subjects.

In all Cases affecting Ambassadors, other public Ministers and Consuls, and those in which a State shall be Party, the supreme Court shall have original Jurisdiction. In all the other Cases before mentioned, the supreme Court shall have appellate Jurisdiction, both as to Law and Fact, with such Exceptions, and under such Regulations as the Congress shall make.

The Trial of all Crimes, except in Cases of Impeachment, shall be by Jury; and such Trial shall be held in the State where the said Crimes shall have been committed; but when not committed within any State, the Trial shall be at such Place or Places as the Congress may by Law have directed.

Section 3

Treason against the United States shall consist only in levying War against them, or in adhering to their Enemies, giving them Aid and Comfort. No Person shall be convicted of Treason unless on the Testimony of two Witnesses to the same overt Act, or on Confession in open Court.

The Congress shall have Power to declare the Punishment of Treason, but no Attainder of Treason shall work Corruption of Blood, or Forfeiture except during the Life of the Person attainted.

Article IV

Section 1

Full Faith and Credit shall be given in each State to the public Acts, Records, and judicial Proceedings of every other State. And the Congress may by general Laws prescribe the Manner in which such Acts, Records and Proceedings shall be proved, and the Effect thereof.

Section 2

The Citizens of each State shall be entitled to all Privileges and Immunities of Citizens in the several States.

A Person charged in any State with Treason, Felony, or other Crime, who shall flee from Justice, and be found in another State, shall on Demand of the executive Authority of the State from which he fled, be delivered up, to be removed to the State having Jurisdiction of the Crime.

No Person held to Service or Labour in one State, under the Laws thereof, escaping into another, shall, in Consequence of any Law or Regulation therein, be discharged from such Service or Labour, but shall be delivered up on Claim of the Party to whom such Service or Labour may be due.

Section 3

New States may be admitted by the Congress into this Union; but no new State shall be formed or erected within the Jurisdiction of any other State; nor any State be formed by the Junction of two or more States, or Parts of States, without the Consent of the Legislatures of the States concerned as well as of the Congress.

The Congress shall have Power to dispose of and make all needful Rules and Regulations respecting the Territory or other Property belonging to the United States; and nothing in this Constitution shall be so construed as to Prejudice any Claims of the United States, or of any particular State.

Section 4

The United States shall guarantee to every State in this Union a Republican Form of Government, and shall protect each of them against Invasion; and on Application of the Legislature, or of the Executive (when the Legislature cannot be convened), against domestic Violence.

Article V

The Congress, whenever two thirds of both Houses shall deem it necessary, shall propose Amendments to this Constitution, or, on the Application of the Legislatures of two thirds of the several States, shall call a Convention for proposing Amendments, which, in either Case, shall be valid to all Intents and Purposes, as Part of this Constitution, when ratified by the Legislatures of three fourths of the several States, or by Conventions in three fourths thereof, as the one or the other Mode of Ratification may be proposed by the Congress; Provided that no Amendment which may be made prior to the Year One thousand eight hundred and eight shall in any Manner affect the first and fourth Clauses in the Ninth Section of the first Article; and that no State, without its Consent, shall be deprived of its equal Suffrage in the Senate.

Article VI

All Debts contracted and Engagements entered into, before the Adoption of this Constitution, shall be as valid against the United States under this Constitution, as under the Confederation.

This Constitution, and the Laws of the United States which shall be made in Pursuance thereof; and all Treaties made, or which shall be made, under the Authority of the United States, shall be the supreme Law of the Land; and the Judges in every State shall be bound thereby, any Thing in the Constitution or Laws of any State to the Contrary notwithstanding.

The Senators and Representatives before mentioned, and the Members of the several State Legislatures, and all executive and judicial Officers, both of the United States and of the several States, shall be bound by Oath or Affirmation, to support this Constitution; but no religious Test shall ever be required as a Qualification to any Office or public Trust under the United States.

Article VII

The Ratification of the Conventions of nine States, shall be sufficient for the Establishment of this Constitution between the States so ratifying the Same.

The Word, "the," being interlined between the seventh and eighth Lines of the first Page, The Word "Thirty" being partly written on an Erazure in the fifteenth Line of the first Page, The Words "is tried" being interlined between the thirty second and thirty third Lines of the first Page and the Word "the" being interlined between the forty third and forty fourth Lines of the second Page.

Attest William Jackson Secretary

done in Convention by the Unanimous Consent of the States present the Seventeenth Day of September in the **Year of our Lord** *one thousand seven hundred and Eighty seven and of the Independence of the United States of America the Twelfth In witness whereof We have hereunto subscribed our Names,*

G°. Washington

Presidt and deputy from Virginia

New Hampshire

John Langdon

Nicholas Gilman

Massachusetts

Nathaniel Gorham

Rufus King

Connecticut

Wm: Saml. Johnson

Roger Sherman

New York

Alexander Hamilton

New Jersey

Wil: Livingston

David Brearly

Wm. Paterson

Jonathan Dayton

Pennsylvania

B. Franklin

Thomas Mifflin

Robt. Morris

Geo. Clymer

Thos. FitzSimons

Jared Ingersoll

James Wilson

Gouv Morris

Delaware

George Read

Gunning Bedford Jr.

John Dickinson

Richard Bassett

Jacob Broom

Maryland

James McHenry

Dan of St Thos. Jenifer

Daniel Carroll

Virginia

John Blair

James Madison Jr.

North Carolina

Wm. Blount

Richard Dobbs Spaight

Hu Williamson

South Carolina

J. Rutledge

Charles Cotesworth Pinckney

Charles Pinckney

Pierce Butler

Georgia

William Few

Abr. Baldwin

Amendments to the US Constitution

AMENDMENT I

Congress shall make no law respecting an establishment of religion, or prohibiting the free exercise thereof; or abridging the freedom of speech, or of the press; or the right of the people peaceably to assemble, and to petition the Government for a redress of grievances.

AMENDMENT II

A well-regulated Militia, being necessary to the security of a free State, the right of the people to keep and bear Arms, shall not be infringed.

AMENDMENT III

No Soldier shall, in time of peace be quartered in any house, without the consent of the Owner, nor in time of war, but in a manner to be prescribed by law.

AMENDMENT IV

The right of the people to be secure in their persons, houses, papers, and effects, against unreasonable searches and seizures, shall not be violated, and no Warrants shall issue, but upon probable cause, supported by Oath or affirmation, and particularly describing the place to be searched, and the persons or things to be seized.

AMENDMENT V

No person shall be held to answer for a capital, or otherwise infamous crime, unless on a presentment or indictment of a Grand Jury, except in cases arising in the land or naval forces, or in the Militia, when in actual service in time of War or public danger; nor shall any person be subject for the same offence to be twice put in jeopardy of life or limb; nor shall be compelled in any criminal case to be a witness against himself, nor be deprived of life, liberty, or property, without due process of law; nor shall private property be taken for public use, without just compensation.

AMENDMENT VI

In all criminal prosecutions, the accused shall enjoy the right to a speedy and public trial, by an impartial jury of the State and district wherein the crime shall have been committed, which district shall have been previously ascertained by law, and to be informed of the nature and cause of the accusation; to be confronted with the witnesses against him; to have compulsory process for obtaining witnesses in his favor, and to have the Assistance of Counsel for his defence.

AMENDMENT VII

In Suits at common law, where the value in controversy shall exceed twenty dollars, the right of trial by jury shall be preserved, and no fact tried by a jury, shall be otherwise re-examined in any Court of the United States, than according to the rules of the common law.

AMENDMENT VIII

Excessive bail shall not be required, nor excessive fines imposed, nor cruel and unusual punishments inflicted.

AMENDMENT IX

The enumeration in the Constitution, of certain rights, shall not be construed to deny or disparage others retained by the people.

AMENDMENT X

The powers not delegated to the United States by the Constitution, nor prohibited by it to the States, are reserved to the States respectively, or to the people.

AMENDMENT XI

Passed by Congress March 4, 1794

Ratified February 7, 1795

The Judicial power of the United States shall not be construed to extend to any suit in law or equity, commenced or prosecuted against one of the United States by Citizens of another State, or by Citizens or Subjects of any Foreign State.

AMENDMENT XII

Passed by Congress December 9, 1803

Ratified June 15, 1804

The Electors shall meet in their respective states and vote by ballot for President and Vice-President, one of whom, at least, shall not be an inhabitant of the same state with themselves; they shall name in their ballots the person voted for as President, and in distinct ballots the person voted for as Vice-President, and they shall make distinct lists of all persons voted for as President, and of all persons voted for as Vice-President, and of the number of votes for each, which lists they shall sign and certify, and transmit sealed to the seat of the government of the United States, directed to the President of the Senate; -- the President of the Senate shall, in the presence of the Senate and House of Representatives, open all the certificates and the votes shall then be counted; -- The person having the greatest number of votes for President, shall be the President, if such number be a majority of the whole number of Electors appointed; and if no person have such majority, then from the persons having the highest numbers not exceeding three on the list of those voted for as President, the House of Representatives shall choose immediately, by ballot, the President. But in choosing the President, the votes shall be taken by states, the representation from each state having one vote; a quorum for this purpose shall consist of a member or members from two-thirds of the states, and a majority of all the states shall be necessary to a choice. [And if the House of Representatives shall not choose a President whenever the right of choice shall devolve upon them, before the fourth day of March next following, then the Vice-President shall act as President, as in case of the death or other constitutional disability of the President.*

The person having the greatest number of votes as Vice-President, shall be the Vice-President, if such number be a majority of the whole number of Electors appointed, and if no person have a majority, then from the two highest numbers on the list, the Senate shall choose the Vice-President; a quorum for the purpose shall consist of two-thirds of the whole number of Senators, and a majority of the whole number shall be necessary to a choice. But no person constitutionally ineligible to the office of President shall be eligible to that of Vice-President of the United States.

AMENDMENT XIII

Passed by Congress January 31, 1865

Ratified December 6, 1865

Section 1
Neither slavery nor involuntary servitude, except as a punishment for crime whereof the party shall have been duly convicted, shall exist within the United States, or any place subject to their jurisdiction.

Section 2
Congress shall have power to enforce this article by appropriate legislation.

AMENDMENT XIV

Passed by Congress June 13, 1866

Ratified July 9, 1868

Section 1
All persons born or naturalized in the United States, and subject to the jurisdiction thereof, are citizens of the United States and of the State wherein they reside. No State shall make or enforce any law which shall abridge the privileges or immunities of citizens of the United States; nor shall any State deprive any person of life, liberty, or property, without due process of law; nor deny to any person within its jurisdiction the equal protection of the laws.

Section 2

Representatives shall be apportioned among the several States according to their respective numbers, counting the whole number of persons in each State, excluding Indians not taxed. But when the right to vote at any election for the choice of electors for President and Vice-President of the United States, Representatives in Congress, the Executive and Judicial officers of a State, or the members of the Legislature thereof, is denied to any of the male inhabitants of such State, being twenty-one years of age,* and citizens of the United States, or in any way abridged, except for participation in rebellion, or other crime, the basis of representation therein shall be reduced in the proportion which the number of such male citizens shall bear to the whole number of male citizens twenty-one years of age in such State.

Section 3

No person shall be a Senator or Representative in Congress, or elector of President and Vice-President, or hold any office, civil or military, under the United States, or under any State, who, having previously taken an oath, as a member of Congress, or as an officer of the United States, or as a member of any State legislature, or as an executive or judicial officer of any State, to support the Constitution of the United States, shall have engaged in insurrection or rebellion against the same, or given aid or comfort to the enemies thereof. But Congress may by a vote of two-thirds of each House, remove such disability.

Section 4

The validity of the public debt of the United States, authorized by law, including debts incurred for payment of pensions and bounties for services in suppressing insurrection or rebellion, shall not be questioned. But neither the United States nor any State shall assume or pay any debt or obligation incurred in aid of insurrection or rebellion against the United States, or any claim for the loss or emancipation of any slave; but all such debts, obligations and claims shall be held illegal and void.

Section 5

The Congress shall have the power to enforce, by appropriate legislation, the provisions of this article.

AMENDMENT XV

Passed by Congress February 26, 1869

Ratified February 3, 1870

Section 1
The right of citizens of the United States to vote shall not be denied or abridged by the United States or by any State on account of race, color, or previous condition of servitude.

Section 2
The Congress shall have the power to enforce this article by appropriate legislation.

AMENDMENT XVI

Passed by Congress July 2, 1909

Ratified February 3, 1913

The Congress shall have power to lay and collect taxes on incomes, from whatever source derived, without apportionment among the several States, and without regard to any census or enumeration.

AMENDMENT XVII

Passed by Congress May 13, 1912

Ratified April 8, 1913

The Senate of the United States shall be composed of two Senators from each State, elected by the people thereof, for six years; and each Senator shall have one vote. The electors in each State shall have the qualifications requisite for electors of the most numerous branch of the State legislatures.

When vacancies happen in the representation of any State in the Senate, the executive authority of such State shall issue writs of election to fill such vacancies: Provided, That the legislature of any State may empower the executive thereof to make temporary appointments until the people fill the vacancies by election as the legislature may direct.

This amendment shall not be so construed as to affect the election or term of any Senator chosen before it becomes valid as part of the Constitution.

AMENDMENT XVIII

Passed by Congress December 18, 1917

Ratified January 16, 1919

Repealed by the 21st Amendment

Section 1
After one year from the ratification of this article the manufacture, sale, or transportation of intoxicating liquors within, the importation thereof into, or the exportation thereof from the United States and all territory subject to the jurisdiction thereof for beverage purposes is hereby prohibited.

Section 2
The Congress and the several States shall have concurrent power to enforce this article by appropriate legislation.

Section 3
This article shall be inoperative unless it shall have been ratified as an amendment to the Constitution by the legislatures of the several States, as provided in the Constitution, within seven years from the date of the submission hereof to the States by the Congress.

AMENDMENT XIX

Passed by Congress June 4, 1919

Ratified August 18, 1920

The right of citizens of the United States to vote shall not be denied or abridged by the United States or by any State on account of sex.

Congress shall have power to enforce this article by appropriate legislation.

AMENDMENT XX

Passed by Congress March 2, 1932

Ratified January 23, 1933

Section 1

The terms of the President and the Vice President shall end at noon on the 20th day of January, and the terms of Senators and Representatives at noon on the 3d day of January, of the years in which such terms would have ended if this article had not been ratified; and the terms of their successors shall then begin.

Section 2

The Congress shall assemble at least once in every year, and such meeting shall begin at noon on the 3d day of January, unless they shall by law appoint a different day.

Section 3

If, at the time fixed for the beginning of the term of the President, the President elect shall have died, the Vice President elect shall become President. If a President shall not have been chosen before the time fixed for the beginning of his term, or if the President elect shall have failed to qualify, then the Vice President elect shall act as President until a President shall have qualified; and the Congress may by law provide for the case wherein neither a President elect nor a Vice President shall have qualified, declaring who shall then act as President, or the manner in which one who is to act shall be selected, and such person shall act accordingly until a President or Vice President shall have qualified.

Section 4

The Congress may by law provide for the case of the death of any of the persons from whom the House of Representatives may choose a President whenever the right of choice shall have devolved upon them, and for the case of the death of any of the persons from whom the Senate may choose a Vice President whenever the right of choice shall have devolved upon them.

Section 5
Sections 1 and 2 shall take effect on the 15th day of October following the ratification of this article.

Section 6
This article shall be inoperative unless it shall have been ratified as an amendment to the Constitution by the legislatures of three-fourths of the several States within seven years from the date of its submission.

AMENDMENT XXI

Passed by Congress February 20, 1933

Ratified December 5, 1933

Section 1
The eighteenth article of amendment to the Constitution of the United States is hereby repealed.

Section 2
The transportation or importation into any State, Territory, or Possession of the United States for delivery or use therein of intoxicating liquors, in violation of the laws thereof, is hereby prohibited.

Section 3
This article shall be inoperative unless it shall have been ratified as an amendment to the Constitution by conventions in the several States, as provided in the Constitution, within seven years from the date of the submission hereof to the States by the Congress.

AMENDMENT XXII

Passed by Congress March 21, 1947

Ratified February 27, 1951

Section 1

No person shall be elected to the office of the President more than twice, and no person who has held the office of President, or acted as President, for more than two years of a term to which some other person was elected President shall be elected to the office of President more than once. But this Article shall not apply to any person holding the office of President when this Article was proposed by Congress, and shall not prevent any person who may be holding the office of President, or acting as President, during the term within which this Article becomes operative from holding the office of President or acting as President during the remainder of such term.

Section 2

This article shall be inoperative unless it shall have been ratified as an amendment to the Constitution by the legislatures of three-fourths of the several States within seven years from the date of its submission to the States by the Congress.

AMENDMENT XXIII

Passed by Congress June 16, 1960

Ratified March 29, 1961

Section 1

The District constituting the seat of Government of the United States shall appoint in such manner as Congress may direct:

A number of electors of President and Vice President equal to the whole number of Senators and Representatives in Congress to which the District would be entitled if it were a State, but in no event more than the least populous State; they shall be in addition to those appointed by the States, but they shall be considered, for the purposes of the election of President and Vice President, to be electors appointed by a State; and they shall meet in the District and perform such duties as provided by the twelfth article of amendment.

Section 2

The Congress shall have power to enforce this article by appropriate legislation.

AMENDMENT XXIV

Passed by Congress August 27, 1962

Ratified January 23, 1964

Section 1

The right of citizens of the United States to vote in any primary or other election for President or Vice President, for electors for President or Vice President, or for Senator or Representative in Congress, shall not be denied or abridged by the United States or any State by reason of failure to pay poll tax or other tax.

Section 2

The Congress shall have power to enforce this article by appropriate legislation.

AMENDMENT XXV

Passed by Congress July 6, 1965

Ratified February 10, 1967

Section 1

In case of the removal of the President from office or of his death or resignation, the Vice President shall become President.

Section 2

Whenever there is a vacancy in the office of the Vice President, the President shall nominate a Vice President who shall take office upon confirmation by a majority vote of both Houses of Congress.

Section 3

Whenever the President transmits to the President pro tempore of the Senate and the Speaker of the House of Representatives his written declaration that he is unable to discharge the powers and duties of his office, and until he transmits to them a written declaration to the contrary, such powers and duties shall be discharged by the Vice President as Acting President.

Section 4

Whenever the Vice President and a majority of either the principal officers of the executive departments or of such other body as Congress may by law provide, transmit to the President pro tempore of the Senate and the Speaker of the House of Representatives their written declaration that the President is unable to discharge the powers and duties of his office, the Vice President shall immediately assume the powers and duties of the office as Acting President.

Thereafter, when the President transmits to the President pro tempore of the Senate and the Speaker of the House of Representatives his written declaration that no inability exists, he shall resume the powers and duties of his office unless the Vice President and a majority of either the principal officers of the executive department or of such other body as Congress may by law provide, transmit within four days to the President pro tempore of the Senate and the Speaker of the House of Representatives their written declaration that the President is unable to discharge the powers and duties of his office. Thereupon Congress shall decide the issue, assembling within forty-eight hours for that purpose if not in session. If the Congress, within twenty-one days after receipt of the latter written declaration, or, if Congress is not in session, within twenty-one days after Congress is required to assemble, determines by two-thirds vote of both Houses that the President is unable to discharge the powers and duties of his office, the Vice President shall continue to discharge the same as Acting President; otherwise, the President shall resume the powers and duties of his office.

AMENDMENT XXVI

Passed by Congress March 23, 1971

Ratified July 1, 1971

Section 1

The right of citizens of the United States, who are eighteen years of age or older, to vote shall not be denied or abridged by the United States or by any State on account of age.

Section 2

The Congress shall have power to enforce this article by appropriate legislation.

AMENDMENT XXVII

Originally proposed Sept. 25, 1789

Ratified May 7, 1992

No law, varying the compensation for the services of the Senators and Representatives, shall take effect, until an election of representatives shall have intervened.

The Northwest Ordinance

An Ordinance for the government of the Territory of the United States northwest of the River Ohio

Section 1

Be it ordained by the United States in Congress assembled, That the said territory, for the purposes of temporary government, be one district, subject, however, to be divided into two districts, as future circumstances may, in the opinion of Congress, make it expedient.

Section 2

Be it ordained by the authority aforesaid, That the estates, both of resident and nonresident proprietors in the said territory, dying intestate, shall descent to, and be distributed among their children, and the descendants of a deceased child, in equal parts; the descendants of a deceased child or grandchild to take the share of their deceased parent in equal parts among them: And where there shall be no children or descendants, then in equal parts to the next of kin in equal degree; and among collaterals, the children of a deceased brother or sister of the intestate shall have, in equal parts among them, their deceased parents' share; and there shall in no case be a distinction between kindred of the whole and half-blood; saving, in all cases, to the widow of the intestate her third part of the real estate for life, and one third part of the personal estate; and this law relative to descents and dower, shall remain in full force until altered by the legislature of the district. And until the governor and judges shall adopt laws as hereinafter mentioned, estates in the said territory may be devised or bequeathed by wills in writing, signed and sealed by him or her in whom the estate may be (being of full age), and attested by three witnesses; and real estates may be conveyed by lease and release, or bargain and sale, signed, sealed and delivered by the person being of full age, in whom the estate may be, and attested by two witnesses, provided such wills be duly proved, and such conveyances be acknowledged, or the execution thereof duly proved, and be recorded within one year after proper magistrates, courts, and registers shall be appointed for that purpose; and personal property may be transferred by delivery; saving, however to the French and Canadian inhabitants, and other settlers of the Kaskaskies, St. Vincents and the neighboring villages who have heretofore professed themselves citizens of Virginia, their laws and customs now in force among them, relative to the descent and conveyance, of property.

Section 3

Be it ordained by the authority aforesaid, That there shall be appointed from time to time by Congress, a governor, whose commission shall continue in force for the term of three years, unless sooner revoked by Congress; he shall reside in the district, and have a freehold estate therein in 1,000 acres of land, while in the exercise of his office.

Section 4

There shall be appointed from time to time by Congress, a secretary, whose commission shall continue in force for four years unless sooner revoked; he shall reside in the district, and have a freehold estate therein in 500 acres of land, while in the exercise of his office. It shall be his duty to keep and preserve the acts and laws passed by the legislature, and the public records of the district, and the proceedings of the governor in his executive department, and transmit authentic copies of such acts and proceedings, every six months, to the Secretary of Congress: There shall also be appointed a court to consist of three judges, any two of whom to form a court, who shall have a common law jurisdiction, and reside in the district, and have each therein a freehold estate in 500 acres of land while in the exercise of their offices; and their commissions shall continue in force during good behavior.

Section 5

The governor and judges, or a majority of them, shall adopt and publish in the district such laws of the original States, criminal and civil, as may be necessary and best suited to the circumstances of the district, and report them to Congress from time to time: which laws shall be in force in the district until the organization of the General Assembly therein, unless disapproved of by

Congress; but afterwards the Legislature shall have authority to alter them as they shall think fit.

Section 6

The governor, for the time being, shall be commander in chief of the militia, appoint and commission all officers in the same below the rank of general officers; all general officers shall be appointed and commissioned by Congress.

Section 7

Previous to the organization of the general assembly, the governor shall appoint such magistrates and other civil officers in each county or township, as he shall find necessary for the preservation of the peace and good order in the same: After the general assembly shall be organized, the powers and duties of the magistrates and other civil officers shall be regulated and defined by the said assembly; but all magistrates and other civil officers not herein otherwise directed, shall during the continuance of this temporary government, be appointed by the governor.

Section 8

For the prevention of crimes and injuries, the laws to be adopted or made shall have force in all parts of the district, and for the execution of process, criminal and civil, the governor shall make proper divisions thereof; and he shall proceed from time to time as circumstances may require, to lay out the parts of the district in which the Indian titles shall have been extinguished, into counties and townships, subject, however, to such alterations as may thereafter be made by the legislature.

Section 9

So soon as there shall be five thousand free male inhabitants of full age in the district, upon giving proof thereof to the governor, they shall receive authority, with time and place, to elect a representative from their counties or townships to represent them in the general assembly: Provided, That, for every five hundred free male inhabitants, there shall be one representative, and so on progressively with the number of free male inhabitants shall the right of representation increase, until the number of representatives shall amount to twenty five; after which, the number and proportion of representatives shall be regulated by the legislature: Provided, That no person be eligible or qualified to act as a representative unless he shall have been a citizen of one of the United States three years, and be a resident in the district, or unless he shall have resided in the district three years; and, in either case, shall likewise hold in his own right, in fee simple, two hundred acres of land within the same; Provided, also, That a freehold in fifty acres of land in the district, having been a citizen of one of the states, and being resident in the district, or the like freehold and two years residence in the district, shall be necessary to qualify a man as an elector of a representative.

Section 10

The representatives thus elected, shall serve for the term of two years; and, in case of the death of a representative, or removal from office, the governor shall issue a writ to the county or township for which he was a member, to elect another in his stead, to serve for the residue of the term.

Section 11

The general assembly or legislature shall consist of the governor, legislative council, and a house of representatives. The Legislative Council shall consist of five members, to continue in office five years, unless sooner removed by Congress; any three of whom to be a quorum: and the members of the Council shall be nominated and appointed in the following manner, to wit: As soon as representatives shall be elected, the Governor shall appoint a time and place for them to meet together; and, when met, they shall nominate ten persons, residents in the district, and each possessed of a freehold in five hundred acres of land, and return their names to Congress; five of whom Congress shall appoint and commission to serve as aforesaid; and, whenever a vacancy shall happen in the council, by death or removal from office, the house of representatives shall nominate two persons, qualified as aforesaid, for each vacancy, and return their names to Congress; one of whom congress shall appoint and commission for the residue of the term. And every five years, four months at least before the expiration of the time of service of the members of council, the said house shall nominate ten persons, qualified as aforesaid, and return their names to Congress; five of whom Congress shall appoint and commission to serve as members of the council five years, unless sooner removed. And the governor, legislative council, and house of representatives, shall have authority to make laws in all cases, for the good government of the district, not repugnant to the principles and articles in this ordinance established and declared. And all bills, having passed by a majority in the house, and by a majority in the council, shall be referred to the governor for his assent; but no bill, or legislative act whatever, shall be of any force without his assent. The governor shall have power to convene, prorogue, and dissolve the general assembly, when, in his opinion, it shall be expedient.

Section 12

The governor, judges, legislative council, secretary, and such other officers as Congress shall appoint in the district, shall take an oath or affirmation of fidelity and of office; the governor before the president of congress, and all other officers before the Governor. As soon as a legislature shall be formed in the district, the council and house assembled in one room, shall have authority, by joint ballot, to elect a delegate to Congress, who shall have a seat in Congress, with a right of debating but not voting during this temporary government.

Section 13

And, for extending the fundamental principles of civil and religious liberty, which form the basis whereon these republics, their laws and constitutions are erected; to fix and establish those principles as the basis of all laws, constitutions, and governments, which forever hereafter shall be formed in the said territory: to provide also for the establishment of States, and permanent government therein, and for their admission to a share in the federal councils on an equal footing with the original States, at as early periods as may be consistent with the general interest:

Section 14

It is hereby ordained and declared by the authority aforesaid, That the following articles shall be considered as articles of compact between the original States and the people and States in the said territory and forever remain unalterable, unless by common consent, to wit:

Article 1

No person, demeaning himself in a peaceable and orderly manner, shall ever be molested on account of his mode of worship or religious sentiments, in the said territory.

Article 2

The inhabitants of the said territory shall always be entitled to the benefits of the writ of habeas corpus, and of the trial by jury; of a proportionate representation of the people in the legislature; and of judicial proceedings according to the course of the common law. All persons shall be bailable, unless for capital offenses, where the proof shall be evident or the presumption great. All fines shall be moderate; and no cruel or unusual punishments shall be inflicted. No man shall be deprived of his liberty or property, but by the judgment of his peers or the law of the land; and, should the public exigencies make it necessary, for the common preservation, to take any person's property, or to demand his particular services, full compensation shall be made for the same. And, in the just preservation of rights and property, it is understood and declared, that no law ought ever to be made, or have force in the said territory, that shall, in any manner whatever, interfere with or affect private contracts or engagements, bona fide, and without fraud, previously formed.

Article 3

Religion, morality, and knowledge, being necessary to good government and the happiness of mankind, schools and the means of education shall forever be encouraged. *The utmost good faith shall always be observed towards the Indians; their lands and property shall never be taken* *from them without their consent; and, in their property, rights, and liberty, they shall never be invaded or disturbed, unless in just and lawful wars authorized by Congress; but laws founded in justice and humanity, shall from time to time be made for preventing wrongs being done to them, and for preserving peace and friendship with them.*

Article 4

The said territory, and the States which may be formed therein, shall forever remain a part of this Confederacy of the United States of America, subject to the Articles of Confederation, and to such alterations therein as shall be constitutionally made; and to all the acts and ordinances of the United States in Congress assembled, conformable thereto. The inhabitants and settlers in the said territory shall be subject to pay a part of the federal debts contracted or to be contracted, and a proportional part of the expenses of government, to be apportioned on them by Congress according to the same common rule and measure by which apportionments thereof shall be made on the other States; and the taxes for paying their proportion shall be laid and levied by the authority and direction of the legislatures of the district or districts, or new States, as in the original States, within the time agreed upon by the United States in Congress assembled. The legislatures of those districts or new States, shall never interfere with the primary disposal of the soil by the United States in Congress assembled, nor with any regulations Congress may find necessary for securing the title in such soil to the bona fide purchasers. No tax shall be imposed on lands the property of the United States; and, in no case, shall nonresident proprietors be taxed higher than residents. The navigable waters leading into the Mississippi and St. Lawrence, and the carrying places between the same, shall be common highways and forever free, as well to the inhabitants of the said territory as to the citizens of the United States, and those of any other States that may be admitted into the confederacy, without any tax, impost, or duty therefor.

Article 5

There shall be formed in the said territory, not less than three nor more than five States; and the boundaries of the States, as soon as Virginia shall alter her act of cession, and consent to the same, shall become fixed and established as follows, to wit: The western State in the said territory, shall be bounded by the Mississippi, the Ohio, and Wabash Rivers; a direct line drawn from the Wabash and Post Vincents, due North, to the territorial line between the United States and Canada; and, by the said territorial line, to the Lake of the Woods and Mississippi. The middle State shall be bounded by the said direct line, the Wabash from Post Vincents to the Ohio, by the Ohio, by a direct line, drawn due north from the mouth of the Great Miami, to the said territorial line, and by the said territorial line. The eastern State shall be bounded by the last mentioned direct line, the Ohio, Pennsylvania, and the said territorial line: Provided, however, and it is further understood and declared, that the boundaries of these three States shall be subject so far to be altered, that, if Congress shall hereafter find it expedient, they shall have authority to form one or two States in that part of the said territory which lies north of an east and west line drawn through the southerly bend or extreme of Lake Michigan. And, whenever any of the said States shall have sixty thousand free inhabitants therein, such State shall be admitted, by its delegates, into the Congress of the United States, on an equal footing with the original States in all respects whatever, and shall be at liberty to form a permanent constitution and State government: Provided, the constitution and government so to be formed, shall be republican, and in conformity to the principles contained in these articles; and, so far as it can be consistent with the general interest of the confederacy, such admission shall be allowed at an earlier period, and when there may be a less number of free inhabitants in the State than sixty thousand.

Article 6

There shall be neither slavery nor involuntary servitude in the said territory, otherwise than in the punishment of crimes whereof the party shall have been duly convicted: Provided, always, That any person escaping into the same, from whom labor or service is lawfully claimed in any one of the original States, such fugitive may be lawfully reclaimed and conveyed to the person claiming his or her labor or service as aforesaid.

Article 7

Be it ordained by the authority aforesaid, That the resolutions of the 23rd of April, 1784, relative to the subject of this ordinance, be, and the same are hereby repealed and declared null and void.

*Done by the United States, in Congress assembled, the 13th day of July, in the **year of our Lord** 1787, and of their sovereignty and independence the twelfth.*

The Articles of Confederation were designed to install some form of a functioning government. There were benefits and drawbacks to this document which ultimately led to the creation of the US Constitution which is the foundation of our system of government and the law of the United States of America.

The difference in the punctuation and the spelling used by the authors of these documents has been left in the wording to maintain their historical accuracy.

With George Washington chosen as Convention President, the Constitutional Convention began in Philadelphia with 56 delegates and the drafting of the US Constitution was begun in May 1787. Several different men were involved in this convention and they were involved with directly or they exuded influence on the wording of the Constitution as well as what was included and what was to be excluded from this document.

In the following chapters many of these men will be discussed as to their contribution and what their true words were when speaking about the founding of the United States and its design intent.

The words of these men will also be revealed as to their true thoughts about whether or not this nation was designed and its foundation rests on their belief and understanding of God and Godly principles or if they never made such statements.

The intent of this book is to bring to the light the true words of the Founders of the United States of America. I included the documents directly associated with the origin of this nation and those documents express the beliefs of the Founders and of the States in the Union. This book will meet that challenge.

Part Two

God and Country

In the past most of the children growing up in the US public school system were taught that the pilgrims came to the New World as religious refugees who fled European nations because of persecution for their religious faith.

The story of the Mayflower landing at Plymouth Rock in 1620 and the beginnings of new lives in an open land, free from the bonds of European monarchies and corrupt church leaders. These historical truths are a constant and they can never be changed because the truth is constant and it never can be altered or erased.

The Founding Fathers, just as every man, woman and child born and raised in an 18th century were a product of their time. Just as with any person born during any decade and century, people will witness the influences of their parents, their teachers, their clergy and their particular way of living. It is undeniable; those men were the product of their time. The truly remarkable thing about these men is that they had a voracious appetite and desire to expand their intellect through the various teachings of the day. They wanted to learn and to understand the different philosophies that were popular during their particular period of time.

Belief in God, Godly values and principles were taught in the schools, the homes and of course the churches in the hamlets, villages and towns in the British colonies of the New World. I had a history professor at one time who told the class that "in order to understand history we must be able to project our self into that time in history". We cannot understand how they thought and why they thought as they did if we cannot relate our self to that period in time. My hope is that anyone reading this book is that if they want to understand the

Founders and that period in history then they will learn how to think as they once thought.

A good quality dictionary will be perhaps the greatest tool to understand their use of words. Many of the words used by the Founders have become lost to our modern day vocabularies.

The internet is the next greatest tool but it is a tool that has to be used cautiously because the internet is filled with misinformation and outright lies. Again that is the main purpose of this book because those lies have fooled so many people into believing the internet instead of researching and learning the truth.

Use the National Archives online, the Library of Congress; both are credible websites about the Founders. Another good source is the Avalon Project.

Credible websites about the Founders would be websites whose purpose has been to catalogue the papers of the Founders and make those archives available online to researchers.

This book will ask and then answer these questions about the founding of this nation and about the Founding Fathers.

What did the Founders really say about God, their belief or lack of belief in God?

Did the Founders ever link the founding of the United States to their faith in God?

Were the Founders as many people believe, to be deists?

Was the US to be governed by religion?

Many of the Founders did openly express their thoughts about God, the Holy Bible and their belief in the Christian faith and in the Word of God.

Yes, many of the Founders did openly and publicly speak about the founding of the United States being linked to their faith in God.

This fact must be noted.

The Founding Fathers did not hate organized religion. The Founding Fathers witnessed what happens when some people who have power become corrupt.

They despised the corruption brought upon the Christian faith by corrupt men who sought power, control and wealth by obtaining influence over the lives of other people.

Throughout this book you will read credible evidence that the Founders believed that the United States is a gift from God. This book will include quotes from certain Founding Fathers where they outright state that the foundation of the United States rests upon their understanding and belief of God and His Word.

No. There is no evidence that as adults, any of the Founding Fathers were practicing deists.

The truth is that the Founders could not have been practicing deists because they attributed the founding of the United States of America to God the Creator. This is the same God of the Christian faith and their expressed belief as such contradicts the definition of a deist.

No. The United States of America was never designed to be governed by religion.

The United States was in part established as a haven for those persecuted for their religious beliefs and even their lack of religious beliefs. This is the reason for their statement that no religious test will be required to obtain public office. This is not evidence that they believed that God has no place in the US government; this statement merely extends the First Amendment rights to non-religious persons living in the United States.

What did the Founders really say about God, their belief or lack of belief in God?

Our third President, Thomas Jefferson of Virginia was a very private man, especially when it came to his faith in God. President Jefferson kept his beliefs mostly to himself but from time to time he would share with his friends, insight into his thoughts and beliefs.

*"The varieties in the structure & action of the human mind, as in those of the body, are the work of our **Creator**, against which it cannot be a religious duty to erect the standard of uniformity. The practice of morality being necessary for the well-being of society, **He** has taken care to impress its precepts so indelibly on our hearts, that they shall not be effaced by the whimsies of our brain."*

*"Hence we see good men in all religions, and as many in one as another. It is then a matter of principle with me to avoid disturbing the tranquility of others by the expression of any opinion on the innocent questions on which we schismatize, & think it enough to hold fast to those moral precepts which are of the essence of **Christianity**, & of all other religions. Nowhere are these to be found in greater purity than in the discourses of the great reformer of religion whom we follow."*

Thomas Jefferson letter to James Fishback, September 27, 1809

First Prayer of the Continental Congress, 1774

*"**O Lord our Heavenly Father, high and mighty King of kings, and Lord of lords**, who dost from thy throne behold all the dwellers on earth and reignest with power supreme and uncontrolled over all the Kingdoms, Empires and Governments; look down in mercy, we beseech Thee, on these our American States, who have fled to Thee from the rod of the oppressor and thrown themselves on Thy gracious protection, desiring to be henceforth dependent only on Thee. To Thee have they appealed for the righteousness of their cause; to Thee do they now look up for that countenance and support, which Thou alone canst give. Take them, therefore, **Heavenly Father**, under Thy nurturing care; give them wisdom in Council and valor in the field;*

defeat the malicious designs of our cruel adversaries; convince them of the unrighteousness of their Cause and if they persist in their sanguinary purposes, of own unerring justice, sounding in their hearts, constrain them to drop the weapons of war from their unnerved hands in the day of battle!

*Be Thou present, **O God of wisdom**, and direct the councils of this honorable assembly; enable them to settle things on the best and surest foundation. That the scene of blood may be speedily closed; that order, harmony and peace may be effectually restored, and truth and justice, religion and piety, prevail and flourish amongst the people. Preserve the health of their bodies and vigor of their minds; shower down on them and the millions they here represent, such temporal blessings as Thou seest expedient for them in this world and crown them with everlasting glory in the world to come. All this we ask in the name and through the merits of **Jesus Christ, Thy Son and our Savior.***"

Amen.

Reverend Jacob Duché, Rector of Christ Church of Philadelphia, Pennsylvania

September 7, 1774, 9 o'clock a.m.

Office of the US Chaplain, US House of Representatives

Even as recently as 1983 has the United States Supreme Court weighed in on the question of prayer in our government.

United States Supreme Court

"The opening of sessions of legislative and other deliberative public bodies with prayer is deeply embedded in the history and tradition of this country. From colonial times through the founding of the Republic and ever since, the practice of legislative prayer has coexisted with the principles of disestablishment and religious freedom... In light of the unambiguous and unbroken history of more than 200 years, there can be no doubt that the

practice of opening legislative sessions with prayer has become part of the fabric of our society."

Marsh v. Chambers, **463 U.S. 783, 787, 792 (1983)**

Proclamations

Proclamation Appointing a Day of Thanksgiving and Prayer, 11 November 1779

Proclamation Appointing a Day of Thanksgiving and Prayer

*Whereas the Honourable the General Congress, impressed with a grateful sense of the goodness of **Almighty God**, in blessing the greater part of this extensive continent with plentiful harvests, crowning our arms with repeated successes, conducting us hitherto safely through the perils with which we have been encompassed and manifesting in multiplied instances his divine care of these infant states, hath thought proper by their act of the 20th day of October last, to recommend to the several states that Thursday the 9th of December next be appointed a day of public and solemn thanksgiving and prayer, which act is in these words, to wit.*

*Whereas it becomes us humbly to approach the throne of **Almighty God**, with gratitude and praise, for the wonders which **His goodness** has wrought in conducting our forefathers to this western world; for **His** protection to them and to their posterity, amidst difficulties and dangers; for raising us their children from deep distress, to be numbered among the nations of the earth; and for arming **the hands of just and mighty Princes in our deliverance**; and especially for that **He** hath been pleased to grant us the enjoyment of health and so to order the revolving seasons, that the earth hath produced her increase in abundance, blessing the labors of the husbandman, and spreading plenty through the land; that **He** hath prospered our arms and those of our ally, been a shield to our troops in the hour of danger, pointed their swords to victory, and led them in triumph over the bulwarks of the foe; that **He** hath gone with those who went out into the wilderness against the savage tribes; that **He** hath stayed the hand of the spoiler, and turned back **His** meditated destruction; that **He** hath prospered our commerce, and given success to those who sought the enemy on the face of the deep; and above all, that **He** hath diffused the glorious light of the gospel, whereby, through the* merits of **our gracious Redeemer**, *we may become the heirs of His eternal glory.*

Therefore,

*Resolved, that it be recommended to the several states to appoint THURSDAY the 9th of December next, to be a **day of public and solemn THANKSGIVING to Almighty God**, for **his** mercies, and of PRAYER, for the continuance of his favour and protection to these United States;*

*To beseech **Him** that **He** would be graciously pleased to influence our public Councils, and bless them with wisdom from on high, with unanimity, firmness and success; that **He** would go forth with our hosts and crown our arms with victory;*

*That **He would grant to his church**, the plentiful effusions of divine grace, and pour out **His holy spirit on all Ministers of the gospel**; That **He would bless and prosper the means of education, and spread the light of Christian knowledge through the remotest corners of the earth**;*

*That **He** would smile upon the labors of his people, and cause the earth to bring forth her fruits in abundance, that we may with gratitude and gladness enjoy them;*

*That **He would take into His holy protection**, our illustrious ally, **give Him victory over His enemies**, and **render Him finally great, as the Father of His people**, and **the protector of the rights of mankind**; that He would **graciously be pleased to turn the hearts of our enemies**, and to **dispense the blessings of peace to contending nations**.*

*That **He** would in mercy look down upon us, pardon all our sins, and receive us into **his** favour; and finally, **that He would establish the independence of these United States upon the basis of religion and virtue, and support and protect them in the enjoyment of peace, liberty and safety.***

*I do therefore by authority from the General Assembly issue this my proclamation, hereby appointing Thursday the 9th day of December next, a day of public and solemn thanksgiving and prayer to **Almighty God**,* *earnestly recommending to all the good people of this commonwealth, to set apart the said day for those purposes, and to the several Ministers of religion to meet their respective societies thereon, to assist them in their prayers, edify them with their discourses, and generally to perform the sacred duties of their function, proper for the occasion.*

*Given under my hand and the seal of the commonwealth, at Williamsburg, this 11th day of November, in the **year of our Lord**, 1779, and in the fourth of the commonwealth*

THOMAS JEFFERSON

By the United States in Congress assembled,

PROCLAMATION

*It being the indispensable duty of all nations, not only to offer up their supplications to **Almighty God**, the giver of all good, for **His** gracious assistance in a time of distress, but also in a solemn and public manner, to give **Him** praise for **His** goodness in general, and especially for great and signal interpositions of **His Providence** in their behalf; therefore, the Unites States in Congress assembled, taking into their consideration the many instances of **Divine goodness** to these States in the course of the important conflict, in which they have been so long engaged, – the present happy and promising state of public affairs, and the events of the war in the course of the year now drawing to a close; particularly the harmony of the public Councils which is so necessary to the success of the public cause, – the perfect union and good understanding which has hitherto subsisted between them and their allies, notwithstanding the artful and unwearied attempts of the common enemy to divide them, – the success of the arms of the United States and those of their allies, – and the acknowledgment of their Independence by another European power, whose friendship and commerce must be of great and lasting advantage to these States;*

*Do hereby recommend it to the inhabitants of these States in general, to observe and request the several states to interpose their authority, in appointing and commanding the observation of THURSDAY the TWENTY-EIGHTH DAY OF NOVEMBER next as a day of SOLEMN THANKSGIVING to **GOD** for all **His** mercies; and they do further recommend to all ranks to testify their gratitude to **God** for **His** goodness by a cheerful obedience to **His** laws and by promoting, each in his station, and by his influence, the practice of true and undefiled religion, which is the great foundation of public prosperity and national happiness.*

*Done in Congress at Philadelphia, the eleventh day of October, in the year of our **LORD**, one thousand seven hundred and eighty-two, and of our Sovereignty and Independence, the seventh*

Thanksgiving Proclamation

Issued by President George Washington, at the request of Congress, on October 3, 1789

By the President of the United States of America, a Proclamation

Whereas it is the duty of all nations to acknowledge the providence of **Almighty God**, *to obey* **His** *will, to be grateful for* **His** *benefits, and humbly to implore* **His** *protection and favor; and — Whereas both Houses of Congress have, by their joint committee, requested me "to recommend to the people of the United States a day of public thanksgiving and prayer, to be observed by acknowledging with grateful hearts the many and signal favors of* **Almighty God**, *especially by affording them an opportunity peaceably to establish a form of government for their safety and happiness:*

Now, therefore, I do recommend and assign Thursday, the 26th day of November next, to be devoted by the people of these States to the service of that great and glorious **Being who is the beneficent author of all the good** *that was, that is, or that will be; that we may then all unite in rendering unto* **Him** *our sincere and humble thanks for* **His** *kind care and protection of the people of this country previous to their becoming a nation; for the signal and manifold mercies and the favor, able interpositions of* **His** *providence in the course and conclusion of the late war; for the great degree of tranquility, union, and plenty which we have since enjoyed; for the peaceable and rational manner in which we have been enabled to establish constitutions of government for our safety and happiness, and particularly the national one now lately instituted; for the civil and religious liberty with which we are blessed, and the means we have of acquiring and diffusing useful knowledge; and, in general, for all the great and various favors which* **He** *has been pleased to confer upon us.*

And also that we may then unite in most humbly offering our prayers and supplications to the **great Lord and Ruler of Nations**, *and beseech* **Him** *to pardon our national and other transgressions; to enable us all, whether in public or private stations, to perform our several and relative duties properly* *and punctually; to render our National Government a blessing to all the people by constantly being a Government of wise, just, and constitutional laws, discreetly and faithfully executed and obeyed; to protect and guide all sovereigns and nations (especially such as have shown kindness to us), and to bless them with good governments, peace, and concord; to promote the knowledge and practice of true religion and virtue, and the increase of science among them and us; and, generally, to grant unto all mankind such a degree of temporal prosperity as* **He** *alone knows to be best.*

Given under my hand at the City of New York the third day of October in the **year of our Lord** *1789.*

George Washington

BY HIS EXCELLENCY SAMUEL HUNTINGTON, ESQUIRE

Governor and Commander in Chief of the State of CONNECTICUT

A PROCLAMATION

Considering the indispensable duty of a people, to acknowledge the overruling hand of divine providence, and their constant dependence upon the supreme being, for all the favor and blessings they may enjoy, or hope to receive; and that notwithstanding the many mercies and signal instances of divine favor conferred upon the inhabitants of this land, yet the prevalence of vice and wickedness give us just reason to fear the divine displeasure and chastisement for our many offenses, unless prevented by speedy repentance and reformation.

*I have therefore thought fit by and with the advice of council, to appoint, and do, hereby appoint WEDNESDAY the Twenty-Second Day of April next, to be observed as a Day of FASTING, HUMILIATION, and PRAYER, throughout this state; earnestly exhorting ministers and people of all denominations to assemble for divine worship; that we may with becoming humility, and united hearts, confess and bewail our manifold sins and transgressions, and by repentance and reformation obtain pardon and forgiveness of all our offenses, through the merits and mediation of **Jesus Christ** our only savior. Also, to offer up fervent supplications to **almighty God** the **father of mercies**, that **he** may bless the United States of America, gives wisdom and integrity to our national council, direct their proceedings at this important crisis, in such manner as shall best promote the union, prosperity and happiness of the nation: –*

*That it may graciously pleas **him** to smile upon and bless the people of this state, inspire our civil rulers with wisdom and integrity becoming their station: bless **his** sacred ambassadors, and cause pure and undefiled religion to flourish, grant us health and plenty; prosper us in all our lawful employments, and crown the year with his goodness; succeed the means of education, extend the peaceful influence of the redeemer's kingdom, and* *dispose all nations to live as brethren in peace and amity, and fill the world with the knowledge and glory of **God**.*

And all servile labor is forbidden on said day.

Given at Norwich, the 28th day of March, in the thirteenth year of the independence of the United States of America,

Annoque Domini 1789.

SAMUEL HUNTINGTON

By His Excellency's Command,

George Wyllys, Sec'ry

BY HIS EXCELLENCY

John Hancock, Esquire,

GOVERNOR of the COMMONWEALTH of MASSACHUSETTS

A PROCLAMATION

For a Day of Public FASTING, HUMILIATION, AND PRAYER

WHEREAS it hath been the Practice of the People inhabiting the Territory of this Commonwealth, from their first Settlement, at this Season of the Year, unitedly to acknowledge their entire Dependence on the **SUPREME BEING,** *and to humble themselves under a Sense of their utter unworthiness of his Favors, by Reason of their Transgression; and whereas the Practice appears to have a Tendency to cultivate the Fear of* **God,** *and a due Regard to* **HIS LAWS:**

I HAVE THEREFORE THOUGHT FIT, by, and with the Advice of the COUNCIL, to appoint, and I hereby do appoint, THURSDAY, the Eleventh Day of April next, to be observed throughout this Commonwealth, as Day of solemn FASTING, HUMILIATION and PRAYER: –

Calling upon Ministers, and People of every Denomination, to assemble on that Day, in their respective Congregations; that with true contrition of Heart we may confess our Sins; resolve to forsake them, and implore the Divine forgiveness, through the Merits and Mediation of **JESUS CHRIST,** *our* **SAVIOUR.**

Humbly supplicate the **Supreme Ruler of the Universe** *to prosper the Administration of the Federal Government, and that of this Commonwealth, and the other States in the Union; enduing them with Firmness, Wisdom, Unanimity and Public Spirit; and leading them in their respective public Councils, to such Determinations as shall be adapted to Promote the great end of Government:*

The Welfare and Happiness of the People:

To restore and maintain Peace in our Borders: Continue Health among us, and give us Wisdom to improve **HIS Blessings**, for **HIS Glory**, and our own Good:

To smile upon our Agriculture, and mercifully prevent the diminishing the Fruits of the Earth, by devouring Insects, unseasonable Weather, or other Judgments; that so our Land may abundantly yield its Increase:

That **HE** would protect and prosper our Navigation, Trade, Fishery, and all the Works of our Hands:

To confirm and continue our invaluable Religious and Civil Liberties:

To prosper the University, and other Seminaries and Means of Education:

To cause Industry, Frugality, and all Moral and Christian Virtues to prevail among us:

To bless the Allies of the United States, and particularly to afford **his Almighty** Aid to the French Nation, and still Guide them into such Measures, as shall tend effectually to establish a Government founded upon Reason, Justice, and the Welfare of the People.

And finally to over-rule all the Commotions in the World, to the spreading the true Religion of our Lord **JESUS CHRIST**, in its Purity and Power, among all the People of the Earth.

And I do earnestly recommend that all unnecessary Labour and Recreation may be suspended on the said Day.

GIVEN at the COUNCIL-CHAMBER, in Boston, the Fourth Day of MARCH, in the **Year of our LORD**, One Thousand Seven Hundred and Ninety-Three, and in the Seventeenth Year of the Independence of the United States of America!

JOHN HANCOCK

By His Excellency's Command, with the Advice and Consent of the COUNCIL,

JOHN AVERY, jun. Secretary.

Commonwealth of Massachusetts

GOD Save the Commonwealth of MASSACHUSETTS!

John Hancock was one of the signers of the Declaration of Independence, his signature being the most famous because his was the largest signature to that document. John Hancock was also a delegate to the Constitutional Convention in 1787 and later became a popular political leader and the Governor of Massachusetts when this proclamation was made in 1793.

Published

BY AUTHORITY,

A PROCLAMATION:

By the PRESIDENT of the UNITED STATES OF AMERICA

When we review the calamities, which afflict so many other nations, the present condition of the United States affords much matter of consolation and satisfaction.

*Our exemption hitherto from foreign war – an increasing prospect of the continuance of that exemption – the great degree of internal tranquility we have enjoyed – the recent confirmation of that tranquility by the suppression of an insurrection which so wantonly threatened it – the happy course of public affairs in general – the unexampled prosperity of all classes of our citizens; are circumstances which peculiarly mark our situation with indications of the **Divine** beneficence towards us. In such a state of things it is, in an especial manner, our duty as people, with devout reverence and affectionate gratitude, to acknowledge our many and great obligations to **Almighty God** and to implore **Him** to continue and confirm the blessings we experience.*

*Deeply penetrated with this sentiment, I, George Washington, President of the United States, do recommend to all religious societies and denominations, and to all persons whomsoever, within the United States, to set apart and observe Thursday, the nineteenth day of February next, as a day of public thanksgiving and prayer: and on that day to meet together and render their sincere and hearty thanks to the great **Ruler of nations** for the manifold and signal mercies which distinguish our lot as a nation. particularly for the possession of constitutions of government which unite and, by their union, establish liberty with order; for the preservation of peace, foreign and domestic; and for the seasonable control, which has been given to a spirit of disorder, in the suppression of the late insurrection; and generally for the* *prosperous course of our affairs, public and private; and, at the same time, humbly and fervently to beseech the kind **Author** of these blessings. graciously to prolong them to us – to imprint on our hearts a deep and solemn sense of our obligations to **Him** for them – to teach us rightly to estimate their immense value – to preserve us from the arrogance of prosperity and from hazarding the advantages we enjoy by delusive pursuits – to dispose us to merit the continuance of **His** favors by not abusing them, by our gratitude for them, and by a correspondent conduct as citizens and as men – to render this country, more and more, a propitious asylum for the unfortunate of other countries – to extend among us true and useful knowledge – to diffuse and establish habits of sobriety, order, morality, and piety – and, finally, to impart all blessings we possess or ask for ourselves, to the whole family of mankind.*

In testimony whereof, I have caused the seal of the United States of America, to be affixed to these presents, and signed the same with my hand.

Done, at the city of Philadelphia, the first day of January, 1795, and of the independence of the United States of America, the nineteenth

Go Washington,

President of the United States

EDMUND RANDOLPH, Secretary of State

By the Governor

A Proclamation

For a Day of PUBLIC FASTING, HUMILIATION and PRAYER

THE **supreme Ruler of the Universe**, *having been pleased, in the course of* **his** *Providence, to establish the Independence of the United States of America, and to cause them to assume their rank, amount the nations of the Earth, and bless them with Liberty, Peace and Plenty; we ought to be led by Religious feelings of Gratitude; and to walk before* **Him**, *in all Humility, according to his most* **Holy Law**.

But, as the depravity of our Hearts has, in so many instances drawn us aside from the path of duty, so that we have frequently offended our **Divine and Merciful Benefactor**; *it is therefore highly incumbent on us, according to the ancient and laudable practice of our pious Ancestors, to open the year by a public and solemn Fast.*

That with true repentance and contrition of Heart, we may unitedly implore the forgiveness of our Sins, through the merits of **Jesus Christ**, *and humbly supplicate our* **Heavenly Father**, *to grant us the aids of* **his Grace**, *for the amendment of our Hearts and Lives, and vouchsafe* **his** *smiles upon our temporal concerns:*

I HAVE therefore thought fit to appoint, and with the advice and consent of the Council, I do hereby appoint Thursday, the Second Day of April next, to be observed as a Day of Public Fasting, Humiliation and Prayer throughout this Commonwealth:

Calling upon the Ministers of the Gospel, of every Denomination, with their respective Congregations, to assemble on that Day, and devoutly implore the Divine forgiveness of our Sins,

To pray that the Light of the Gospel, and the rights of Conscience, may be continued to the people of United America; and that **his Holy Word** *may be improved by them, so that the name of* **God** *may be exalted, and their own Liberty and Happiness secured.*

*That **he** would be graciously pleased to bless our Federal Government; that by a wise administration, it may be a sure guide and safe protection in national concerns, for the people who have established, and who support it*

*That **He** would continue to us the invaluable Blessings of Civil Liberty; guarding us against intestine commotions; and enabling the United States, in the exercise of such Governmental powers, as are devolved upon them, so that the honor and dignity of our Nation, upon the Sea and the Land, may be supported, and Peace with the other Powers of the World, upon safe and honorable terms, may be maintained.*

*That **he** would direct the administration of our Federal and State Governments, so that the lives, liberties and property of all the Citizens, and the just rights of the People, as Men and Citizens, may be forever acknowledged, and at all times defended, by Constitutions, founded upon equal rights; and by good and wholesome Laws, wisely and judiciously administered and duly executed.*

*That **he** would enable Legislators and Magistrates of this Commonwealth, to discharge the important duties incumbent on them, that the People may have good reason to feel themselves happy and safe, and lead quiet and peaceable lives in all **Godliness and Honesty**.*

*That **he** would incline the Natives of the Wilderness, to listen to reasonable offers of Peace, that tranquility and security may be established on the Frontiers Of our Country.*

*That **he** would graciously regard the Lives and Health of the People of this and our sister States, and preserve them from contagious and wasting diseases:*

*To crown the ensuing Year with Plenty and Prosperity, by **his** blessing on our Husbandry, our Fisheries, our Commerce, and all the labor of our Hands*

*To affect our minds with a sense of our entire dependence upon **Him**, and of **his** great goodness towards us, that when we may present ourselves before*

*Him, at the close of the Year, with our thank-offerings, our Hearts may by his grace, be prepared to do it in a manner acceptable to **Him**.*

*That **He** would be graciously pleased to establish the French Republic, and prosper others who are contending for the Rights of Men, and dispose all Nations to favor the same principles, and return to Peace and Friendship.*

*That **He** would in his great Mercy, remember the unhappy state of our Fellow-Citizens and others, who are groaning under bondage, in a foreign Land.*

*That **He** would soften the Hearts of those who have led them captive, inclining that People to show them favor during their Captivity, and in **His** own due time open a door for their relief:*

*And finally, that **He** would over-rule all the confusions that are in the Earth, of the speedy establishment of the Redeemer's Kingdom, which consisteth in Righteousness and Peace.*

And I do recommend to the People of this Commonwealth, to abstain from all unnecessary Labor and Recreation on the said Day.

*GIVEN at the Council-Chamber, in Boston, this Twenty-eighth Day of February, in the **Year of our Lord**, One Thousand Seven Hundred and Ninety-five, and in the Nineteenth Year of the Independence of the United States of America*

SAMUEL ADAMS

Attest: John Avery, jun. Secretary, Commonwealth of Massachusetts

GOD Save the COMMONWEALTH of MASSACHUSETTS!

By the President of the United States of America

A PROCLAMATION

*AS the safety and prosperity of nations ultimately and essentially depend on
the protection and blessing of **Almighty God**; and the national
acknowledgment of this truth is not only an indispensable duty which the
people owe to **Him**, but a duty whose natural influence is favorable to the
promotion of that morality and piety, without which social happiness cannot
exist, nor the blessings of a free government be enjoyed; and as this duty, at
all times incumbent, is so especially in seasons of difficulty and of danger,
when existing or threatening calamities, the just judgments of **God** against
prevalent iniquity are a loud call to repentance and reformation; and as the
United States of America are at present placed in a hazardous and afflictive
situation, by the unfriendly disposition, conduct and demands of a foreign
power, evinced by repeated refusals to receive our messengers of reconciliation
and peace, by depredations on our commerce, and the infliction of injuries on
very many of our fellow citizens, while engaged in their lawful business on
the seas:*

*Under these considerations it has appeared to me that the duty of imploring
the **mercy and benediction of Heaven** on our country, demands at this time
a special attention from its inhabitants.*

*I HAVE therefore thought it fit to recommend, that Wednesday, the 9th day
of May next be observed throughout the United States, as a day of Solemn
Humiliation, Fasting and Prayer.*

*That the citizens of these states, abstaining on that day from their customary
worldly occupations, offer their devout addresses to the **Father of Mercies**,
agreeably to those forms or methods which they have severally adopted as the
most suitable and becoming:*

*That all religious congregations do, with the deepest humility, acknowledge
before **GOD** the manifold sins and transgressions with which we are justly
chargeable as individuals and as a nation; beseeching him, at the same time, of
his infinite Grace, through the **Redeemer of the world**, freely to remit all*

134

*our offences, and to incline us, by **his holy spirit**, to that sincere repentance and reformation which may afford us reason to hope for his inestimable favor and heavenly benediction;*

That it be made the subject of particular and earnest supplication, that our country may be protected from all the dangers which threaten it; that our civil and religious privileges may be preserved inviolate, and perpetuated to the latest generations;

That our public councils and magistrates may be especially enlightened and directed at this critical period; that the American people may be united in those bonds of amity and mutual confidence, and inspired with that vigor and fortitude by which they have in times past been so highly distinguished, and by which they have obtained such invaluable advantages:

That the health of the inhabitants of our land may be preserved, and their agriculture, commerce, fisheries, arts and manufactures be blessed and prospered: **That the principles of genuine piety and sound morality may influence the minds and govern the lives of every description of our citizens; and that the blessings of peace, freedom, and pure religion, may be speedily extended to all the nations of the earth.**

*And finally I recommend, that on the said day; the duties of humiliation and prayer be accompanied by fervent Thanksgiving to the **bestower of every good gift**, not only for having hitherto protected and preserved the people of these United States in the independent enjoyment of their religious and civil freedom, but also for having prospered them in a wonderful progress of population, and for conferring on them many and great favours conducive to the happiness and prosperity of a nation.*

*Given under my hand and seal of the United States of America, at Philadelphia, this twenty-third day of March, in the **year of our Lord** one thousand seven hundred and ninety-eight, and of the Independence of the said States the twenty-second.*

By the President, JOHN ADAMS

TIMOTHY PICKERING, Secretary of State

The Columbian Centinel, April 4, 1798

GENERAL FAST

By the President of the United States of America,

A Proclamation

*As no truth is more clearly taught in the Volume of Inspiration, nor any more fully demonstrated by the experience of all ages, than that a deep sense and a due acknowledgment of the governing providence of a **Supreme Being**, and of the accountableness of men to **Him** as the searcher of hearts and righteous distributor of rewards and punishments, are conducive, equally, to the happiness and rectitude of individuals, and to the well-being of communities; as it is, also, most reasonable, in itself, that men who are made capable of social acts and relations, who owe their improvements to the social state, and who derive their enjoyments from it, should, as a society, make their acknowledgments of dependence and obligation to **Him** who hath endowed them with these capacities and elevated them in the scale of existence by these distinctions; as it is, likewise, a plain dictate of duty, and a strong sentiment of nature, that in circumstances of great urgency and seasons of imminent danger, earnest and particular supplications should be made to **Him** who is able to defend or to destroy; as, moreover, the most precious interests of the people of the United States are still held in jeopardy, by the hostile designs and insidious acts of a foreign nation, as well as by the dissemination among them of those principles subversive of the foundations of all religious, moral, and social obligations, that have produced incalculable mischief and misery in other countries; and as, in fine, the observance of special seasons for public religious solemnities, is happily calculated to avert the evils which we ought to deprecate, and to excite to the performance of the duties which we ought to discharge, - by calling and fixing the attention of the people at large to the momentous truths already recited, by affording opportunity to teach and inculcate them, by animating devotion and giving to it the character of a national act:*

For these reasons I have thought proper to recommend, and I do hereby recommend accordingly, that Thursday, the Twenty-fifth day of April next, be *observed throughout the United States of America as a **day of solemn humiliation, fasting, and prayer**.*

That the citizens on that day abstain as far as may be from their secular occupations, devote the time to the sacred duties of religion in public and in private:

*That they call to mind our numerous offenses against the **most High God**, confess them before **Him** with the sincerest penitence, implore **His** pardoning mercy, through the **great Mediator and Redeemer**, for our past transgressions, and that, through the grace of **His Holy Spirit**, we may be disposed and enabled to yield a more suitable obedience to **His** righteous requisitions in time to come:*

*That **He** would interpose to arrest the progress of that impiety and licentiousness in principle and practice, so offensive to **Himself** and so ruinous to mankind:*

*That **He** would make us deeply sensible that "righteousness exalteth a nation, but sin is a reproach to any people":*

*That **He** would turn us from our transgressions and turn **His** displeasure from us:*

*That **He** would withhold us from unreasonable discontent, - from disunion, faction, sedition, and insurrection:*

*That **He** would preserve our country from the desolating sword:*

*That **He** would save our cities and towns from a repetition of those awful pestilential visitations under which they have lately suffered so severely, and that the health of our inhabitants, generally, may be precious in **His** sight:*

*That **He** would favor us with fruitful seasons, and so bless the labors of the husbandman as that there may be food in abundance for man and beast:*

*That **He** would prosper our commerce, manufactures, and fisheries, and give success to the people in all their lawful industry and enterprise: That **He*** would smile on our colleges, academies, schools, and seminaries of learning, and make them nurseries of sound science, morals, and religion:

That **He** would bless all magistrates, from the highest to the lowest, give them the true spirit of their station, make them a terror to evil doers and a praise to them that do well:

That **He** would preside over the councils of the nation at this critical period, enlighten them to a just discernment of the public interest, and save them from mistake, division, and discord:

That **He** would succeed our preparations for defense, and bless our armaments by land and by sea:

That **He** would put an end to the effusion of human blood, and the accumulation of human misery, among the contending nations of the earth, by disposing them to justice, to equity, to benevolence, and to peace:

And that **He** would extend the blessings of knowledge, of true liberty, and of pure and undefiled religion, throughout the world.

And I do, also, recommend that with these acts of humiliation, penitence, and prayer, fervent thanksgiving to the **Author of all good** be united, for the countless favors which **He** is still continuing to the people of the United States, and which render their condition as a nation eminently happy, when compared with the lot of others.

Signed John Adams

Massachusetts Mercury, March 19, 1799

By the President of the United States of America,

A Proclamation

*WHEREAS the Congress of the United States, by a joint resolution of the two Houses, have signified a request, that a day may be recommended, to be observed by the People of the United States, with religious solemnity, as a day of public Humiliation, and Prayer; and whereas such a recommendation will enable the several religious denominations and societies so disposed, to offer, at one and the same time, their common vows and adorations to **Almighty God**, on the solemn occasion produced by the war, in which **he** has been pleased to permit the injustice of a foreign power to involve these United States;*

*I do therefore recommend the third Thursday in August next, as a convenient day to be set apart for the devout purposes of rendering to the **Sovereign of the Universe and the Benefactor of mankind**, the public homage due to his holy attributes; of acknowledging the transgressions which might justly provoke the manifestations of His divine displeasures; of seeking **His merciful forgiveness, His assistance in the great duties of repentance and amendment**; and especially of offering fervent supplications, that in the present season of calamity and war, **He** would take the American People under **his** peculiar care and protection; that **he** would guide their public councils, animate their patriotism, and bestow **His** blessing on their arms; that **He** would inspire all nations with a love of justice and of concord, and with a reverence for the unerring precept of our holy religion, to do to others as they would require others to do to them; and finally, that , turning the hearts of our enemies from the violence and injustice which sway their councils against us, **He would hasten a restoration of the blessings of Peace**.*

*Given at Washington the 9th day of July, in the **year of our Lord** one thousand eight hundred and twelve.*

James Madison.

By the President

James Monroe,

Secretary of State

The Independent Chronicle, July 20, 1812

On August 20, 1812 in Massachusetts, Henry Colman preached a sermon in relation to the Day of Fast proclamation issued by President Madison.

Presidential Proclamation

July 23, 1813

*Whereas the Congress of the United States, by a joint resolution of the two Houses, have signified a request that a day may be recommended, to be observed by the people of the U. States with religious solemnity, as a day of Public Humiliation and Prayer; and whereas in times of public calamity, such as that of the war, brought on the U. States by the injustice of a foreign government, it is especially becoming, that the hearts of all should be touched with the same, and the eyes of all be turned to that **Almighty Power, in whose hand are the welfare and the destiny of nations**:*

*I do, therefore, issue this my Proclamation, recommending to all, who shall be piously disposed to unite their hearts and voices in addressing, at one and the same time, their vows and adorations, to the **great Parent and Sovereign of the Universe, that they assemble on the second Thursday of September next, in their respective religious congregations, to render him thanks for the many blessings He has bestowed on the people of the United States; that He has blessed them with a land capable of yielding all the necessaries and requisites of human life, with ample means for convenient exchanges with foreign countries; that He has blessed the labours employed in its cultivation and improvement; that He is now blessing the exertions to extend and establish the arts and manufactures, which will secure within ourselves supplies too important to remain dependent on the precarious policy, on the peaceable dispositions of other nations, and particularly that He has blessed the United States with a political constitution founded on the will and authority of the whole people, and guaranteeing to each individual the security,** not only of his person and his property, but of those sacred rights of conscience, so essential to his present happiness, and so dear to his future hopes: that with those expressions of devout thankfulness be joined supplications to the same **Almighty Power**, that **He** would look down with compassion on our infirmities, that **He** would pardon our manifold transgressions, and awaken and strengthen in all the wholesome purposes of repentance and amendment; that in this season of trial and calamity, **He*** *would preside in a particular manner, over our public councils, and inspire all citizens with a love of their country, and with those fraternal affections and that mutual confidence, which have so happy a tendency to make us safe at home and respected abroad; and that, as **He** was graciously pleased, heretofore, to smile on our struggles against the attempts of the government of the empire, of which these states then made a part, to wrest from them the rights and privileges to which they were entitled in common with every other part, and to raise them to the station of an independent and sovereign people; so he would now be pleased, in like manner, to bestow **His** blessing on our arms in resisting the hostile and persevering efforts of the same power, to degrade us on the ocean, the common inheritance of all, from rights and immunities, belonging and essential to the American people, as a co-equal member of the great community of independent nations; and that, inspiring our enemies with moderation, with justice and with that spirit of reasonable accommodation, which our country has continued to manifest, we may be enabled to beat our swords into plough shares, and to enjoy in peace, every man, the fruits of his honest industry, and the rewards of **His** lawful enterprize.*

*If the public homage of a people can ever be worthy the favorable regard of the **Holy and Omniscient Being** to whom it is addressed, it must be that, in which those who join in it are guided only by their free choice, by the impulse of their hearts and the dictates of their consciences; and such a spectacle must be interesting to all **Christian nations**; as proving that religion, that **gift of Heaven** for the good of man, freed from all coercive edicts, from that unhallowed connexion with the powers of this world, which corrupts religion into an instrument or an usurper of the policy of the state, and, making no appeal but to reason, to the heart and to the conscience, can spread its benign influence everywhere, and can attract to the **Divine Altar** those free-will offerings of humble supplication, thanksgiving and praise, which alone can be acceptable to **Him** whom no hypocrisy can deceive, and no forced sacrifices propitiate.*

Upon these principles, and with these views, the good people of the U. States are invited, in conformity with the resolution aforesaid, to dedicate the day above named, to the religious solemnities therein recommended.

*Given at Washington, this twenty-third day of July in the **year of our Lord** one thousand eight hundred and thirteen.*

James Madison

A PROCLAMATION

BY THE PRESIDENT

*The two Houses of the National Legislature having, by a joint resolution, expressed their desire, that in the present time of public calamity and war, a day may be recommended to be observed by the people of the United States as a Day of Public Humiliation and Fasting and of Prayer to **Almighty God**, for the safety and welfare of these States, **His** blessing on their arms, and a speedy restoration of peace. – I have deemed it proper by this Proclamation, to recommend that Thursday the Twelfth of January next be set apart as a day on which all may have an opportunity of voluntarily offering, at the same time, in their respective religious assemblies, their humble adoration to the **Great Sovereign of the Universe**, of confessing their sins and transgressions, and of strengthening their vows of repentance and amendment.*

*They will be invited by the same solemn occasion, to call to mind the distinguished favors conferred on the American people, in the general health which has been enjoyed; in the abundant fruits of the season; in the progress of the arts, instrumental to their comfort, their prosperity, and their security; and in the victories which have so powerfully contributed to the defense and protection of our country – a devout thankfulness for all which ought to be mingled with their supplications to the **Beneficent Parent of the human race**, that **He** would be graciously pleased to pardon all their offenses against **Him**; to support and animate them in the discharge of their respective duties; to continue to them the precious advantages flowing from political institutions so auspicious to their safety against dangers from abroad, to their tranquility at home, and to their liberties, civil and religious; and that **He** would, in a special manner, preside over the nation, in its public councils and constituted authorities, giving wisdom to its measures and success to its arms, in maintaining its rights, and in overcoming all hostile designs and attempts against it; and, finally, that by inspiring the enemy with dispositions favorable to a just and reasonable Peace, its blessings may be speedily and happily restored.*

Given under my hand at the city of Washington, the 16th day of November, 1814, and of the Independence of the United States the 38th.

JAMES MADISON, President of the United States of America

The Yankee, November 25, 1814

Subsequent proclamations were issued by President James Buchanan on December 14, 1860 and by President Abraham Lincoln on March 30, 1863.

James Buchanan, President of the United States of America.

A Proclamation for a Day of Humiliation, Fasting, & Prayer

To the People of the United States, a Recommendation

Numerous appeals have been made to me by pious and patriotic associations and citizens, in view of the present distracted and dangerous condition of our country, to recommend that a day be set apart for Humiliation, Fasting and Prayer throughout the Union.

*In compliance with their request and my own sense of duty, I designate Friday, the 4th of January 1861, for this purpose, and recommend that the People assemble on that day, **according to their several forms of worship, to keep it as a solemn Fast.***

The Union of the States is at the present moment threatened with alarming and immediate danger; panic and distress of a fearful character prevails throughout the land; our laboring population are without employment, and consequently deprived of the mans of earning their bread.

Indeed, hope seems to have deserted the minds of men. All classes are in a state of confusion and dismay, and the wisest counsels of our best and purest men are wholly disregarded.

*In this the hour of our calamity and peril, to whom shall we resort for relief but to the **God** of our fathers?*

*His omnipotent arm only can save us from the awful effects of our own crimes and follies — our own ingratitude and guilt towards our **Heavenly Father**.*

*Let us, then, with deep contrition and penitent sorrow, unite in humbling ourselves before the **Most High**, in confessing our individual and national sins, and in acknowledging the injustice of our punishment.*

147

*Let us implore **Him** to remove from our hearts that false pride of opinion which would impel us to persevere in wrong for the sake of consistency, rather than yield a just submission to the unforeseen exigencies by which we are now surrounded.*

*Let us with deep reverence beseech **Him** to restore the friendship and good will which prevailed in former days among the people of the several States; and, above all, to save us from the horrors of civil war and "blood-guiltiness."*

*Let our fervent prayers ascend to **His Throne** that **He** would not desert us in this hour of extreme peril, but remember us as **He** did our fathers in the darkest days of the revolution; and preserve our Constitution and our Union, the work of their hands, for ages yet to come.*

*An **Omnipotent Providence** may overrule existing evils for permanent good. **He** can make the wrath of man to praise **Him**, and the remainder of wrath **He** can restrain. — Let me invoke every individual, in whatever sphere of like **He** may be placed, to feel a personal responsibility to **God** and his country for keeping this day holy, and for contributing all in **His** power to remove our actual and impending calamities.*

James Buchanan

Washington, Dec. 14, 1860

Proclamation of Thanksgiving

Washington, D.C.
October 3, 1863

By the President of the United States of America

A Proclamation

The year that is drawing towards its close, has been filled with the blessings of fruitful fields and healthful skies. To these bounties, which are so constantly enjoyed that we are prone to forget the source from which they come, others have been added, which are of so extraordinary a nature, that they cannot fail to penetrate and soften even the heart which is habitually insensible to the ever watchful providence of **Almighty God.**

In the midst of a civil war of unequalled magnitude and severity, which has sometimes seemed to foreign States to invite and to provoke their aggression, peace has been preserved with all nations, order has been maintained, the laws have been respected and obeyed, and harmony has prevailed everywhere except in the theatre of military conflict; while that theatre has been greatly contracted by the advancing armies and navies of the Union.

Needful diversions of wealth and of strength from the fields of peaceful industry to the national defence have not arrested the plough, the shuttle or the ship; the axe has enlarged the borders of our settlements, and the mines, as well of iron and coal as of the precious metals, have yielded even more abundantly than heretofore. Population has steadily increased, notwithstanding the waste that has been made in the camp, the siege and the battle-field; and the country, rejoicing in the consciousness of augmented strength and vigor, is permitted to expect continuance of years with large increase of freedom. No human counsel hath devised nor hath any mortal hand worked out these great things. They are the gracious gifts of the **Most High God,** *who, while dealing with us in anger for our sins, hath nevertheless remembered mercy.*

It has seemed to me fit and proper that they should be solemnly, reverently and gratefully acknowledged as with one heart and one voice by the whole American People.

*I do therefore invite my fellow citizens in every part of the United States, and also those who are at sea and those who are sojourning in foreign lands, to set apart and observe the last Thursday of November next, as a day of Thanksgiving and Praise to our **beneficent Father who dwelleth in the Heavens.***

*And I recommend to them that while offering up the ascriptions justly due to **Him** for such singular deliverances and blessings, they do also, with humble penitence for our national perverseness and disobedience, commend to **His** tender care all those who have become widows, orphans, mourners or sufferers in the lamentable civil strife in which we are unavoidably engaged, and fervently implore the interposition of the **Almighty Hand** to heal the wounds of the nation and to restore it as soon as may be consistent with the **Divine** purposes to the full enjoyment of peace, harmony, tranquility and Union.*

In testimony whereof, I have hereunto set my hand and caused the Seal of the United States to be affixed.

*Done at the City of Washington, this Third day of October, in the **year of our Lord** one thousand eight hundred and sixty-three, and of the Independence of the United States the Eighty-eighth.*

By the President: Abraham Lincoln

**William H. Seward,
Secretary of State**

The proclamation declared by President Lincoln led to the establishment of a National Day of Thanksgiving.

On November 28, 1861 President Lincoln had ordered all government departments be closed in observance of a day of thanksgiving.

A magazine editor by the name of Sarah Josepha Hale, wrote a letter to President Lincoln, dated September 28, 1863 requesting that President Lincoln, *"day of our annual Thanksgiving made a National and fixed Union Festival."*

"You may have observed that, for some years past, there has been an increasing interest felt in our land to have the Thanksgiving held on the same day, in all the States; it now needs National recognition and authoritive fixation, only, to become permanently, an American custom and institution."

So as seen through these presidential proclamations, the Founding Fathers in the role of national leader did in FACT call upon the nation to fast and come to God of the Christian faith to come to the aid of the United States.

Throughout these Presidential & Governor Proclamations, these documents are filled with request s upon the nation to come together on the assigned day to refrain from work during that day to fast and to pray to our Almighty God in thanksgiving for the blessings on the United States; to pray to our Almighty God for His guidance on our nation and to ask forgiveness for the sins of the nation.

For those unfamiliar with fasting, this is a practice in the Christian faith where people deny themselves food and water; sometimes just food and they kneel in prayer for God to intervene in a time of need.

The fact that these men all called upon a national prayer to God demonstrates that they were NOT deists and that they founded this nation as a NATION UNDER GOD.

Our Founding Fathers embraced the Word of God, the very same words from the Holy Bible taught to them by their family members and taught from the pulpit of their chosen church.

The Holy Bible was not used just to teach the Word of God but the Bible was used to teach values and principles such as "love thy neighbor" and other such important values such as honesty and integrity.

These same Christian values are the genesis of our founding documents.

Unfortunately this nation is filled with people who do not understand the foundation of the United States is the Word of God.

The United States of America is a nation of freedom and the freedom to choose.

Not one person in this country is required to believe in God; they have the right to not believe in God and they have the right to hold their own personal beliefs…but their beliefs cannot change the truth of our founding.

Deism

In understanding the Founding Fathers of the United States the philosophy of deism is constantly misapplied as being their accepted and practiced philosophy. Some of the leading founders, George Washington and Benjamin Franklin have been erroneously labeled as deists because of their rare use of the word in recorded documentation.

In order to understand what a deist is and what they believe all we need to do is go to the dictionary for a concise definition of the word.

Deism: (dē'ĭz'əm) n.

*"A religious belief holding that **God** created the universe and established rationally comprehensible moral and natural laws but does not intervene in human affairs through miracles or supernatural revelation."*

A deist believes, by the very definition of the word "that God does not intervene in human affairs through miracles or supernatural revelation". By reading the words of the Founders and their national proclamations it is IMPOSSIBLE for them to be a practicing deist.

This book is not about religious beliefs but a book about the Founders and what they said about God and the United States. Without a doubt, some readers of this book will at minimum take exception with my assertion that the main Founding Fathers of the United States were not deists.

What the words of the Founding Fathers DO PROVE is that the majority of them openly expressed the connection between their belief in God and the founding of the United States of America.

Congress cannot pass a law to establish religion.

In Europe the monarchs used the churches to spread corruption and for control of the people. The founders were keenly aware of the pitfalls of a government-controlled religion because it was happening in Europe in their lifetime and before.

This nation was founded upon the principles of Christianity.

The Founders believed that our rights come from God, not men. The freedom of religion in this country is in support of their belief that all people received their rights from God and not men. This is a Christian nation which invites and protects the freedom to choose one's belief and live as they choose so long as it does not infringe on another person's freedom.

Not deism...John Adams Fast Day Proclamation (1798), *"acknowledge before **God** the manifold sins and transgressions with which we are justly chargeable as individuals and as a nation; beseeching him at the same time, of **His** infinite grace, through the **Redeemer of the World**, freely to remit all our offences, and to incline us, by **His Holy Spirit**, to that sincere repentance and reformation which may afford us reason to hope for his inestimable favor and heavenly benediction."*

Not deism...Benjamin Franklin's speech to the 1787 Constitutional Convention, *"the longer I live, the more convincing proofs I see of this Truth--that **God** governs in the Affairs of Men." "I also believe, that "without his concurring Aid, we shall succeed in this political Building no better than the Builders of Babel."*

Not deism...Washington's Prayer (George Washington) 1783, *"dispose us all, to do Justice, to love mercy, and to demean ourselves with that Charity, humility and pacific temper of mind, which were the Characteristicks of the **Divine Author** of our blessed Religion, and without an humble imitation of whose example in these things, we can never hope to be a happy Nation."*

Not deism...*"**God** who gave us life gave us liberty. And can the liberties of a nation be thought secure if we have removed their only firm basis: a* *conviction in the minds of men that these liberties are the gift of **God**? That they are not to be violated but with **His** wrath? Indeed, I tremble for my country when I reflect that **God** is just; that His justice cannot sleep forever."*

*The **God** who gave us life gave us liberty at the same time: the hand of force may destroy, but cannot disjoin them."*

Thomas Jefferson

The atheists and the deniers of true US history will cling to their rhetoric and their agenda, even when proven wrong but for those who believe in the truth and who value the truth they can always know this: THE TRUTH ALWAYS WINS.

Again this book is to share these few treasures of fact so that the reader will have the facts with them and this book also gives the reader a starting point to conduct their own historical research.

Dr. Franklin's Motion for Prayers in the Convention

June 28, 1787

Mr. President

The small Progress we have made after 4 or 5 Weeks close Attendance and continual Reasonings with each other, our different Sentiments on almost every Question, several of the last producing as many Noes as Ayes, is methinks a melancholy Proof of the Imperfection of the Human Understanding.

We indeed seem to feel our own Want of political Wisdom, since we have been running all about in search of it. We have gone back to ancient History for Models of Government, and examin'd the different Forms of those Republicks, which, having been originally form'd with the Seeds of their own Dissolution, now no longer exist. And we have view'd modern States all round Europe, but find none of their Constitutions suitable to our Circumstances.

*In this Situation of this Assembly, groping, as it were, in the dark, to find Political Truth, and scarce able to distinguish it when presented to us, how has it happened, Sir, that we have not, hitherto once thought of humbly applying to the **Father of Lights** to illuminate our Understandings?*

*In the Beginning of the Contest with Britain, when we were sensible of Danger, we had daily Prayers in this Room for the **Divine Protection**! Our Prayers, Sir, were heard; and they were graciously answered. All of us, who were engag'd in the Struggle, must have observ'd frequent Instances of a **Superintending Providence** in our Favour.*

*To that kind Providence we owe this happy Opportunity of Consulting in Peace on the Means of establishing our future national Felicity. And have we now forgotten that **powerful Friend**? or do we imagine we no longer need its Assistance?*

*I have lived, Sir, a long time; and the longer I live, the more convincing Proofs I see of this Truth, That **GOD** governs in the Affairs of Men! And if a Sparrow cannot fall to the Ground without **his** Notice, is it probable that an Empire can rise without **his** Aid?*

*We have been assured, Sir, in the Sacred Writings, that "except the **Lord** build the House, they labor in vain that build it." I firmly believe this; and I also believe that without **his** concurring Aid, we shall succeed in this political Building no better than the Builders of Babel: We shall be divided by our little partial local Interests, our Projects will be confounded and we ourselves shall become a Reproach and a Byeword down to future Ages. And what is worse, Mankind may hereafter, from this unfortunate Instance, despair of establishing Government by human Wisdom, and leave it to Chance, War and Conquest. I therefore beg leave to move,*

*That henceforth Prayers, imploring the **Assistance of Heaven**, and its Blessing on our Deliberations, be held in this Assembly every Morning before we proceed to Business; and that one or more of the Clergy of this City be requested to officiate in that Service.*

The Franklin Papers

The false allegation that many of the Founding Fathers were practitioners of Christian deism

The argument from some people is that the founders, particularly Jefferson and Franklin were followers of deism but a simple quick search proves that this allegation is untrue.

"Christian Deists believe that God does take an ongoing interest in the world and humanity but God does not control the world or humanity." source: the Christian Deism/archives website.

But in 1779, Thomas Jefferson included this thought in a Thanksgiving Proclamation that he ordered to be issued and he signed.
"To beseech **Him** *that* **He** *would be graciously pleased to influence our public Councils, and bless them with wisdom from on high, with unanimity, firmness and success; that* **He** *would go forth with our hosts and crown our arms with victory;"*

If Thomas Jefferson was a Christian deist, how could he believe that God does not influence the world or humanity but yet in his proclamation of 1779, Thomas Jefferson asks that the public pray for God to influence their public councils and crown them with victory?

More from the Christian deism website under, *"What is a Christian Deist?"*

"If God directly intervened in human events, we would no longer be "free agents in a free world. We would be like puppets controlled by God."
More from Jefferson's Proclamation of 1779:
"That **He** *would take into* **His** *holy protection, our illustrious ally, give him victory over his enemies, and render him finally great, as the father of his people, and the protector of the rights of mankind; that* **He** *would graciously be pleased to turn the hearts of our enemies, and to dispense the blessings of peace to contending nations."*
"That **He** *would in mercy look down upon us, pardon all our sins, and receive us into* **His** *favour; and finally, that* **He** *would establish the independence of*

these United States upon the basis of religion and virtue, and support and protect them in the enjoyment of peace, liberty and safety."

If Thomas Jefferson were a Christian deist, why would he believe that God would intervene in human events when the belief of a Christian deist is the opposite of that?

Even by the standards of "Christian deist", the Founding fathers don't meet their criteria.

Thomas Jefferson made reference to *the "venerated reformer of human errors"* which is Jesus Christ.

What the definition is of venerated?

Veneration (noun)

Definition of veneration

1: *"respect or awe inspired by the dignity, wisdom, dedication, or talent of a person."*

2: *"the act of venerating."*

3: *"the condition of one that is venerated."*

Venerate (verb)

Venerated; venerating

Definition of venerate (transitive verb)

1: *"to regard with reverential respect or with admiring deference."*

2: *"to honor (an icon, a relic, etc.) with a ritual act of devotion."*

Reformer (noun)

Definition of reformer

1: *"one that works for or urges reform."*

Reform (verb) reformed; reforming; reforms

Reformer (transitive verb)

Definition of reform (transitive verb)

1. a: *"to put or change into an improved form or condition."*

b: *"to amend or improve by change of form or removal of faults or abuses."*

2. *"to put an end to (an evil) by enforcing or introducing a better method or course of action."*

3. *"to induce or cause to abandon evil ways."*

Jesus Christ is the VENERATED REFORMER of human errors.

This contradicts the belief of Christian deism.

"Christian Deists do not worship Jesus as God and do not believe in the theory of atonement that claims that Jesus had to die as a sacrifice to pay the "death penalty" for humankind and save them from the "wrath" of God."

"God can care for the poor through charitable persons and through programs designed by compassionate leaders and legislators."

This is the opposite in what the founders believed.

We have to read this very carefully to prevent misunderstanding what Jefferson said in the context that he meant this comment to be understood.

*"The truth is that the greatest enemies to the doctrines of **Jesus** are those calling themselves the expositors of them, who have perverted them for the structure of a system of fancy absolutely incomprehensible, and without any foundation in **His** genuine words. And the day will come when the mystical generation of **Jesus**, by **the Supreme Being as His father** in the womb of a*

virgin will be classed with the fable of the generation of Minerva in the brain of Jupiter."

"But we may hope that the dawn of reason and freedom of thought in these United States will do away all this artificial scaffolding, and restore to us the primitive and genuine doctrines of this the most venerated reformer of human errors." **Thomas Jefferson letter to John Adams April 11, 1823**

By quickly reading this statement made by Thomas Jefferson, any person could misunderstand what the meaning of this statement really meant.

What is an expositor and what does using this word mean in the context that it was used by Thomas Jefferson.

Definition of expositor,

Expositor (noun)

Definition of expositor, 14th century.

"a person who explains."

Exposition (noun)

Definition of exposition, 14th century.

1: *"a setting forth of the meaning or purpose (as of writing)."*

2a: *"discourse or an example of it designed to convey information or explain what is difficult to understand."*

Expository (adjective)

Definition of expository, 1628.

"of, relating to, or containing exposition."

The Aitken Bible

The Bible of the Revolution

"The United States in Congress assembled highly approve the pious and laudable undertaking of Mr. Aitken, as subservient to the interest of religion, as well as an instance of the progress of arts in this country, and being satisfied from the above report of his care and accuracy in the execution of the work, they recommend this edition of the Bible to the inhabitants of the United States, and hereby authorize him to publish this recommendation in the manner he shall think proper."

CHA. THOMSON, Sec'ry

Congressional Resolution, September 10, 1782

Because of the war with England by 1777 it became virtually impossible to import new Bibles to the American colonies. On September 11, 1777 the chaplain of the Continental Congress, Dr. Patrick Allison reported a shortage of Bibles. Dr. Allison stated that Bibles were needed because "the use of the Bible is so universal and its importance so great" and so Congress took action to remedy the shortage. Therefore Congress passed a resolution to purchase 20,000 Bibles in the English language and have them imported from Holland. This too proved to be a difficult if not entirely impossible feat so the Continental Congress began to search for another way to supply the colonies with much needed and requested Bibles.

Enter Robert Aitken, a printer from Philadelphia who petitioned the Continental Congress to support him printing the much needed Bibles. Robert Aitken was well-known with the Congress and his credentials as a printer of quality easily convinced the Congress to authorize him and compensate him for printing copies of a complete Bible. Aitken had previously published the Journals of Congress for the First

Continental Congress among other publications for other authors such as Thomas Paine.

On September 10, 1782 Congress passed a resolution for the first edition printing of what was to become known as the Aitken Bible.

The Aitken Bible was well received in the American colonies with George Washington too, being very appreciative of the Aitken Bible.

It is said that General Washington remarked to a friend that he wished that Congress had thought to supply his soldiers with a copy of the Aitken Bible in appreciation and support for their sacrifice to gain freedom from England.

Part Three

The Treaty of Tripoli

There is an intentional effort by the atheists and the deniers of true US history to perpetuate the lie that the United States was not founded by Christians or that the US was founded upon Christian principles. The people in those groups have spread their lies because of their spin of Article 11 of the Treaty of Tripoli. To understand the truth of Article 11 we must visit the historical facts surrounding the reasons for the US making a treaty with the Mussleman pirates (Muslim pirates) and the sequence of events which followed.

As the United States was a new and very young nation its strength and influence with foreign nations and leaders was minimal. Although the US had defeated England and its military, without assistance by France with soldiers, equipment and financial aid there is little reason to believe that the American colonies would have won their war for independence.

The first administration under George Washington was struggling in their efforts to stabilize the United States and international trade was the key to the economy's stability. Merchant ships under the American flag sailing in foreign national and international waters were becoming targets for Muslim pirates.

Not only were these pirates seizing American merchant ships but the ship's crews were being held for ransom. Losing merchants ships and the ship's cargo was damaging to US companies but the capture of US sailors and holding them for ransom was something that the US government would not tolerate.

John Adams, Thomas Jefferson and Ben Franklin were given full power and authority by the US government to negotiate a treaty with the government of Morocco to end Muslim piracy.

Although an agreement had been reached with the pirates in 1785 Algerian pirates captured two American ships with their crew and demanded a ransom of $60,000 to be paid for their safe release.

Thomas Jefferson did not support paying tribute to pirates nor did Jefferson believe that American citizens would be in favor of paying an annual tribute. Jefferson felt that if the pirates refused to end taking American merchant ships and crews then the US government should go to war against the Mussleman pirates and end their piracy once and for all.

To Horatio Gates

Paris Dec. 13, 1784

Dear General

"I duly received the letter you were so good as to write me from New York. We have here under our contemplation the future miseries of human nature, like to be occasioned by the ambition of a young man, who has been taught to view his subjects as his cattle. The pretensions he sets up to the navigation of the Scheld would have been good if natural right had been left uncontrolled. But it is impossible for express compact to have taken away a right more effectually than it has the Emperor's. There are numbers here (but not of the cabinet) who still believe he will retract. But I see no one circumstance on which to found such a belief. Nothing has happened but what he must have foreseen and calculated on. And in fact all his movements indicate war.

The Dutch are truly animated and ready to place their existence on the stake now contended for. The spring which brings genial happiness to all other beings will probably open the sluices of calamity on our wretched fellow creatures on this side the Atlantic. France, Holland, Prussia and Turkey, against the two empires I think will be an overmatch. England will be neuter from interest as well as impotence. The disposition of her inhabitants is very unfriendly to us. It remains to see whether their ministers suffer themselves to be led by passion also.

I think it probable we shall go over there for a short time. An American vessel (a Virginian) has been lately taken by a frigate of the emperor of Morocco, who has five of them cruising in the Atlantic. This brig had just left Cadiz. Our trade to Portugal, Spain, and the Mediterranean is annihilated unless we do something decisive. Tribute or war is the usual alternative of these pirates.

If we yield the former, it will require sums which our people will feel. Why not begin a navy then and decide on war? We cannot begin in a better cause nor against a weaker foe.

You will have heard that the E. of Shelburne is made Marquis of Lansdown and Ld. Temple Marquis of Buckingham. There is no appearance however of the former coming into the ministry which seems absolutely firm."

I am with great esteem Dear General Your friend & servt,

Thomas Jefferson

The government of the United States continued to negotiate treaties which did not stop the pirates from seizing American ships and crews. Ransoms were paid and what continued to occur is very much like how the modern day US government handles criminals on foreign soil, pay them and try to appease them.

Thomas Jefferson never supported payment of ransom and it was obvious that no treaty would end the piracy.

Treaty with Morocco June 28 and July 15, 1786

To all Persons to whom these Presents shall come or be made known- Whereas the United States of America in Congress assembled by their Commission bearing date the twelvth day of May One thousand Seven hundred and Eighty four thought proper to constitute John Adams, Benjamin Franklin and Thomas Jefferson their Ministers Plenipotentiary, giving to them or a Majority of them full Powers to confer, treat & negotiate with the Ambassador, Minister or Commissioner of His Majesty the Emperor of Morocco concerning a Treaty of Amity and Commerce, to make & receive propositions for such Treaty and to conclude and sign the same, transmitting it to the United States in Congress assembled for their final Ratification, And by one other (commission bearing date the Eleventh day of March One thousand Seven hundred & Eighty five did further empower the said Ministers Plenipotentiary or a majority of them, by writing under the* hands and Seals to appoint such Agent in the said Business as they might think proper with Authority under the directions and Instructions of the said Ministers to commence & prosecute the said Negotiations & Conferences for the said Treaty provided that the said Treaty should be signed by the said Ministers:

And Whereas, We the said John Adams & Thomas Jefferson two of the said Ministers Plenipotentiary (the said Benjamin Franklin being absent) by writing under the Hand and Seal of the said John Adams at London October the fifth, One thousand Seven hundred and Eighty five, & of the said Thomas Jefferson at Paris October the Eleventh of the same Year, did appoint Thomas Barclay, Agent in the Business aforesaid, giving him the Powers therein, which by the said second Commission we were authorized to give, and the said Thomas Barclay in pursuance thereof, hath arranged Articles for a Treaty of Amity and Commerce between the United States of America and His Majesty the Emperor of Morocco, which Articles written in the Arabic Language, confirmed by His said Majesty the Emperor of Morocco & seal'd with His Royal Seal, being translated into the Language of the said United States of America, together with the Attestations thereto annexed are in the following Words, To Wit.

In the name of Almighty God,

This is a Treaty of Peace and Friendship established between us and the United States of America, which is confirmed, and which we have ordered to be written in this Book and sealed with our Royal Seal at our Court of Morocco on the twenty fifth day of the blessed Month of Shaban, in the Year One thousand two hundred, **trusting in God** *it will remain permanent.*

1. We declare that both Parties have agreed that this Treaty consisting of twenty five Articles shall be inserted in this Book and delivered to the Honorable Thomas Barclay, the Agent of the United States now at our Court, with whose Approbation it has been made and who is duly authorized on their Part, to treat with us concerning all the Matters contained therein.

2. If either of the Parties shall be at War with any Nation whatever, the other Party shall not take a Commission from the Enemy nor fight under their Colors.

3. If either of the Parties shall be at War with any Nation whatever and take a Prize belonging to that Nation, and there shall be found on board Subjects or Effects belonging to either of the Parties, the Subjects shall be set at Liberty and the Effects returned to the Owners. And if any Goods belonging to any Nation, with whom either of the Parties shall be at War, shall be loaded on Vessels belonging to the other Party, they shall pass free and unmolested without any attempt being made to take or detain them.

4. A Signal or Pass shall be given to all Vessels belonging to both Parties, by which they are to be known when they meet at Sea, and if the Commander of a Ship of War of either Party shall have other Ships under his Convoy, the Declaration of the Commander shall alone be sufficient to exempt any of them from examination.

5. If either of the Parties shall be at War, and shall meet a Vessel at Sea, belonging to the other, it is agreed that if an examination is to be made, it shall be done by sending a Boat with two or three Men only, and if any Gun shall be Bred and injury done without Reason, the offending Party shall make good all damages.

6. *If any Moor shall bring Citizens of the United States or their Effects to His Majesty, the Citizens shall immediately be set at Liberty and the Effects restored, and in like Manner, if any Moor not a Subject of these Dominions shall make Prize of any of the Citizens of America or their Effects and bring them into any of the Ports of His Majesty, they shall be immediately released, as they will then be considered as under His Majesty's Protection.*

7. *If any Vessel of either Party shall put into a Port of the other and have occasion for Provisions or other Supplies, they shall be furnished without any interruption or molestation.*

If any Vessel of the United States shall meet with a Disaster at Sea and put into one of our Ports to repair, she shall be at Liberty to land and reload her cargo, without paying any Duty whatever.

9. *If any Vessel of the United States shall be cast on Shore on any Part of our Coasts, she shall remain at the disposition of the Owners and no one shall attempt going near her without their Approbation, as she is then considered particularly under our Protection; and if any Vessel of the United States shall be forced to put into our Ports, by Stress of weather or otherwise, she shall not be compelled to land her Cargo, but shall remain in tranquility until the Commander shall think proper to proceed on his Voyage.*

10. *If any Vessel of either of the Parties shall have an engagement with a Vessel belonging to any of the* **Christian** *Powers within gunshot of the Forts of the other, the Vessel so engaged shall be defended and protected as much as possible until she is in safety; And if any American Vessel shall be cast on shore on the Coast of Wadnoon or any coast thereabout, the People belonging to her shall be protected, and assisted until by the help of* **God**, *they shall be sent to their Country.*

11. *If we shall be at War with any* **Christian** *Power and any of our Vessels sail from the Ports of the United States, no Vessel belonging to the enemy shall follow until twenty four hours after the Departure of our Vessels; and the same Regulation shall be observed towards the American Vessels sailing from our Ports.-be their enemies Moors or* **Christians**.

12. If any Ship of War belonging to the United States shall put into any of our Ports, she shall not be examined on any Pretense whatever, even though she should have fugitive Slaves on Board, nor shall the Governor or Commander of the Place compel them to be brought on Shore on any pretext, nor require any payment for them.

13. If a Ship of War of either Party shall put into a Port of the other and salute, it shall be returned from the Fort, with an equal Number of Guns, not with more or less.

14. The Commerce with the United States shall be on the same footing as is the Commerce with Spain or as that with the most favored Nation for the time being and their Citizens shall be respected and esteemed and have full Liberty to pass and repass our Country and Sea Ports whenever they please without interruption.

15. Merchants of both Countries shall employ only such interpreters, & such other Persons to assist them in their Business, as they shall think proper. No Commander of a Vessel shall transport his Cargo on board another Vessel, he shall not be detained in Port, longer than he may think proper, and all persons employed in loading or unloading Goods or in any other Labor whatever, shall be paid at the Customary rates, not more and not less.

16. In case of a War between the Parties, the Prisoners are not to be made Slaves, but to be exchanged one for another, Captain for Captain, Officer for Officer and one private Man for another; and if there shall prove a deficiency on either side, it shall be made up by the payment of one hundred Mexican Dollars for each Person wanting; And it is agreed that all Prisoners shall be exchanged in twelve Months from the Time of their being taken, and that this exchange may be effected by a Merchant or any other Person authorized by either of the Parties.

17. Merchants shall not be compelled to buy or Sell any kind of Goods but such as they shall think proper; and may buy and sell all sorts of Merchandise but such as are prohibited to the other **Christian Nations**.

18. All goods shall be weighed and examined before they are sent on board, and to avoid all detention of Vessels, no examination shall afterwards be made, unless it shall first be proved, that contraband Goods have been sent on board, in which Case the Persons who took the contraband Goods on board shall be punished according to the Usage and Custom of the Country and no other Person whatever shall be injured, nor shall the Ship or Cargo incur any Penalty or damage whatever.

19. No vessel shall be detained in Port on any presence whatever, nor be obliged to take on board any Article without the consent of the Commander, who shall be at full Liberty to agree for the Freight of any Goods he takes on board.

20. If any of the Citizens of the United States, or any Persons under their Protection, shall have any disputes with each other, the Consul shall decide between the Parties and whenever the Consul shall require any Aid or Assistance from our Government to enforce his decisions it shall be immediately granted to him.

21. If a Citizen of the United States should kill or wound a Moor, or on the contrary if a Moor shall kill or wound a Citizen of the United States, the Law of the Country shall take place and equal Justice shall be rendered, the Consul assisting at the Tryal, and if any Delinquent shall make his escape, the Consul shall not be answerable for him in any manner whatever.

22. If an American Citizen shall die in our Country and no Will shall appear, the Consul shall take possession of his Effects, and if there shall be no Consul, the Effects shall be deposited in the hands of some Person worthy of Trust, until the Party shall appear who has a Right to demand them, but if the Heir to the Person deceased be present, the Property shall be delivered to him without interruption; and if a Will shall appear, the Property shall descend agreeable to that Will, as soon as the Consul shall declare the Validity thereof.

23. The Consuls of the United States of America shall reside in any Sea Port of our Dominions that they shall think proper; And they shall be respected and enjoy all the Privileges which the Consuls of any other Nation enjoy, and

if any of the Citizens of the United States shall contract any Debts or engagements, the Consul shall not be in any Manner accountable for them, unless he shall have given a Promise in writing for the payment or fulfilling thereof, without which promise in Writing no Application to him for any redress shall be made.

*24. If any differences shall arise by either Party infringing on any of the Articles of this Treaty, Peace and Harmony shall remain notwithstanding in the fullest force, until a friendly Application shall be made for an Arrangement, and until that Application shall be rejected, no appeal shall be made to Arms. And if a War shall break out between the Parties, Nine Months shall be granted to all the Subjects of both Parties, to dispose of their Effects and retire with their Property. And it is further declared that whatever indulgences in Trade or otherwise shall be granted to any of the **Christian** Powers, the Citizens of the United States shall be equally entitled to them.*

*25. This Treaty shall continue in full Force, with the help of **God** for Fifty Years.*

We have delivered this Book into the Hands of the before-mentioned Thomas Barclay on the first day of the blessed Month of Ramadan, in the Year One thousand two hundred.

I certify that the annexed is a true Copy of the Translation made by Issac Cardoza Nunez, Interpreter at Morocco, of the treaty between the Emperor of Morocco and the United States of America.

THOS BARCLAY

Or Ouadnoun, on the Atlantic coast, about latitude 29Â° N.

This treaty is quite lengthy to read but it has been included in its entirety to maintain its context and in proof that what atheist and deniers claim is true about Article 11 of the Treaty of Tripoli is in reality FALSE.

There were subsequent treaties made with the Mussleman pirates before the Treaty of Tripoli was written and signed. In 1805 the US government entered into a new treaty called the Treaty of Peace and Amity which replaced the Treaty of Tripoli which removed and nullified Article 11.

We will now reveal and examine the Treaty of Tripoli (Treaty of Peace and Friendship) and the Treaty of Peace and Amity.

Treaty of Peace and Friendship between the United States of America and the Bey and Subjects of Tripoli of Barbary, 1797

ARTICLE 1

There is a firm and perpetual Peace and friendship between the United States of America and the Bey and subjects of Tripoli of Barbary, made by the free consent of both parties, and guaranteed by the most potent Dey & regency of Algiers.

ARTICLE 2

If any goods belonging to any nation with which either of the parties is at war shall be loaded on board of vessels belonging to the other party they shall pass free, and no attempt shall be made to take or detain them.

ARTICLE 3

If any citizens, subjects or effects belonging to either party shall be found on board a prize vessel taken from an enemy by the other party, such citizens or subjects shall be set at liberty, and the effects restored to the owners.

ARTICLE 4

Proper passports are to be given to all vessels of both parties, by which they are to be known. And, considering the distance between the two countries, eighteen months from the date of this treaty shall be allowed for procuring such passports. During this interval the other papers belonging to such vessels shall be sufficient for their protection.

ARTICLE 5

A citizen or subject of either party having bought a prize vessel condemned by the other party or by any other nation, the certificate of condemnation and bill of sale shall be a sufficient passport for such vessel for one year; this being a reasonable time for her to procure a proper passport.

ARTICLE 6

Vessels of either party putting into the ports of the other and having need of provisions or other supplies, they shall be furnished at the market price. And if any such vessel shall so put in from a disaster at sea and have occasion to repair, she shall be at liberty to land and reembark her cargo without paying any duties. But in no case shall she be compelled to land her cargo.

ARTICLE 7

Should a vessel of either party be cast on the shore of the other, all proper assistance shall be given to her and her people; no pillage shall be allowed; the property shall remain at the disposition of the owners, and the crew protected and succored till they can be sent to their country.

ARTICLE 8

If a vessel of either party should be attacked by an enemy within gun-shot of the forts of the other she shall be defended as much as possible. If she be in port she shall not be seized or attacked when it is in the power of the other party to protect her. And when she proceeds to sea no enemy shall be allowed to pursue her from the same port within twenty four hours after her departure.

ARTICLE 9

The commerce between the United States and Tripoli,-the protection to be given to merchants, masters of vessels and seamen,- the reciprocal right of establishing consuls in each country, and the privileges, immunities and jurisdictions to be enjoyed by such consuls, are declared to be on the same footing with those of the most favoured nations respectively.

ARTICLE 10

The money and presents demanded by the Bey of Tripoli as a full and satisfactory consideration on his part and on the part of his subjects for this treaty of perpetual peace and friendship are acknowledged to have been received by him previous to his signing the same, according to a receipt which is hereto annexed, except such part as is promised on the part of the United

States to be delivered and paid by them on the arrival of their Consul in Tripoli, of which part a note is likewise hereto annexed. And no presence of any periodical tribute or farther payment is ever to be made by either party.

ARTICLE 11

As the government of the United States of America is not in any sense founded on the Christian Religion, as it has in itself no character of enmity against the laws, religion or tranquility of Mussleman,-and as the said States never have entered into any war or act of hostility against any Mehomitan nation, it is declared by the parties that no pretext arising from religious opinions shall ever produce an interruption of the harmony existing between the two countries.

ARTICLE 12

In case of any dispute arising from a notation of any of the articles of this treaty no appeal shall be made to arms, nor shall war be declared on any pretext whatever. But if the (consul residing at the place where the dispute shall happen shall not be able to settle the same, an amicable reference shall be made to the mutual friend of the parties, the Dey of Algiers, the parties hereby engaging to abide by his decision. And he by virtue of his signature to this treaty engages for himself and successors to declare the justice of the case according to the true interpretation of the treaty, and to use all the means in his power to enforce the observance of the same.

Signed and sealed at Tripoli of Barbary the 3d day of Jumad in the year of the Higera 1211-corresponding with the 4th day of Novr. 1796 by

JUSSUF BASHAW MAHOMET Bey

SOLIMAN Kaya

MAMET Treasurer

GALIL Genl of the Troops

AMET Minister of Marine

MAHOMET Coml of the city

AMET Chamberlain

MAMET Secretary

ALLY-Chief of the Divan

Signed and sealed at Algiers the 4th day of Argib 1211-corresponding with the 3d day of January 1797 by

HASSAN BASHAW Dey

and by the Agent plenipotentiary of the United States of America

[Seal] Joel BARLOW

[The "Receipt"]

Praise be to God &c-

The present writing done by our hand and delivered to the American Captain O'Brien makes known that he has delivered to us forty thousand Spanish dollars,-thirteen watches of gold, silver & pinsbach,-five rings, of which three of diamonds, one of sapphire and one with a watch in it, One hundred & forty piques of cloth, and four caftans of brocade,-and these on account of the peace concluded with the Americans.

Given at Tripoli in Barbary the 20th day of Jumad 1211, corresponding with the 21st day of Novr 1796-

(Signed) JUSSUF BASHAW-Bey **whom God Exalt**

The foregoing is a true copy of the receipt given by Jussuf Bashaw- Bey of Tripoli-

(Signed) HASSAN BASHAW-Dey of Algiers

The foregoing is a literal translation of the writing in Arabic on the opposite page.

JOEL BARLOW

[The " Note "]

On the arrival of a consul of the United States in Tripoli he is to deliver to Jussuf Bashaw Bey-

Twelve thousand Spanish dollars

Five hawsers-8 Inch

Three cables-10 Inch

Twenty five barrels tar

Twenty five dÂ° pitch

Ten dÂ° rosin

Five hundred pine boards

Five hundred oak dÂ°

Ten masts (without any measure mentioned, suppose for vessels from 2 to 300 ton)

Twelve yards

Fifty bolts canvas

Four anchors

And these when delivered are to be in full of all demands on his part or on that of his successors from the United States according as it is expressed in the tenth article of the following treaty. And no farther demand of tributes, presents or payments shall ever be made.

Translated from the Arabic on the opposite page, which is signed & sealed by Hassan Bashaw Dey of Algiers-the 4th day of Argib 1211-or the 3d day of June 1797-by-

Joel BARLOW

[Approval of Humphreys]

To all to whom these Presents shall come or be made known.

Whereas the Underwritten David Humphreys hath been duly appointed Commissioner Plenipotentiary by Letters Patent, under the Signature of the President and Seal of the United States of America, dated the 30th of March 1795, for negotiating and concluding a Treaty of Peace with the Most Illustrious the Bashaw, Lords and Governors of the City & Kingdom of Tripoli; whereas by a Writing under his Hand and Seal dated the 10th of February 1796, he did (in conformity to the authority committed to me therefor) constitute and appoint Joel Barlow and Joseph Donaldson Junior Agents jointly and separately in the business aforesaid; whereas the annexed Treaty of Peace and Friendship was agreed upon, signed and sealed at Tripoli of Barbary on the 4th Of November 1796, in virtue of the Powers aforesaid and guaranteed by the Most potent Dey and Regency of Algiers; and whereas the same was certified at Algiers on the 3d of January 1797, with the Signature and Seal of Hassan Bashaw Dey, and of Joel Barlow one of the Agents aforesaid, in the absence of the other.

Now Know ye, that I David Humphreys Commissioner Plenipotentiary aforesaid, do approve and conclude the said Treaty, and every article and clause therein contained, reserving the same nevertheless for the final Ratification of the President of the United States of America, by and with the advice and consent of the Senate of the said United States.

In testimony whereof I have signed the same with my Name and Seal, at the City of Lisbon this 10th of February 1797.

[Seal] DAVID HUMPHREYS

Treaty of Tripoli

Treaty of Peace and Friendship, Signed at Tunis August 28, 1797

God is infinite.

*Under the auspices of the greatest, the most powerful of all the princes of the Ottoman nation who reign upon the earth, our most glorious and most august Emperor, who commands the two lands and the two seas, Selim Khan I the victorious, son of the Sultan Moustafa, whose realm may **God** prosper until the end of ages, the support of kings, the seal of justice, the Emperor of emperors.*

*The most illustrious and most magnificent Prince Hamuda Pasha, Bey, who commands the Odgiak of Tunis, the abode of happiness; and the most honored Ibrahim Dey; and Suleiman, Agha of the Janizaries and chief of the Divan; and all the elders of the Odgiak; and **the most distinguished and honored President of the Congress of the United States of America, the most distinguished among those who profess the religion of the Messiah, of whom may the end be happy.***

We have concluded between us the present Treaty of Peace and Friendship, all the articles of which have been framed by the intervention of Joseph Stephen Famin, French merchant resident at Tunis, Charge d'Affaires of the United States of America; which stipulations and conditions are comprised in twenty-three articles, written and expressed in such manner as to leave no doubt of their contents, and in such way as not to be contravened.

ARTICLE 1

There shall be a perpetual and constant peace between the United States of America and the magnificent Pasha, Bey of Tunis, and also a permanent friendship, which shall more and more increase.

ARTICLE 2

If a vessel of war of the two nations shall make prize of an enemy vessel in which may be found effects, property, and subjects of the two contracting parties, the whole shall be restored; the Bey shall restore the property and subjects of the United States, and the latter shall make a reciprocal restoration; it being understood on both sides that the just right to what is claimed shall be proved.

ARTICLE 3

Merchandise belonging to any nation which may be at war with one of the contracting parties, and loaded on board of the vessels of the other, shall pass without molestation and without any attempt being made to capture or detain it.

ARTICLE 4

On both sides sufficient passports shall be given to vessels, that they may be known and treated as friendly; and considering the distance between the two countries, a term of eighteen months is given, within which term respect shall be paid to the said passports, without requiring the conge or document (which at Tunis is called testa), but after the said term the conge shall be presented.

ARTICLE 5

If the corsairs of Tunis shall meet at sea with ships of war of the United States having under their escort merchant vessels of their nation, they shall not be searched or molested; and in such case the commanders shall be believed upon their word, to exempt their ships from being visited and to avoid quarantine. The American ships of war shall act in like manner towards merchant vessels escorted by the corsairs of Tunis.

ARTICLE 6

If a Tunisian corsair shall meet with an American merchant vessel and shall visit it with her boat, she shall not exact anything, under pain of being severely punished; and in like manner, if a vessel of war of the United States shall meet with a Tunisian merchant vessel, she shall observe the same rule. In case a slave shall take refuge on board of an I American vessel of war, the Consul shall be required to cause him to be restored; and if any of their prisoners shall escape on board of the Tunisian vessels, they shall be restored;

but if any slave shall take refuge in any American merchant vessel, and it shall be proved that the vessel has departed with the said slave, then he shall be returned, or his ransom shall be paid.

ARTICLE 7

An American citizen having purchased a prize-vessel from our Odgiak, may salt our passport, which we will de liver for the term of one year, by force of which our corsairs which may meet with her shall respect her; the Consul on his part shall furnish her with a bill of sale; and considering the distance of the two countries, this term shall suffice to obtain a passport in form. But after the expiration of this term, if our corsairs shall meet with her without the passport of the United States, she shall be stopped and declared good prize, as well the vessel as the cargo and crew.

ARTICLE 8

If a vessel of one of the contracting parties shall be obliged to enter into a port of the other and may have need of provisions and other articles, they shall be granted to her without any difficulty, at the price current at the place; and if such a vessel shall have suffered at sea and shall have need of repairs, she shall be at liberty to unload and reload her cargo without being obliged to pay any duty; and the captain shall only be obliged to pay the wages of those whom he shall have employed in loading and unloading the merchandise.

ARTICLE 9

If, by accident and by the permission of **God**, a vessel of one of the contracting parties shall be cast by tempest upon the coasts of the other and shall be wrecked or otherwise damaged, the commandant of the place shall render all possible assistance for its preservation, without allowing any person to make any opposition; and the proprietor of the effects shall pay the costs of salvage to those who may have been employed.

ARTICLE 10

In case a vessel of one of the contracting parties shall be attacked by an enemy under the cannon of the forts of the other party, she shall be defended and protected as much as possible; and when she shall set sail, no enemy shall be permitted to pursue her from the same port, or any other neighboring port, for forty-eight hours after her departure.

ARTICLE 11

When a vessel of war of the United States of America shall enter the port of Tunis, and the Consul shall request that the castle may salute her, the number of guns shall be fired which he may request; and if the said Consul does not want a salute, there shall be no question about it.

But in case he shall desire the salute, and the number of guns shall be fired which he may have requested, they shall be counted and returned by the vessel in as many barrels of cannon powder.

The same shall be done with respect to the Tunisian corsairs when they shall enter any port of the United States.

ARTICLE 12

When citizens of the United States shall come within the dependencies of Tunis to carry on commerce there, the same respect shall be paid to them which the merchants of other nations enjoy; and if they wish to establish themselves within our ports, no opposition shall be made thereto; and they shall be free to avail themselves of such interpreters as they may judge necessary, without any obstruction, in conformity with the usages of other nations; and if a Tunisian subject shall go to establish himself within the dependencies of the United States, he shall be treated in like manner.

If any Tunisian subject shall freight an American vessel and load her with merchandise, and shall afterwards want to unlace or ship them on board of another vessel, we will not permit him until the matter is determined by a reference of merchants, who shall decide upon the case; and after the decision, the determination shall be conformed to.

No captain shall be detained in port against his consent, except when our ports are shut for the vessels of all other nations, which may take place with respect to merchant vessels but not to those of war.

The subjects of the two contracting powers shall be under the protection of the Prince and under the jurisdiction of the chief of the place where they may be, and no other persons shall have authority over them. If the commandant of the place does not conduct himself agreeably to justice, a representation of it shall be made to us.

In case the Government shall have need of an American merchant vessel, it shall cause it to be freighted, and then a suitable freight shall be paid to the captain, agreeably to the intention of the Government, and the captain shall not refuse it.

ARTICLE 13

If among the crews of merchant vessels of the United States, there shall be found subjects of our enemies, they shall not be made slaves, on condition that they do not exceed a third of the crew; and when they do exceed a third, they shall be made slaves. The present article only concerns the sailors, and not the passengers, who shall not be in any manner molested.

ARTICLE 14

A Tunisian merchant who may go to America with a vessel of any nation so ever, loaded with merchandise which is the production of the kingdom of Tunis, shall pay duty (small as it is) like the merchants of other nations; and the American merchants shall equally pay, for the merchandise of their country which they may bring to Tunis under their flag, the same duty as the Tunisians pay in America.

But if an American merchant, or a merchant of any other nation, shall bring American merchandise under any other flag, he shall pay six (1) per cent duty. In like manner, if a foreign merchant shall bring the merchandise of his country under the American flag, he shall also pay six (1) per cent.

ARTICLE 15

It shall be free for the citizens of the United States to carry on what commerce they please in the kingdom of Tunis, without any opposition, and they shall be treated like the merchants of other nations; but they shall not carry on commerce in wine, nor in prohibited articles; and if any one shall be detected in a contraband trade, he shall be punished according to the laws of the country. The commandants of ports and castles shall take care that the captains and sailors shall not load prohibited articles; but if this should happen, those who shall not have contributed to the smuggling shall not be molested nor searched, no more than shall the vessel and cargo; but only the offender, who shall be demanded to be punished. No captain shall be obliged to receive merchandise on board of his vessel, nor to unlace the same against his will, until the freight shall be paid.

ARTICLE 16

The merchant vessels of the United States which shall cast anchor in the road of the Gouletta, or any other port of the Kingdom of Tunis, shall be obliged to pay the same anchorage for entry and departure which French vessels pay, to wit: Seventeen plasters and a half, money of Tunis, for entry, if they import merchandise; and the same for departure, if they take away a cargo; but they shall not be obliged to pay anchorage if they arrive in ballast and depart in the same manner.

ARTICLE 17

Each of the contracting parties shall be at liberty to establish a consul in the dependencies of the other; and if such consul does not act in conformity with the usages of the country, like others, the government of the place shall inform his Government of it, to the end that he may be changed and replaced; but he shall enjoy, as well for himself as his family and suite, the protection of the government. And he may import for his own use all his provisions and furniture without paying any duty; and if he shall import merchandise (which it shall be lawful for him to do), he shall pay duty for it.

ARTICLE 18

If the subjects or citizens of either of the contracting parties, being within the possessions of the other, contract debts or enter into obligations, neither the consul nor the nation, nor any subjects or citizens thereof, shall be in any manner responsible, except they or the consul shall have previously become bound in writing; and without this obligation in writing they cannot be called upon for indemnity or satisfaction.

ARTICLE 19

In case of a citizen or subject of either of the contracting parties dying within the possessions of the other, the consul or the vakil shall take possession of his effects (if he does not leave a will), of which he shall make an inventory; and the government of the place shall have nothing to do therewith. And if there shall be no consul, the effects shall be deposited in the hands of a confidential person of the place, taking an inventory of the whole that they may eventually be delivered to those to whom they of right belong.

ARTICLE 20

The consul shall be the judge in all disputes between his fellow citizens or subjects, as also between all other persons who may be immediately under his protection; and in all cases wherein he shall require the assistance of the government where he resides to sanction his decisions, it shall be granted to him.

ARTICLE 21

If a citizen or subject of one of the parties shall kill, wound, or strike a citizen or subject of the other, justice shall be done according to the laws of the country where the offense shall be committed. The consul shall be present at the trial; but if any offender shall escape, the consul shall be in no manner responsible for it.

ARTICLE 22

If a dispute or lawsuit on commercial or other civil matters shall happen, the trial shall be had in the presence of the consul, or of a confidential person of his choice, who shall represent him and endeavor to accommodate the difference which may have happened between the citizens or subjects of the two nations.

ARTICLE 23

If any difference or dispute shall take place concerning the infraction of any article of the present treaty on either side, peace and good harmony shall not be interrupted until a friendly application shall have been made for satisfaction; and resort shall not be had to arms therefor, except where such application shall have been rejected; and if war be then declared, the term of one year shall be allowed to the citizens or subjects of the contracting parties to arrange their affairs and to withdraw themselves with their property.

The agreements and terms above concluded by the two contracting parties shall be punctually observed with the will of the Most High. And for the maintenance and exact observance of the said agreements, we have caused their contents to tee here transcribed, in the present month of Rabia Elul, of the Hegira **one thousand two hundred and twelve, corresponding with the month of August of the (Christian year one thousand seven hundred and ninety-seven).**

The BEY'S signature

[Seal]

IBRAHIM DEY'S signature [Seal]

The AGHA SULEIMAN'S signature [Seal]

To all to whom these Presents shall come or be made known.

Whereas the Underwritten David Humphreys hath been duly appointed (commissioner Plenipotentiary by letters patent under the signature of the

President and seal of the United States of America, dated the 30th day of March 1795, for negotiating and concluding a Treaty of Amity and (commerce with the Most Excellent & Illustrious Lord the Bey and Supreme (commander of the State of Tunis; whereas in conformity to the necessary authority committed to him therefor, he did constitute and appoint Joel Barlow an Agent in the business aforesaid; and whereas the annexed Treaty was in consequence thereof agreed upon, in the manner and at the time therein mentioned through the intervention of Joseph Stephen Famin invested with full Powers for the said purpose.

Now, know ye, that I David Humphreys Commissioner Plenipotentiary aforesaid, do approve and conclude the said Treaty and every article and clause therein contained, reserving the same nevertheless for the final Ratification of the President of the United States of America, by and with the advice and consent of the Senate of the said United States.

In Testimony whereof I have signed the same with my name & affixed thereto my Seal, at the City of Madrid this fourteenth day of November 1797.

[Seal] DAVID HUMPHREYS

Whereas the President of the United States of America, by his Letters patent, under his signature and the seal of State, dated [Seal] the 18th day of December 1798, vested Richard O'Brien,

William Eaton and James Leander Cathcart, or any two of them in the absence of the third, with full powers to confer, negotiate and conclude with the Bey and Regency of Tunis, on certain alterations in the treaty between the United States and the government of Tunis, concluded by the intervention of Joseph Etienne Famin on behalf of the United States, in the month of August 1797; we the underwritten William Eaton and James Leander Cathcart (Richard O'Brien being absent) have concluded on and entered in the foregoing treaty certain alterations in the eleventh, twelfth and fourteenth articles, and do agree to said treaty with said alterations: reserving the same nevertheless for the final ratification of the President of the United States, by and with the advice and consent of the Senate.

In Testimony whereof we annex our names and the Consular seal of the United States. Done in Tunis the twenty sixth day of March in the year of the Christian Era one thousand seven hundred and ninety nine, and of American Independence the twenty third.

(signed) WILLIAM EATON

JAMES LEAR CATHCART

Treaty of Peace and Amity

Signed at Tripoli June 4, 1805

Treaty of Peace and Amity between the United States of America and the Bashaw, Bey and Subjects of Tripoli in Barbary

ARTICLE 1st

There shall be, from the conclusion of this Treaty, a firm, inviolable and universal peace, and a sincere friendship between the President and Citizens of the United States of America, on the one part, and the Bashaw, Bey and Subjects of the Regency of Tripoli in Barbary on the other, made by the free consent of both Parties, and on the terms of the most favoured Nation. And if either party shall hereafter grant to any other Nation, any particular favour or privileged in Navigation or Commerce, it shall immediately become common to the other party, freely, where it is freely granted, to such other Nation, but where the grant is conditional it shall be at the option of the contracting parties to accept, alter or reject, such conditions in such manner, as shall be most conducive to their respective Interests.

ARTICLE 2d

The Bashaw of Tripoli shall deliver up to the American Squadron now off Tripoli, all the Americans in his possession; and all the Subjects of the Bashaw of Tripoli now in the power of the United States of America shall be delivered up to him; and as the number of Americans in possession of the Bashaw of Tripoli amounts to Three Hundred Persons, more or less; and the number of Tripolino Subjects in the power of the Americans to about, One Hundred more or less; The Bashaw of Tripoli shall receive from the United States of America, the sum of Sixty Thousand Dollars, as a payment for the difference between the Prisoners herein mentioned.

ARTICLE 3rd

All the forces of the United States which have been, or may be in hostility against the Bashaw of Tripoli, in the Province of Derne, or elsewhere within the Dominions of the said Bashaw shall be withdrawn therefrom, and no supplies shall be given by or in behalf of the said United States, during the continuance of this peace, to any of the Subjects of the said Bashaw, who may be in hostility against him in any part of his Dominions; And the Americans will use all means in their power to persuade the Brother of the said Bashaw, who has co-operated with them at Derne &c, to withdraw from the Territory of the said Bashaw of Tripoli; but they will not use any force or improper means to effect that object; and in case he should withdraw himself as aforesaid, the Bashaw engages to deliver up to him, his Wife and Children now in his powers

ARTICLE 4th

If any goods belonging to any Nation with which either of the parties are at war, should be loaded on board Vessels belonging to the other party they shall pass free and unmolested, and no attempt shall be made to take or detain them.

ARTICLE 5th

If any Citizens, or Subjects with or their effects belonging to either party shall be found on board a Prize Vessel taken from an Enemy by the other party, such Citizens or Subjects shall be liberated immediately and their effects so captured shall be restored to their lawful owners or their Agents.

ARTICLE 6th

Proper passports shall immediately be given to the vessels of both the contracting parties, on condition that the Vessels of War belonging to the Regency of Tripoli on meeting with merchant Vessels belonging to (citizens of the United States of America, shall not be permitted to visit them with more than two persons besides the rowers, these two only shall be permitted to go on board said Vessel, without first obtaining leave from the Commander of said Vessel, who shall compare the passport, and immediately permit said Vessel proceed on her voyage; and should any of the said Subjects of Tripoli insult or molest the Commander or any other person on board Vessel so visited; or plunder any of the property contained in the full complaint being made by the Consul of the United States America resident at Tripoli and on his producing sufficient proof substantiate the fact, The Commander or Rais of said Tripoline ship or Vessel of War, as well as the Offenders shall be punished in the most exemplary manner.

All Vessels of War belonging to the United States of America meeting with a Cruiser belonging to the Regency of Tripoli, and having seen her passport and Certificate from the Consul of the United States of America residing in the Regency, shall permit her to proceed on her Cruise unmolested, and without detention. No pas port shall be granted by either party to any Vessels, but such as are absolutely the property of Citizens or Subjects of said contracting parties, on any presence whatever.

ARTICLE 7th

A Citizen or Subject of either of the contracting parties having bought a Prize Vessel condemned by the other party, or by any other Nation, the Certificate of condemnation and Bill of Sale she be a sufficient passport for such Vessel for two years, which, considering the distance between the two Countries, is no more than a reason able time for her to procure proper passports.

ARTICLE 8th

Vessels of either party, putting into the ports of the other, and having need of provisions or other supplies, they shall be furnish at the Market price, and if any such Vessel should so put in from disaster at Sea, and have occasion to repair; she shall be at liberty to land and reembark her Cargo, without paying any duties; but in no case shall she be compelled to land her Cargo.

ARTICLE 9th

Should a Vessel of either party be cast on the shore of the other all proper assistance shall be given to her and her Crew. No pillar shall be allowed, the property shall remain at the disposition of its owners, and the Crew protected and succored till they can be sent to their Country.

ARTICLE 10th

If a Vessel of either party, shall be attacked by an Enemy within Gun shot of the Forts of the other, she shall be defended as much as possible; If she be in port, she shall not be seized or attacked when it is in the power of the other party to protect her; and when she proceeds to Sea, no Enemy shall be allowed to pursue her from the same port, within twenty four hours after her departure.

ARTICLE 11th

The Commerce between the United States of America and the Regency of Tripoli; The Protections to be given to Merchants, Masters of Vessels and Seamen; The reciprocal right of establishing Consuls in each Country; and the privileges, immunities and jurisdictions to be enjoyed by such Consuls, are declared to be on the same footing, with those of the most favoured Nations respectively.

ARTICLE 12th

The Consul of the United States of America shall not be answerable for debts contracted by Citizens of his own Nation, unless, he previously gives a written obligation so to do.

ARTICLE 13th

On a Vessel of War, belonging to the United States of America, anchoring before the City of Tripoli, the Consul is to inform the Bashaw of her arrival, and she shall be saluted with twenty one Guns, which she is to return in the same quantity or number.

ARTICLE 14th

As the Government of the United States of America, has in itself no character of enmity against the Laws, Religion or Tranquility of Musselmen, and as the said States never have entered into any voluntary war or act of hostility against any Mahometan Nation, except in the defence of their just rights to freely navigate the High

Seas: It is declared by the contracting parties that no pretext arising from Religious Opinions, shall ever produce an interruption of the Harmony existing between the two Nations; And the Consuls and Agents of both Nations respectively, shall have liberty to exercise his Religion in his own house; all slaves of the same Religion shall not be Impeded in going to said Consuls house at hours of Prayer. The Consuls shall have liberty and personal security given them to travel within the Territories of each other, both by land and sea, and shall not be prevented from going on board any Vessel that they may think proper to visit; they shall have likewise the liberty to appoint their own Drogoman and Brokers.

ARTICLE 15th

In case of any dispute arising from the violation of any of the articles of this Treaty, no appeal shall be made to Arms, nor shall War be declared on any pretext whatever; but if the Consul residing at the place, where the dispute shall happen, shall not be able to settle the same; The Government of that Country shall state their grievances in writing, and transmit it to the Government of the other, and the period of twelve calendar months shall be allowed for answers to be returned; during which time no act of hostility shall be permitted by either party, and in case the grievances are not redressed, and War should be the event, the Consuls and Citizens or Subjects of both parties reciprocally shall be permitted to embark with their effects unmolested, on board of what vessel or Vessels they shall think proper.

ARTICLE 16th

If in the fluctuation of Human Events, a War should break out between the two Nations; The Prisoners captured by either party shall not be made Slaves; but shall be exchanged Rank for Rank; and if there should be a deficiency on either side, it shall be made up by the payment of Five Hundred Spanish Dollars for each Captain, Three Hundred Dollars for each Mate and Supercargo and One hundred Spanish Dollars for each Seaman so wanting. And it is agreed that Prisoners shall be exchanged in twelve months from the time of their capture, and that this Exchange may be affected by any private Individual legally authorized by either of the parties.

ARTICLE 17th

If any of the Barbary States, or other powers at War with the United States of America, shall capture any American Vessel, and send her into any of the ports of the Regency of Tripoli, they shall not be permitted to sell her, but shall be obliged to depart the Port on procuring the requisite supplies of Provisions; and no duties shall be exacted on the sale of Prizes captured by Vessels sailing under the Flag of the United States of America when brought into any Port in the Regency of Tripoli.

ARTICLE 18th

If any of the Citizens of the United States, or any persons under their protection, shall have any dispute with each other, the Consul shall decide between the parties; and whenever the Consul shall require any aid or assistance from the Government of Tripoli, to enforce his decisions, it shall immediately be granted to him. And if any dispute shall arise between any Citizen of the United States and the Citizens or Subjects of any other Nation, having a Consul or Agent in Tripoli, such dispute shall be settled by the Consuls or Agents of the respective Nations.

ARTICLE 19th

If a Citizen of the United States should kill or wound a Tripoline, or, on the contrary, if a Tripoline shall kill or wound a Citizen of the United States, the law of the Country shall take place, and equal justice shall be rendered, the Consul assisting at the trial; and if any delinquent shall make his escape, the Consul shall not be answerable for him in any manner whatever.

ARTICLE 20th

Should any Citizen of the United States of America die within the limits of the Regency of Tripoli, the Bashaw and his Subjects shall not interfere with the property of the deceased; but it shall be under the immediate direction of the Consul, unless otherwise disposed of by will. Should there be no Consul, the effects shall be deposited in the hands of some person worthy of trust, until the party shall appear who has a right to demand them, when they shall render an account of the property. Neither shall the Bashaw or his Subjects give hindrance in the execution of any will that may appear.

Whereas, the undersigned, Tobias Lear, Consul General of the United States of America for the Regency of Algiers, being duly appointed Commissioner, by letters patent under the signature of the President, and Seal of the United States of America, bearing date at the City of Washington, the 18" day of November 1803 for negotiating and concluding a Treaty of Peace, between the United States of America, and the Bashaw, Bey and Subjects of the Regency of Tripoli in Barbary-

Now Know Ye, That I, Tobias Lear, Commissioner as aforesaid, do conclude the foregoing Treaty, and every article and clause therein contained; reserving the same nevertheless for the final ratification of the President of the United States of America, by and with the advice and consent of the Senate of the said United States.

Done at Tripoli in Barbary, the fourth day of June, in the year One thousand, eight hundred and five; corresponding with the sixth day of the first month of Rabbia 1220.

[Seal] TOBIAS LEAR

Having appeared in our presence, Colonel Tobias Lear, Consul General of the United States of America, in the Regency of Algiers, and Commissioner for negotiating and concluding a Treaty of Peace and Friendship between Us and the United States of America, bringing with him the present Treaty of Peace with the within Articles, they were by us minutely examined, and we do hereby accept, confirm and ratify them, Ordering all our Subjects to fulfill entirely their contents, without any violation and under no pretext.

In Witness whereof We, with the heads of our Regency, Subscribe it.

Given at Tripoli in Barbary the sixth day of the first month of Rabbia 1220, corresponding with the 4th day of June 1805.

(L. S.) JUSUF CARAMANLY Bashaw

(L. S.) MOHAMET CARAMANLY Bey

(L. S.) MOHAMET Kahia

(L. S.) HAMET Rais de Marino

(L. S.) MOHAMET DGHIES First Alinister

(L. S.) SARAH Aga of Divan

(L. S.) SEEIM Hasnadar

(L. S.) MURAT Dqblartile

(L. S.) MURAT RAIS Admiral

(L. S.) SOEIMAN Kehia

(L. S.) ABDAEEA Basa Aga

(L. S.) MAHOMET Scheig al Belad

(L. S.) ALEI BEN DIAB First Secretary

[Receipt]

We hereby acknowledge to have received from the hands of Colonel Tobias Lear the full sum of sixty thousand dollars, mentioned as Ransom for two hundred Americans, in the Treaty of Peace concluded between Us and the United States of America on the Sixth day of the first Month of Rabbia 1220- and of all demands against the said United States.

Done this twenty first day of the first month of Rabbia 1220

(L. S.) Signed (JOSEPH CARMANALY) Bashaw

Treaty of Peace

Signed Algiers June 30 and July 3, 1815

Treaty of peace concluded between His United States of America and his Highness Omar Bashaw Dey of Algiers.

David Humphreys served from the ranks up in the American Revolution and eventually was promoted to the rank of colonel. Colonel Humphreys served with distinction and eventually was appointed aid-de-camp to General George Washington. After the war Colonel Humphreys became George Washington's private secretary travelling with General and Mrs. Washington and he lived at Mount Vernon for a while.

David Humphreys was the first person appointed by the newly formed American government to serve as a minister to Portugal. The title Commissioner Plenipotentiary is a title which basically defined as a minister or diplomat conferred with full power. It was during his assignment as Minister to Portugal that Humphreys negotiated the first ransom for US sailors from the Dey of Tripoli.

Joel Barlow, Yale graduate and poet served in the American Revolution as a chaplain in the 4th Massachusetts Brigade during the final years of the revolution. Known mainly as a poet and a satirist, Joel Barlow is best known for his writings *The Hasty-Pudding* and *The Vision of Columbus* and was a member of the *Hartford Wits*. Barlow also wrote a poem about the evils of slavery entitled *The Prospect for Peace*.

In 1786 Joel Barlow became a lawyer and in 1788 Barlow went to France. Joel Barlow wrote the poem *The Vision of Columbus* which he dedicated to the King of France, Louis XVI but later called for the King's beheading.

Always known as being radical in his thoughts about religion, politics and social matters, Barlow was a candidate for the French Assembly and in 1792 he accepted honorary French citizenship.

Joel Barlow was involved with the Scioto Company which was exposed for fraudulent land deeds. Though Barlow is believed to have been unaware of the company's fraud, this scandal damaged his reputation in the United States.

Joel Barlow and his wife moved to London because of his loss of popularity where he wrote *"Advice to the Privileged Orders* and *The Conspiracy of Kings"*. Barlow's writing of the *Advice* offended the British government, the writing was banned in England and the government attempted to arrest Barlow. Joel Barlow left his wife in London, fled England for France to avoid his trouble in England. Barlow was in France during its revolution against their monarchy and the imprisonment of his friend Thomas Paine.

In 1796, Joel Barlow was sent to Algiers to gain the release of US sailors held for ransom by Muslim pirates and to negotiate treaties with the Muslim pirates. It is during his time in Algiers that Barlow authored the controversial Article 11 in the Treaty of Tripoli.

The fact of the matter of the meaning of Article 11 is found in its wording. Article 11 does in fact say the following, *"As the Government of the United States of America is not, in any sense, founded on the Christian religion; as it has in itself no character of enmity against the laws, religion, or tranquility, of Mussulmen [Muslims]; and as the said States never entered into any war or act of hostility against any Mahometan [Muslim] nation, it is declared by the parties that no pretext arising from religious opinions shall ever produce an interruption of the harmony existing between the two countries."*

The distinction is that the Government of the US is NOT founded on religion of any type; that much is true. The US Congress cannot establish a national religion of church but the US Constitution does not forbid the individual States from this practice.

It should also be pointed out that the US government is not the nation, We the People are the nation and this nation is comprised of those people and the individual States which are united together to form a nation.

In 1797 the Treaty of Tripoli was drawn in another attempt to negotiate peace with the pirates along the Barbary Coast. This is the treaty which contains the infamous Article 11 where it states *"As the government of the United States of America is not in any sense founded on the **Christian Religion**,-as it has in itself no character of enmity against the laws, religion or tranquility of Mussleman,-and as the said States never have entered into any war or act of hostility against any Mehomitan nation, it is declared by the parties that no pretext arising from religious opinions shall ever produce an interruption of the harmony existing between the two countries."*

The problem the atheists have is endless though because they attempt to revise history at every opportunity just as they have attempted to rewrite Article 11.

There is also the not so small matter that below the seal and the receipt are the words, *"**Praise be to God"**** which quite clearly refutes the assertion that the United States did not view the United States as a nation under God.

In addition to that, it is quite obvious that the United States government had no issue with signing a treaty with the words ***"Praise be to God"*** next to the signature of one of its representatives, the receipt and the seal finalizing the treaty between the United States and the Musselmen pirates.

Joel Barlow was known for his radical views on religion and government. Barlow supported the French nationals revolting against their king and the French Revolution has been associated with the cathedrals of France having been violated with pagan rituals and orgies in order to defile Houses of God.

The Jakobins in France led the bloody revolution and they held strong hatred for Christianity.

The Jakobins ordered that all symbols of the Catholic Church and Christianity be removed from everywhere and the Notre Dame Cathedral became known as "the temple of reason" because the new religion of France was named the "religion of reason". This new religion was also known as the *"Cult of the Supreme Being"* established by Maximillien Robespierre, rooted in paganism and atheism.

The revolutionaries in France were definitely fascist and they wore a red cap to symbolize their allegiance to the revolution. The red cap was born out of paganism and the myth of Mithra.

These actions and policies are known as the dechristiaization of France.

These changes in the religious culture of France would seemingly be reflective of Joel Barlow's radical opinions and beliefs.

Before it was ratified, the Treaty of Tripoli was read before the US Senate. Secretary of War James McHenry protested the wording of Article 11.

In a letter to Secretary of the Treasury Oliver Wolcott, Jr. dated September 26, 1800 McHenry wrote,

"The Senate, my good friend, and I said so at the time, ought never to have ratified the treaty alluded to, with the declaration that 'the government of the United States, is not, in any sense, founded on the Christian religion.' What else is it founded on? This act always appeared to me like trampling upon the cross. I do not recollect that Barlow was even reprimanded for this outrage upon the government and religion."

It should be pointed out that the treaty in Arabic did not include the controversial Article 11.

Another fact is that all previous treaties including the Treaty of Peace and Friendship signed at Tunis August 28, 1797, originally in Turkish begin with the words *"God is infinite"*.

The agreements and terms above concluded by the two contracting parties shall be punctually observed with the will of the Most High. And for the maintenance and exact observance of the said agreements, we have caused their contents to be here transcribed, **in the present month of Rabia Elul, of the Hegira one thousand two hundred and twelve, corresponding with the month of August of the (Christian year one thousand seven hundred and ninety-seven).**

The treaties arranged by the emissaries of the US government and accepted by the Barbary pirates all invoke God and Christians into the wording.

To quote the treaty's final words, **"In Testimony whereof we annex our names and the Consular seal of the United States. Done in Tunis the twenty sixth day of March in the year of the Christian Era one thousand seven hundred and ninety nine, and of American Independence the twenty third.)**

Words clarify sentences and we should pay close attention to what words are used and how those words are used.

On July 4th, 1805 a new treaty was signed, the Treaty of Peace and Amity replaced the Treaty of Tripoli and the 1805 treaty did not include the phrase *"not, in any sense, founded on the Christian religion."*

Atheists will ONLY refer to and as they refer incorrectly Article 11 which was written and inserted by Joel Barlow as being WRITTEN and AGREED TO by John Adams.

John Adams is NOT THE AUTHOR of Article 11.

Article 11 was protested for being included in the English version; it WAS NOT included in the Arabic version.

Article 11 was removed when a new treaty was authored and signed in 1805.

Militant atheists clearly fear that the truth about the Treaty of Tripoli and the other treaties concerning the Musselmen pirates will become known and taught to US school children.

Darkness of truth is the ally of militant atheists.

Part Four

Early American Education

*"Education is useless without the Bible. The Bible was America's basic text book in all fields. **God's Word**, contained in the Bible, has furnished all necessary rules to direct our conduct."*

Noah Webster, 1828

A DEFENCE OF THE USE OF THE BIBLE IN SCHOOLS

By Dr. Benjamin Rush

Dear Sir:

It is now several months since I promised to give you my reasons for preferring the Bible as a schoolbook to all other compositions. Before I state my arguments, I shall assume the five following propositions:

I. That Christianity is the only true and perfect religion; and that in proportion as mankind adopt its principles and obey its precepts they will be wise and happy.

2. That a better knowledge of this religion is to be acquired by reading the Bible than in any other way.

3. That the Bible contains more knowledge necessary to man in his present state than any other book in the world.

4. That knowledge is most durable and religious instruction most useful, when imparted in early life.

5. That the Bible, when not read in schools, is seldom read in any subsequent period of life.

My arguments in favor of the use of the Bible as a schoolbook are founded.

I. In the constitution of the human mind.

1. The memory is the first faculty which opens in the minds of children. Of how much consequence, then, must it be to impress it with the great truths of Christianity, before it is preoccupied with less interesting subjects.

*2. There is a peculiar aptitude in the minds of children for religious knowledge. I have constantly found them, in the first six or seven years of their lives, more inquisitive upon religious subjects than upon any others. And an ingenious instructor of youth has informed me that he has found young children more capable of receiving just ideas upon the most difficult tenets of religion than upon the most simple branches of human knowledge. It would be strange if it were otherwise, for **God** creates all **His** means to suit **His** ends. There must, of course, be a fitness between the human mind and the truths which are essential to its happiness.*

3. The influence of early impressions is very great upon subsequent life; and in a world where false prejudices do so much mischief, it would discover great weakness not to oppose them by such as are true. I grant that many men have rejected the impressions derived from the Bible; but how much so ever these impressions may have been despised, I believe no man was ever early instructed in the truths of the Bible without having been made wiser or better by the early operation of these impressions upon his mind. Every just principle that is to be found in the writings of Voltaire is borrowed from the Bible; and the morality of Deists, which has been so much admired and praised where it has existed, has been, I believe, in most cases, the effect of habits produced by early instruction in the principles of Christianity.

4. We are subject, by a general law of our natures, to what is called habit. Now, if the study of the Scriptures be necessary to our happiness at any time of our life, the sooner we begin to read them, the more we shall probably be attached to them; for it is peculiar to all the acts of habit, to become easy, strong, and agreeable by repetition.

5. It is a law in our natures that we remember longest the knowledge we acquire by the greatest number of our senses. Now, a knowledge of the contents of the Bible is acquired in school by the aid of the eye and the ear, for children, after getting their lessons, read or repeat them to their instructors in an audible voice; of course, there is a presumption that this knowledge will be retained much longer than if it had been acquired in any other way.

6. The interesting events and characters recorded and described in the Old and New Testaments are calculated, above all others, to seize upon all the faculties of the mind of children. The understanding, the memory, the imagination, the passions, and the moral powers are all occasionally addressed by the various incidents which are contained in those divine books, insomuch that not to be delighted with them is to be devoid of every principle of pleasure that exists in a sound mind.

7. There is in man a native preference of truth to fiction. Lord Shaftesbury says that "truth is so congenial to our mind that we love even the shadow of it"; and Horace, in his rules for composing an epic poem, established the same law in our natures by advising that "fictions in poetry should resemble truth."

Now, the Bible contains more truth than any other book in the world; so true is the testimony that it bears of **God in His** works of creation, providence, and redemption that it is called truth itself, by way of preeminence above other things that are acknowledged to be true. How forcibly are we struck with the evidence of truth in the history of the Jews, above what we discover in the history of other nations. Where do we find a hero or an historian record his own faults or vices except in the Old Testament? Indeed, my friend, from some accounts which I have read of the American Revolution, I begin to grown skeptical to all history except that which is contained in the Bible. Now, if this book be known to contain nothing but what is materially true, the mind will naturally acquire a love for it from this circumstance; and from this affection for the truths of the Bible, it will acquire a discernment of truth in other books, and a preference of it in all the transactions of life.

8. There is wonderful property in the memory which enables it in old age to recover the knowledge acquired in early life after it had been apparently forgotten for forty or fifty years. Of how much consequence, then, must it be

to fill the mind with that species of knowledge in childhood and youth which, when recalled in the decline of life, will support the soul under the infirmities of age and smooth the avenues of approaching death.

The Bible is the only book which is capable of affording this support to old age; and it is for this reason that we find it resorted to with so much diligence and pleasure by such old people as have read it in early life. I can recollect many instances of this kind in persons who discovered no special attachment to the Bible in the meridian of their days, who have, notwithstanding, spent the evening of life in reading no other book.

The late Sir John Pringle, physician to the queen of Great Britain, after passing a long life in camps and at court, closed it by studying the Scriptures. So anxious was he to increase his knowledge in them that he wrote to Dr. Michaelis, a learned professor of divinity in Germany, for an explanation of a difficult text of Scripture a short time before his death.

II. My second argument in favor of the use of the Bible in schools is founded upon an implied command of **God** and upon the practice of several of the wisest nations of the world.

In the sixth chapter of Deuteronomy, we find the following words, which are directly to my purpose: **"And thou shalt love the Lord thy God with all thine heart, and with all thy soul, and with all thy might. And these words, which I command thee this day, shall be in thine heart: And thou shalt teach them diligently unto thy children, and shalt talk of them when thou sittest in thine house, and when thou walkest by the way, and when thou liest down, and when thou risest up."**

It appears, moreover, from the history of the Jews, that they flourished as a nation in proportion as they honored and read the books of Moses, which contained the only revelation that **God** had made to the world. The law was not only neglected, but lost, during the general profligacy of manner which accompanied the long and wicked reign of Manasseh. But the discovery of it amid the rubbish of the temple by Josiah and its subsequent general use were followed by a return of national virtue and prosperity. We read further of the wonderful effects which the reading of the law by Ezra, after his return from his captivity in Babylon, had upon the Jews. They showed the sincerity of their repentance by their general reformation.

The learning of the Jews, for many years, consisted in a knowledge of the Scriptures. These were the textbooks of all the instruction that was given in the schools of their Prophets. It was by means of this general knowledge of their law that those Jews who wandered from Judea into other countries carried with them and propagated certain ideas of the true **God** among all the civilized nations upon the face of the earth. And it was from the attachment they retained to the Old Testament that they procured a translation of it into the Greek language, after they had lost the Hebrew tongue by their long absence from their native country. The utility of this translation, commonly called the Septuagint, in facilitating the progress of the Gospel is well known to all who are acquainted with the history of the first age of the Christian church.

But the benefits of an early and general acquaintance with the Bible were not confined to the Jewish nation; they have appeared in many countries in Europe since the Reformation. The industry and habits of order which distinguish many of the German nations are derived from their early instruction in the principles of Christianity by means of the Bible.

In Scotland and in parts of New England, where the Bible has been long used as a schoolbook, the inhabitants are among the most enlightened in religions and science, the most strict in morals, and the most intelligent in human affairs of any people whose history has come to my knowledge upon the surface of the globe.

I wish to be excused from repeating here that if the Bible did not convey a single direction for the attainment of future happiness, it should be read in our schools in preference to all other books from its containing the greatest portion of that kind of knowledge which is calculated to produce private and public temporal happiness.

We err, not only in human affairs but in religion likewise, only because we do not "know the Scriptures" and obey their instructions. Immense truths, I believe, are concealed in them. The time, I have no doubt, will come when posterity will view and pity our ignorance of these truths as much as we do the ignorance sometimes manifested by the disciples of our **Saviour**, who knew nothing of the meaning of those plain passages in the Old Testament which were daily fulfilling before their eyes. But further, we err, not only in religion but in philosophy likewise, because we "do not know or believe the Scriptures." The sciences have been compared to a circle, of which religion composes a part. To understand any one of them perfectly, it is necessary to have some knowledge of them all. Bacon, Boyle, and Newton included the Scriptures in the inquiries to which their universal geniuses disposed them, and their philosophy was aided by their knowledge in them. A striking agreement has been lately discovered between the history of certain events recorded in the Bible and some of the operations and productions of nature, particularly those which are related in Whitehurst's observation on the deluge, in Smith's account of the origin of the variety of color in the human species, and in Bruce's travels. It remains yet to be shown how many other events related in the Bible accord with some late important discoveries in the principles of medicine. The events and the principles alluded to mutually establish the truth of each other.

I know it is said that the familiar use of the Bible in our schools has a tendency to lessen a due reverence for it. But this objection, by proving too much, proves nothing. If familiarity lessens respect for divine things, then all those precepts of our religion which enjoin the daily or weekly worship of the Deity are improper. The Bible was not intended to represent a Jewish ark; and **it is an anti-Christian idea to suppose that it can be profaned by being carried into a schoolhouse, or by being handled by children.**

It is also said that a great part of the Old Testament is no way interesting to mankind under the present dispensation of the Gospel. But I deny that any of the books of the Old Testament are not interesting to mankind under the Gospel dispensation. Most of the characters, events, and ceremonies mentioned in them are personal, providential, or instituted types of the Messiah, all of which have been, or remain yet, to be fulfilled by **Him**.

It is from an ignorance or neglect of these types that we have so many Deists in Christendom, for so irrefragably do they prove the truth of Christianity that I am sure a young man who had been regularly instructed in their meaning could never doubt afterwards of the truth of any of its principles. *If any obscurity appears in these principles, it is only, to use the words of the poet, because they are dark with excessive brightness.*

*I know there is an objection among many people to teaching children doctrines of any kind, because they are liable to be controverted. But let us not be wiser than our **Maker**. If moral precepts alone could have reformed mankind, the mission of the **Son of God** into our world would have been unnecessary. **He** came to promulgate a system of doctrines, as well as a system of morals. The perfect morality of the Gospel rests upon a doctrine which, though often controverted, has never been refuted; I mean the vicarious life and death of the **Son of God**. This sublime and ineffable doctrine delivers us from the absurd hypothesis of modern philosophers concerning the foundation of moral obligation, and fixes it upon the eternal and self-moving principle of LOVE. It concentrates a whole system of ethics in a single text of Scripture:* **"A new commandment I give unto you, that ye love one another, even as I have loved you."**

*By withholding the knowledge of this doctrine from children, we deprive ourselves of the best means of awakening moral sensibility in their minds. We do more; we furnish an argument for withholding from them a knowledge of the morality of the Gospel likewise; for this, in many instances, is as supernatural and therefore as liable to be controverted, as any of the doctrines or miracles which are mentioned in the New Testament. The miraculous conception of the **Saviour** of the world by a virgin is not more opposed to the ordinary course of natural events, nor is the doctrine of the atonement more above human reason, than those moral precepts which command us to love our enemies or to die for our friends.*

I cannot but suspect that the present fashionable practice of rejecting the Bible from our schools has originated with Deists. And they discover great ingenuity in this new mode of attacking Christianity. If they proceed in it, they will do more in half a century in extirpating our religion than Bolingbroke or Voltaire could have effected in a thousand years.

*But passing by all other considerations, and contemplating merely the political institutions of the United States, I lament that we waste so much time and money in punishing crimes and take so little pains to prevent them. **We profess to be republicans, and yet we neglect the only means of establishing and perpetuating our republican forms of government; that is, the universal education of our youth in the principles of Christianity by means of the Bible; for this divine book, above all others, favors that equality among mankind, that respect for just laws, and all those sober and frugal virtues which constitute the soul of republicanism.***

Perhaps an apology may be necessary for my having presumed to write upon a subject so much above my ordinary studies. My excuse for it is that I thought a single mite from a member of a profession which has been frequently charged with skepticism in religion might attract the notice of persons who had often overlooked the more ample contributions, upon this subject, of gentlemen in other professions.

With great respect, I am, etc.

Benjamin Rush, 1830

"Every civil government is based upon some religion or philosophy of life. Education in a nation will propagate the religion of that nation. In America, the foundational religion was Christianity. And it was sown in the hearts of Americans through the home and private and public schools for centuries. Our liberty, growth, and prosperity was the result of a Biblical philosophy of life. Our continued freedom and success is dependent on our educating the youth of America in the principles of Christianity."

Noah Webster, 1828

The New England Primer

1687

The *New England Primer* was created as a learning tool for children living in the American colonies. The Primer originated from the *English Protestant Tutor* written by Benjamin Harris and is considered to teach against Catholicism.

The Primer used patriotism in the new nation of the United States of America. Examples of duty to country were taught by using George Washington as an example of patriotism.

The Primer consisted of a single sheet of paper on a flat wooden board coated in shellac for protection. The contents of the Primer comprised of the alphabet, vowels, consonants, and word sounds using teachings from the *King James Holy Bible*.

Prayers and lessons in Christian morals were taught from the lessons of Jesus Christ and God's commands. Topics included abstaining from sinful behaviors, respect for one's parents and elders and honesty. The Primer contained the standard prayer of that time, *"Now I lay me down to sleep, I pray thee, **Lord**, my soul to keep; If I should die before I wake, I pray thee, **Lord**, my soul to take."*

The New England Primer was used in schoolhouses until well into the 19th century.

The American Spelling Book

Also known as

The Blue-Back Speller

1787

The American Spelling Book aka the *Blue-Back Speller* was the creation of Noah Webster Jr. and was first used in the 1790s as an additional learning tool for teachers and students in American schoolhouses.

The Blue-Back Speller became the most widely used textbook in schools throughout the States. The Speller focused on teaching morality and patriotism through its lessons and it included the Catechism.

Noah Webster was concerned with American school children receiving the best education possible while making the lessons simpler for the teachers to teach. He believed that the most effective method of teaching was to break words and sentences down into their basic construction.

The lessons in the Blue-Back Speller came from the teachings in the Holy Bible. Much like the New England Primer the Speller used Biblical instructions on morality, respect and Godliness to teach children how to read, spelling, proper sentence structure and word pronunciation. The Blue-Back Speller used words commonly associated with spiritual teachings; examples of the words used are tithe, God, Lord, sin, thee, thy, bad and harm.

The Blue-Back Speller also taught lessons about God's Law and duty to God through writings that contained several short paragraphs, much like a poem.

This is an example of the teachings from Webster's book:

Lesson 1 *"NO man may put off the **law of God**,"*

Reformation came to the US educational system beginning in the mid-19th century. Schools began to use books such as the *McGuffey Reader* to teach children how to be self-disciplined, success through achievement, sobriety in life and virtue through honesty and integrity.

The McGuffey Reader became the most popular textbook for schools in America selling more than 12 million copies over a span of 80 years.

The schoolhouses of the new nation were mostly one-room buildings where students of all grade levels attended school.

During the 17th, 18th & 19th centuries, it was more common for men to be educators than women.

Known as schoolmasters, men were regarded as the most qualified to be teachers and disciplinarians in the schools.

Some schools employed women to teach small children beginning lessons before those students graduated to the next grade levels.

Through Biblically inspired lessons, US schoolchildren were taught how to read, write and spell because this was believed to be the best method at the time.

God was welcome in our schools and students were taught by using stories from the Bible and the Word of God not just for the basics of education but for the important lessons in how to live their life, with principles and honor.

On the Education of Youth in America

Another defect in our schools, which, since the revolution, is become inexcusable, is the want of proper books. The collections which are now used consist of essays that respect foreign and ancient nations. The minds of youth are perpetually led to the history of Greece and Rome or to Great Britain; boys are constantly repeating the declamations of Demosthenes and Cicero, or debates upon some political question in the British Parliament. These are excellent specimens of good sense, polished stile and perfect oratory; but they are not interesting to children. They cannot be very useful, except to young gentlemen who want them as models of reasoning and eloquence, in the pulpit or at the bar.

But every child in America should be acquainted with his own country.

He should read books that furnish him with ideas that will be useful to him in life and practice. As soon as he opens his lips, he should rehearse the history of his own country; he should lisp the praise of liberty, and of those illustrious heroes and statesmen, who have wrought a revolution in her favor.

A selection of essays, respecting the settlement and geography of America; the history of the late revolution and of the most remarkable characters and events that distinguished it, and a compendium of the principles of the federal and provincial governments, should be the principal school book in the United States.

These are interesting objects to every man; they call home the minds of youth and fix them upon the interests of their own country, and they assist in forming attachments to it, as well as in enlarging the understanding.

"It is observed by the great Montesquieu, that the laws of education ought to be relative to the principles of the government."

In despotic governments, the people should have little or no education, except what tends to inspire them with a servile fear. Information is fatal to despotism.

In monarchies, education should be partial, and adapted to the rank of each class of citizens. But "in a republican government," says the same writer, "the whole power of education is required." Here every class of people should know and love the laws. This knowledge should be diffused by means of schools and newspapers; and an attachment to the laws may be formed by early impressions upon the mind.

*Two regulations are essential to the continuance of republican governments':
Such a distribution of lands and such principles of descent and alienation, as
shall give every citizen a power of acquiring what his industry merits. Such a
system of education as gives every citizen an opportunity of acquiring
knowledge and fitting himself for places of trust. These are fundamental
articles; the sine qua non of the existence of the American republics.*

*Hence the absurdity of our copying the manners and adopting the institutions
of Monarchies.*

*In several States, we find laws passed, establishing provision for colleges and
academies, where people of property may educate their sons; but no provision
is made for instructing the poorer rank of people, even in reading and writing.
Yet in these same States, every citizen who is worth a few shillings annually
is entitled to vote for legislators. This appears to me a most glaring solecism
in government. The constitutions are republican, and the laws of education
are monarchical. The former extend civil rights to every honest industrious
man; the latter deprive a large proportion of the citizens of a most valuable
privilege.*

*In our American republics, where [government] is in the hands of the people,
knowledge should be universally diffused by means of public schools. Of such
consequence is it to society, that the people who make laws, should be well
informed, that I conceive no Legislature can be justified in neglecting proper
establishments for this purpose.*

*When I speak of a diffusion of knowledge, I do not mean merely knowledge of
spelling books, and the **New Testament**. An acquaintance with ethics, and
with the general principles of law, commerce, money and government, is
necessary for the yeomanry of a republican state. This acquaintance they
might obtain by means of books calculated for schools, and read by the
children, during the winter months, and by the circulation of public papers.*

*"In Rome it was the common exercise of boys at school, to learn the laws of
the twelve tables by heart, as they did their poets and classic authors." What
an excellent practice this in a free government!*

It is said, indeed by many, that our common people are already too well informed. Strange paradox! The truth is, they have too much knowledge and spirit to resign their share in government, and are not sufficiently informed to govern themselves in all cases of difficulty.

There are some acts of the American legislatures which astonish men of information; and blunders in legislation are frequently ascribed to bad intentions. But if we examine the men who compose these legislatures, we shall find that wrong measures generally proceed from ignorance either in the men themselves, or in their constituents. They often mistake their own interest, because they do not foresee the remote consequences of a measure.

It may be true that all men cannot be legislators; but the more generally knowledge is diffused among the substantial yeomanry; the more perfect will be the laws of a republican state.

Every small district should be furnished with a school, at least four months in a year; when boys are not otherwise employed. This school should be kept by the most reputable and well informed man in the district. Here children should be taught the usual branches of learning; submission to superiors and to laws; the moral or social duties; the history and transactions of their own country; the principles of liberty and government. Here the rough manners of the wilderness should be softened, and the principles of virtue and good behaviour inculcated. The virtues of men are of more consequence to society than their abilities; and for this reason, the heart should be cultivated with more assiduity than the head.

*Such a general system of education is neither impracticable nor difficult; and excepting the formation of a federal government that shall be efficient and permanent, it demands the first attention of American patriots. Until such a system shall be adopted and pursued; until the Statesman and **Divine** shall unite their efforts in forming the human mind, rather than in loping its excrescences, after it has been neglected; until Legislators discover that the only way to make good citizens and subjects, is to nourish them from infancy; and until parents shall be convinced that the worst of men are not the proper teachers to make the best; mankind cannot know to what a degree of perfection* *society and government may be carried. America affords the fairest opportunities for making the experiment, and opens the most encouraging prospect'of success."*

Noah Webster, 1788

Part Five

Separation of Church and State

The belief that the US Constitution actually contains the phrase, "Separation of Church and State" is controversial in the least. Those on the side of the argument who claim that those words actually exist and are enforceable always refer to two sources as evidence in support of their assertion, the Danbury Baptist letters and the Establishment Clause.

The Danbury Baptist Association letter

Letter from the Danbury Baptists

The address of the Danbury Baptist Association in the State of Connecticut assembled October 7, 1801.

To Thomas Jefferson, Esq., President of the United States of America

Sir,

Among the many millions in America and Europe who rejoice in your election to office, we embrace the first opportunity which we have enjoyed in our collective capacity, since your inauguration, to express our great satisfaction in your appointment to the Chief Magistracy in the United States. And though the mode of expression may be less courtly and pompous than what many others clothe their addresses with, we beg you, sir, to believe, that none is more sincere.

*Our sentiments are uniformly on the side of religious liberty: that Religion is at all times and places a matter between **God** and individuals, that no man ought to suffer in name, person, or effects on account of his religious opinions, [and] that the legitimate power of civil government extends no further than to punish the man who works ill to his neighbor. But sir, our constitution of government is not specific. Our ancient charter, together with the laws made* coincident therewith, were adapted as the basis of our government at the time of our revolution. And such has been our laws and usages, and such still are, [so] that Religion is considered as the first object of Legislation, and therefore what religious privileges we enjoy (as a minor part of the State) we enjoy as favors granted, and not as inalienable rights. And these favors we receive at the expense of such degrading acknowledgments, as are inconsistent with the rights of freemen. It is not to be wondered at therefore, if those who seek after power and gain, under the pretense of government and Religion, should reproach their fellow men, [or] should reproach their Chief Magistrate, as an enemy of religion, law, and good order, because he will not, dares not, assume the prerogative of **Jehovah** and make laws to govern the **Kingdom of Christ**.

Sir, we are sensible that the President of the United States is not the National Legislator and also sensible that the national government cannot destroy the laws of each State, but our hopes are strong that the sentiment of our beloved President, which have had such genial effect already, like the radiant beams of the sun, will shine and prevail through all these States--and all the world-- until hierarchy and tyranny be destroyed from the earth. Sir, when we reflect on your past services, and see a glow of philanthropy and goodwill shining forth in a course of more than thirty years, we have reason to believe that **America's God** has raised you up to fill the Chair of State out of that goodwill which he bears to the millions which you preside over. May **God** strengthen you for the arduous task which providence and the voice of the people have called you--to sustain and support you and your Administration against all the predetermined opposition of those who wish to rise to wealth and importance on the poverty and subjection of the people.

And may the **Lord** preserve you safe from every evil and bring you at last to **his Heavenly Kingdom** through **Jesus Christ our Glorious Mediator**.

Signed in behalf of the Association,

Neh,h Dodge }

Eph'm Robbins} The Committee

Stephen S. Nelson}

Thomas Jefferson's reply

January 1, 1802

To messers. Nehemiah Dodge, Ephraim Robbins, & Stephen S. Nelson, a committee of the Danbury Baptist association in the state of Connecticut.

Gentlemen

The affectionate sentiments of esteem and approbation which you are so good as to express towards me, on behalf of the Danbury Baptist association, give me the highest satisfaction. my duties dictate a faithful and zealous pursuit of the interests of my constituents, & in proportion as they are persuaded of my fidelity to those duties, the discharge of them becomes more and more pleasing.

*Believing with you that religion is a matter which lies solely between Man & his **God**, that he owes account to none other for his faith or his worship, that the legitimate powers of government reach actions only, & not opinions, I contemplate with sovereign reverence that act of the whole American people which declared that their legislature should "make no law respecting an establishment of religion, or prohibiting the free exercise thereof," thus building a wall of separation between Church & State. Adhering to this expression of the supreme will of the nation in behalf of the rights of conscience, I shall see with sincere satisfaction the progress of those sentiments which tend to restore to man all his natural rights, convinced he has no natural right in opposition to his social duties.*

I reciprocate your kind prayers for the protection & blessing of the common father and creator of man, and tender you for yourselves & your religious association, assurances of my high respect & esteem.

Thomas Jefferson

The First Amendment aka The Establishment Clause

"Congress shall make no law respecting an establishment of religion, or prohibiting the free exercise thereof..."

The words "Separation of Church and State" do not exist anywhere in the US Constitution.

The First Amendment prohibits the US Congress from making any law which will establish a religion and the US Congress is prohibited from infringing on the right of all American citizens to practice their religious or spiritual faith.

The Founding Fathers believed in a ***Nation under God*** where liberty and freedom are exercised by everyone regardless of faith and including those of no faith in God.

Thomas Jefferson was a man of faith in God and a man who believed that Jesus Christ was a real man who taught important and valuable lessons to mankind through the Word of God.

Atheism and communism go hand-in-hand.

One of the tenets of communism is to remove God from the public view and through that removal of God; morality is redefined no longer by God's Laws but by human emotion human rationale.

The De-Christianization of the world was implemented through the French Revolution and it was propagated by the self-proclaimed "intellectuals" born out of the Enlightenment Period.

Part 6

State Constitutions

A fact not widely known is that Forty-seven of the Fifty States reference God in their State Constitution. Most of these State Constitutions reference God in their Preamble which is the section at the beginning of a Constitution that explains the intent and purpose of the document.

In June, 2015 the Oklahoma State Supreme Court decided that a stone monument display of the 10 Commandments could not be displayed on the Capital grounds because the monument violated the First Amendment to the US Constitution & the Oklahoma State Constitution.

Yet if asked, it is doubtful that any of the opponents to this monument can name the church this monument established nor can any person identify any tax levied by the State, any city, any township, any municipality or any county to support a church or any religious affiliation.

The Preamble of the Oklahoma Constitution invokes God into the intent and purpose of their State Constitution.

James Madison is known as the father of the U.S. Constitution. He was also the fourth President of the United States. He was the primary author of the Bill of Rights and as Secretary of State under Thomas Jefferson, James Madison helped engineered the Louisiana Purchase of 1803.

Madison believed Christianity to be the foundation upon which a just government must be built.

"We the Subscribers say, that the General Assembly of this Commonwealth have no such authority: And that no effort may be omitted on our part against so dangerous an usurpation, we oppose to it, this remonstrance; earnestly praying, as we are in duty bound, that the **Supreme Lawgiver of the Universe**, *by illuminating those to whom it is addressed, may on the one hand, turn their Councils from every act which would affront* **His** *holy prerogative, or violate the trust committed to them: and on the other, guide them into every measure which may be worthy of* **His** *blessing, may redound to their own praise, and may establish more firmly the liberties, the prosperity and the happiness of the Commonwealth."* **James Madison, Memorial & Remonstrance, June 1785**

In 1788, Madison stated: *"The belief in* **God** *all powerful wise and good, is so essential to the moral order of the world and to the happiness of man, that arguments which enforce it cannot be drawn from too many sources nor adapted with too much solicitude to the different characters and capacities to be impressed with it."* **James Madison, 1788**

"The constitutions of most of our States assert, that all power is inherent in the people; that they may exercise it by themselves, ... or they may act by representatives, freely and equally chosen; that it is their right and duty to be at all times armed; that they are entitled to freedom of person, **freedom of religion,** *freedom of property, and freedom of the press."* **Thomas Jefferson letter to Major John Cartwright, June 5, 1824**

These quotes are further evidence of the belief in our nation's founders in God and the that they believed that this nation being placed under God was integral to our national identity.

James Madison

Memorial and Remonstrance against Religious Assessments

June 20, 1785

To the Honorable the General Assembly of the

Commonwealth of Virginia A Memorial and Remonstrance

We the subscribers, citizens of the said Commonwealth, having taken into serious consideration, a Bill printed by order of the last Session of General Assembly, entitled "A Bill establishing a provision for Teachers of the Christian Religion," and conceiving that the same if finally armed with the sanctions of a law, will be a dangerous abuse of power, are bound as faithful members of a free State to remonstrate against it, and to declare the reasons by which we are determined.

We remonstrate against the said Bill,

*1. Because we hold it for a fundamental and undeniable truth, "that Religion or the duty which we owe to our **Creator** and the manner of discharging it, can be directed only by reason and conviction, not by force or violence."*

[Virginia Declaration of Rights, art. 16] The Religion then of every man must be left to the conviction and conscience of every man; and it is the right of every man to exercise it as these may dictate. This right is in its nature an unalienable right. It is unalienable, because the opinions of men, depending only on the evidence contemplated by their own minds cannot follow the dictates of other men:

*It is unalienable also, because what is here a right towards men, is a duty towards the **Creator**. It is the duty of every man to render to the **Creator** such homage and such only as he believes to be acceptable to him. This duty is precedent, both in order of time and in degree of obligation, to the claims of Civil Society. Before any man can be considered as a member of Civil Society, he must be considered as a subject of the **Governour of the Universe**: And if a member of Civil Society, who enters into any subordinate Association, must* *always do it with a reservation of his duty to the **General Authority**; much more must every man who becomes a member of any particular Civil Society, do it with a saving of his allegiance to the **Universal Sovereign**.*

We maintain therefore that in matters of Religion, no man's right is abridged by the institution of Civil Society and that Religion is wholly exempt from its cognizance. True it is, that no other rule exists, by which any question which may divide a Society, can be ultimately determined, but the will of the majority; but it is also true that the majority may trespass on the rights of the minority.

2. Because if Religion be exempt from the authority of the Society at large, still less can it be subject to that of the Legislative Body. The latter are but the creatures and vicegerents of the former. Their jurisdiction is both derivative and limited: it is limited with regard to the co-ordinate.

3. Departments, more necessarily is it limited with regard to the constituents. The preservation of a free Government requires not merely, that the metes and bounds which separate each department of power be invariably maintained; but more especially that neither of them be suffered to overleap the great Barrier which defends the rights of the people. The Rulers who are guilty of such an encroachment, exceed the commission from which they derive their authority, and are Tyrants. The People who submit to it are governed by laws made neither by themselves nor by an authority derived from them, and are slaves.

3. Because it is proper to take alarm at the first experiment on our liberties. We hold this prudent jealousy to be the first duty of Citizens, and one of the noblest characteristics of the late Revolution. The free-men of America did not wait till usurped power had strengthened itself by exercise, and entangled the question in precedents. They saw all the consequences in the principle, and they avoided the consequences by denying the principle. We revere this lesson too much soon to forget it. Who does not see that the same authority which can establish Christianity, in exclusion of all other Religions, may establish with the same ease any particular sect of Christians, in exclusion of all other Sects? That the same authority which can force a citizen to contribute three

226

pence only of his property for the support of any one establishment, may force him to conform to any other establishment in all cases whatsoever?

4. Because the Bill violates that equality which ought to be the basis of every law, and which is more indispensible, in proportion as the validity or expediency of any law is more liable to be impeached.

If "all men are by nature equally free and independent," [Virginia Declaration of Rights, art. 1] all men are to be considered as entering into Society on equal conditions; as relinquishing no more, and therefore retaining no less, one than another, of their natural rights. Above all are they to be considered as retaining an "equal title to the free exercise of Religion according to the dictates of Conscience." [Virginia Declaration of Rights, art. 16] Whilst we assert for ourselves a freedom to embrace, to profess and to observe the Religion which we believe to be of divine origin, we cannot deny an equal freedom to those whose minds have not yet yielded to the evidence which has convinced us.

If this freedom be abused, it is an offence against **God**, not against man: To **God**, therefore, not to man, must an account of it be rendered. As the Bill violates equality by subjecting some to peculiar burdens, so it violates the same principle, by granting to others peculiar exemptions. Are the Quakers and Menonists the only sects who think a compulsive support of their Religions unnecessary and unwarrantable? Can their piety alone be entrusted with the care of public worship? Ought their Religions to be endowed above all others with extraordinary privileges by which proselytes may be enticed from all others? We think too favorably of the justice and good sense of these denominations to believe that they either covet pre-eminences over their fellow citizens or that they will be seduced by them from the common opposition to the measure.

5. Because the Bill implies either that the Civil Magistrate is a competent Judge of Religious Truth; or that he may employ Religion as an engine of Civil policy. The first is an arrogant pretension falsified by the contradictory opinions of Rulers in all ages, and throughout the world: the second an unhallowed perversion of the means of salvation.

6. *Because the establishment proposed by the Bill is not requisite for the support of the Christian Religion. To say that it is, is a contradiction to the Christian Religion itself, for every page of it disavows a dependence on the powers of this world: it is a contradiction to fact; for it is known that this Religion both existed and flourished, not only without the support of human laws, but in spite of every opposition from them, and not only during the period of miraculous aid, but long after it had been left to its own evidence and the ordinary care of Providence.*

Nay, it is a contradiction in terms; for a Religion not invented by human policy, must have pre-existed and been supported, before it was established by human policy. It is moreover to weaken in those who profess this Religion a pious confidence in its innate excellence and the patronage of its Author; and to foster in those who still reject it, a suspicion that its friends are too conscious of its fallacies to trust it to its own merits.

7. *Because experience witnesseth that ecclesiastical establishments, instead of maintaining the purity and efficacy of Religion, have had a contrary operation. During almost fifteen centuries has the legal establishment of Christianity been on trial.*

What have been its fruits? More or less in all places, pride and indolence in the Clergy, ignorance and servility in the laity, in both, superstition, bigotry and persecution. Enquire of the Teachers of Christianity for the ages in which it appeared in its greatest lustre; those of every sect, point to the ages prior to its incorporation with Civil policy. Propose a restoration of this primitive State in which its Teachers depended on the voluntary rewards of their flocks, many of them predict its downfall.

On which Side ought their testimony to have greatest weight, when for or when against their interest?

8. *Because the establishment in question is not necessary for the support of Civil Government. If it be urged as necessary for the support of Civil Government only as it is a means of supporting Religion, and it be not necessary for the latter purpose, it cannot be necessary for the former. If*

Religion be not within the cognizance of Civil Government how can its legal establishment be necessary to Civil Government? What influence in fact have ecclesiastical establishments had on Civil Society? In some instances they have been seen to erect a spiritual tyranny on the ruins of the Civil authority; in many instances they have been seen upholding the thrones of political tyranny: in no instance have they been seen the guardians of the liberties of the people. Rulers who wished to subvert the public liberty, may have found an established Clergy convenient auxiliaries.

A just Government instituted to secure & perpetuate it needs them not. Such a Government will be best supported by protecting every Citizen in the enjoyment of his Religion with the same equal hand which protects his person and his property; by neither invading the equal rights of any Sect, nor suffering any Sect to invade those of another.

9. Because the proposed establishment is a departure from that generous policy, which, offering an Asylum to the persecuted and oppressed of every Nation and Religion, promised a lustre to our country, and an accession to the number of its citizens. What a melancholy mark is the Bill of sudden degeneracy?

Instead of holding forth an Asylum to the persecuted, it is itself a signal of persecution. It degrades from the equal rank of Citizens all those whose opinions in Religion do not bend to those of the Legislative authority.

Distant as it may be in its present form from the Inquisition, it differs from it only in degree. The one is the first step, the other the last in the career of intolerance. The magnanimous sufferer under this cruel scourge in foreign Regions, must view the Bill as a Beacon on our Coast, warning him to seek some other haven, where liberty and philanthropy in their due extent, may offer a more certain repose from his Troubles.

10. Because it will have a like tendency to banish our Citizens. The allurements presented by other situations are every day thinning their number. To superadd a fresh motive to emigration by revoking the liberty

which they now enjoy, would be the same species of folly which has dishonoured and depopulated flourishing kingdoms.

11. Because it will destroy that moderation and harmony which the forbearance of our laws to intermeddle with Religion has produced among its several sects. Torrents of blood have been spilt in the old world, by vain attempts of the secular arm, to extinguish Religious discord, by proscribing all difference in Religious opinion. Time has at length revealed the true remedy.

Every relaxation of narrow and rigorous policy, wherever it has been tried, has been found to assuage the disease. The American Theatre has exhibited proofs that equal and complete liberty, if it does not wholly eradicate it, sufficiently destroys its malignant influence on the health and prosperity of the State. If with the salutary effects of this system under our own eyes, we begin to contract the bounds of Religious freedom, we know no name that will too severely reproach our folly. At least let warning be taken at the first fruits of the threatened innovation. The very appearance of the Bill has transformed "that Christian forbearance, love and charity," [Virginia Declaration of Rights, art. 16] which of late mutually prevailed, into animosities and jealousies, which may not soon be appeased.

What mischiefs may not be dreaded, should this enemy to the public quiet be armed with the force of a law?

12. Because the policy of the Bill is adverse to the diffusion of the light of Christianity. The first wish of those who enjoy this precious gift ought to be that it may be imparted to the whole race of mankind. Compare the number of those who have as yet received it with the number still remaining under the dominion of false Religions; and how small is the former!

Does the policy of the Bill tend to lessen the disproportion?

No; it at once discourages those who are strangers to the light of revelation from coming into the Region of it; and countenances by example the nations who continue in darkness, in shutting out those who might convey it to them. Instead of Levelling as far as possible, every obstacle to the victorious progress *of Truth, the Bill with an ignoble and unchristian timidity would circumscribe it with a wall of defence against the encroachments of error.*

13. Because attempts to enforce by legal sanctions, acts obnoxious to so great a proportion of Citizens, tend to enervate the laws in general, and to slacken the bands of Society. If it be difficult to execute any law which is not generally deemed necessary or salutary, what must be the case, where it is deemed invalid and dangerous? And what may be the effect of so striking an example of impotency in the Government, on its general authority?

14. Because a measure of such singular magnitude and delicacy ought not to be imposed, without the clearest evidence that it is called for by a majority of citizens, and no satisfactory method is yet proposed by which the voice of the majority in this case may be determined, or its influence secured. "

The people of the respective counties are indeed requested to signify their opinion respecting the adoption of the Bill to the next Session of Assembly."

But the representation must be made equal, before the voice either of the

Representatives or of the Counties will be that of the people. Our hope is that neither of the former will, after due consideration, espouse the dangerous principle of the Bill. Should the event disappoint us, it will still leave us in full confidence, that a fair appeal to the latter will reverse the sentence against our liberties.

15. Because finally, "the equal right of every citizen to the free exercise of his Religion according to the dictates of conscience" is held by the same tenure with all our other rights.

If we recur to its origin, it is equally the gift of nature; if we weigh its importance, it cannot be less dear to us; if we consult the "Declaration of those rights which pertain to the good people of Virginia, as the basis and foundation of Government," it is enumerated with equal solemnity, or rather studied emphasis. Either then, we must say, that the Will of the Legislature is the only measure of their authority; and that in the plenitude of this authority, they may sweep away all our fundamental rights; or, that they are bound to leave this particular right untouched and sacred: Either we must say, that they may control the freedom of the press, may abolish the Trial by Jury, may swallow up the Executive and Judiciary Powers of the State; nay that they may despoil us of our very right of suffrage, and erect themselves into an independent and hereditary Assembly or, we must say, that they have no authority to enact into law the Bill under consideration.

We the Subscribers say, that the General Assembly of this Commonwealth have no such authority: And that no effort may be omitted on our part against so dangerous an usurpation, we oppose to it, this remonstrance; earnestly praying, as we are in duty bound, that the Supreme Lawgiver of the Universe, by illuminating those to whom it is addressed, may on the one hand, turn their Councils from every act which would affront His holy prerogative, or violate the trust committed to them: and on the other, guide them into every measure which may be worthy of His blessing, may redound to their own praise, and may establish more firmly the liberties, the prosperity and the happiness of the Commonwealth.

A Bill Establishing a Provision for Teachers of the Christian Religion

Patrick Henry

January 1, 1784

Whereas the general diffusion of Christian knowledge hath a natural tendency to correct the morals of men, restrain their vices, and preserve the peace of society; which cannot be effected without a competent provision for learned teachers, who may be thereby enabled to devote their time and attention to the duty of instructing such citizens, as from their circumstances and want of education, cannot otherwise attain such knowledge; and it is judged that such provision may be made by the Legislature, without counteracting the liberal principle heretofore adopted and intended to be preserved by abolishing all distinctions of preeminence amongst the different societies or communities of Christians;

Be it therefore enacted by the General Assembly, That for the support of Christian teachers, per centum on the amount, or in the pound on the sum payable for tax on the property within this Commonwealth, is hereby assessed, and shall be paid by every person chargeable with the said tax at the time the same shall become due; and the Sheriffs of the several Counties shall have power to levy and collect the same in the same manner and under the like restrictions and limitations, as are or may be prescribed by the laws for raising the Revenues of this State.

And be it enacted, That for every sum so paid, the Sheriff or Collector shall give a receipt, expressing therein to what society of Christians the person from whom he may receive the same shall direct the money to be paid, keeping a distinct account thereof in his books.

The Sheriff of every County, shall, on or before the___ day of___ in every year, return to the Court, upon oath, two alphabetical lists of the payments to him made, distinguishing in columns opposite to the names of the persons who shall have paid the same, the society to which the money so paid was by them appropriated; and one column for the names where no appropriation shall be made. One of which lists, after being recorded in a book to be kept for that purpose, shall be filed by the Clerk in his office; the other shall by the Sheriff be fixed up in the Court-house, there to remain for the inspection of all concerned.

And the Sheriff, after deducting five per centum for the collection, shall forthwith pay to such person or persons as shall be appointed to receive the same by the Vestry, Elders, or Directors, however denominated of each such society, the sum so stated to be due to that society....

And be it further enacted, That the money to be raised by virtue of this Act, shall be by the Vestries, Elders, or Directors of each religious society, appropriated to a provision for a Minister or Teacher of the Gospel of their denomination, or the providing places of divine worship, and to none other use whatsoever; except in the denominations of Quakers and Menonists, who may receive what is collected from their members, and place it in their general fund, to be disposed of in a manner which they shall think best calculated to promote their particular mode of worship.

And be it enacted, That all sums which at the time of payment to the Sheriff or Collector may not be appropriated by the person paying the same, shall be accounted for with the Court in manner as by this Act is directed; and after deducting for his collection, the Sheriff shall pay the amount thereof upon account certified by the Court to the Auditors of Public Accounts, and by them to the Treasurer) into the public Treasury, to be disposed of under the direction of the General Assembly, for the encouragement of seminaries of learning within the Counties whence such sums shall arise, and to no other use or purpose whatsoever.

THIS Act shall commence, and be in force, from and after the _____ day of

_____ in the year _____

Preambles to each State Constitution

Alabama

"We the people of the State of Alabama, invoking the favor and guidance of **Almighty God**, *do ordain and establish the following Constitution."*

Alaska

"We the people of Alaska, grateful to **God** *and to those who founded our nation and pioneered this great land, in order to secure and transmit to succeeding generations our heritage of political, civil, and religious liberty within the Union of States, do ordain and establish this constitution for the State of Alaska."*

Arizona

"We the people of the State of Arizona, grateful to **Almighty God** *for our liberties, do ordain this Constitution."*

Arkansas

"We, the People of the State of Arkansas, grateful to **Almighty God** *for the privilege of choosing our own form of government; for our civil and religious liberty; and desiring to perpetuate its blessings, and secure the same to ourselves and posterity; do ordain and establish this Constitution."*

California

"We, the People of the State of California, grateful to **Almighty God** *for our freedom, in order to secure and perpetuate its blessings, do establish this Constitution."*

Colorado

"We, the people of Colorado, with profound reverence for the **Supreme Ruler of the Universe**, *in order to form a more independent and perfect government; establish justice; insure tranquility; provide for the common*

defense; promote the general welfare and secure the blessings of liberty to ourselves and our posterity, do ordain and establish this constitution for the "State of Colorado."

Connecticut

*"The People of Connecticut acknowledging with gratitude, the good providence of **God**, in having permitted them to enjoy a free government; do, in order more effectually to define, secure, and perpetuate the liberties, rights and privileges which they have derived from their ancestors; hereby, after a careful consideration and revision, ordain and establish the following constitution and form of civil government."*

Delaware

*"Through **Divine goodness**, all men have by nature the rights of worshiping and serving their **Creator** according to the dictates of their consciences, of enjoying and defending life and liberty, of acquiring and protecting reputation and property, and in general of obtaining objects suitable to their condition, without injury by one to another; and as these rights are essential to their welfare, for due exercise thereof, power is inherent in them; and therefore all just authority in the institutions of political society is derived from the people, and established with their consent, to advance their happiness; and they may for this end, as circumstances require, from time to time, alter their Constitution of government."*

Florida

*"We, the people of the State of Florida, being grateful to **Almighty God** for our constitutional liberty, in order to secure its benefits, perfect our government, insure domestic tranquility, maintain public order, and guarantee equal civil and political rights to all, do ordain and establish this constitution."*

Georgia

*"To perpetuate the principles of free government, insure justice to all, preserve peace, promote the interest and happiness of the citizen and of the family, and transmit to posterity the enjoyment of liberty, we the people of Georgia, relying upon the protection and guidance of **Almighty God**, do ordain and establish this Constitution."*

Hawaii

*"We, the people of Hawaii, grateful for **Divine Guidance**, and mindful of our Hawaiian heritage and uniqueness as an island State, dedicate our efforts to fulfill the philosophy decreed by the Hawaii State motto, "Ua mau ke ea o ka aina i ka pono."*

We reserve the right to control our destiny, to nurture the integrity of our people and culture, and to preserve the quality of life that we desire.

We reaffirm our belief in a government of the people, by the people and for the people, and with an understanding and compassionate heart toward all the peoples of the earth, do hereby ordain and establish this constitution for the State of Hawaii."

Idaho

*"We, the people of the state of Idaho, grateful to **Almighty God** for our freedom, to secure its blessings and promote our common welfare do establish this Constitution."*

Illinois

*"We, the People of the State of Illinois; grateful to **Almighty God** for the civil, political and religious liberty which He has permitted us to enjoy and seeking His blessing upon our endeavors — in order to provide for the health, safety and welfare of the people; maintain a representative and orderly government; eliminate poverty and inequality; assure legal, social and economic justice; provide opportunity for the fullest development of the individual; insure domestic tranquility; provide for the common defense; and*

secure the blessings of freedom and liberty to ourselves and our posterity - do ordain and establish this Constitution for the State of Illinois."

Indiana

"TO THE END, that justice be established, public order maintained, and liberty perpetuated; WE, the People of the State of Indiana, grateful to **ALMIGHTY GOD** for the free exercise of the right to choose our own form of government, do ordain this Constitution."

Iowa

"WE THE PEOPLE OF THE STATE OF IOWA, grateful to the **Supreme Being** for the blessings hitherto enjoyed, and feeling our dependence on Him for a continuation of those blessings, do ordain and establish a free and independent government, by the name of the State of Iowa, the boundaries whereof shall be as follows:"

Kansas

"We, the people of Kansas, grateful to **Almighty God** for our civil and religious privileges, in order to insure the full enjoyment of our rights as American citizens, do ordain and establish this constitution of the state of Kansas, with the following boundaries, to wit: Beginning at a point on the western boundary of the state of Missouri, where the thirty-seventh parallel of north latitude crosses the same; thence running west on said parallel to the twenty-fifth meridian of longitude west from Washington; thence north on said meridian to the fortieth parallel of north latitude; thence east on said parallel to the western boundary of the state of Missouri; thence south with the western boundary of said state to the place of beginning."

Kentucky

"We, the people of the Commonwealth of Kentucky, grateful to **Almighty God** for the civil, political and religious liberties we enjoy, and invoking the continuance of these blessings, do ordain and establish this Constitution."

Louisiana

"We, the people of Louisiana, grateful to **Almighty God** for the civil, political, economic, and religious liberties we enjoy, and desiring to protect individual rights to life, liberty, and property; afford opportunity for the fullest development of the individual; assure equality of rights; promote the health, safety, education, and welfare of the people; maintain a representative and orderly government; ensure domestic tranquility; provide for the common defense; and secure the blessings of freedom and justice to ourselves and our posterity, do ordain and establish this constitution."

Maine

"We the people of Maine, in order to establish justice, insure tranquility, provide for our mutual defense, promote our common welfare, and secure to ourselves and our posterity the blessings of liberty, acknowledging with grateful hearts the goodness of the **Sovereign Ruler of the Universe** in affording us an opportunity, so favorable to the design; and, imploring **God's aid and direction** in its accomplishment, do agree to form ourselves into a free and independent State, by the style and title of the State of Maine and do ordain and establish the following Constitution for the government of the same."

Maryland

"We, the People of the State of Maryland, grateful to **Almighty God** for our civil and religious liberty, and taking into our serious consideration the best means of establishing a good Constitution in this State for the sure foundation and more permanent security thereof, declare"

Massachusetts

"The end of the institution, maintenance, and administration of government, is to secure the existence of the body politic, to protect it, and to furnish the individuals who compose it with the power of enjoying in safety and tranquility their **natural rights**, and the blessings of life: and whenever these *great objects are not obtained, the people have a right to alter the government, and to take measures necessary for their safety, prosperity and happiness.*

The body politic is formed by a voluntary association of individuals: it is a social compact, by which the whole people covenants with each citizen, and each citizen with the whole people, that all shall be governed by certain laws for the common good. It is the duty of the people, therefore, in framing a constitution of government, to provide for an equitable mode of making laws, as well as for an impartial interpretation, and a faithful execution of them; that every man may, at all times, find his security in them.

*We, therefore, the people of Massachusetts, acknowledging, with grateful hearts, the goodness of the great **Legislator of the universe**, in affording us, in the course of **His providence**, an opportunity, deliberately and peaceably, without fraud, violence or surprise, of entering into an original, explicit, and solemn compact with each other; and of forming a new constitution of civil government, for ourselves and posterity; and devoutly imploring **His direction** in so interesting a design, do agree upon, ordain and establish the following Declaration of Rights, and Frame of Government, as the Constitution of the Commonwealth of Massachusetts."*

Michigan

*"We, the people of the State of Michigan, grateful to **Almighty God** for the blessings of freedom, and earnestly desiring to secure these blessings undiminished to ourselves and our posterity, do ordain and establish this constitution."*

Minnesota

*"We, the people of the state of Minnesota, grateful to **God** for our civil and religious liberty, and desiring to perpetuate its blessings and secure the same to ourselves and our posterity, do ordain and establish this Constitution."*

Mississippi

*"We, the people of Mississippi in convention assembled, grateful to **Almighty God** and invoking his blessing on our work, do ordain and establish this constitution."*

Missouri

*"We, the people of Missouri, with profound reverence for the **Supreme Ruler of the Universe**, and grateful for **His goodness**, do establish this Constitution for the better government of the state."*

Montana

*"We the people of Montana grateful to **God** for the quiet beauty of our state, the grandeur of our mountains, the vastness of our rolling plains, and desiring to improve the quality of life, equality of opportunity and to secure the blessings of liberty for this and future generations do ordain and establish this constitution."*

Nebraska

*"We, the people, grateful to **Almighty God** for our freedom, do ordain and establish the following declaration of rights and frame of government, as the Constitution of the State of Nebraska."*

Nevada

*"We the people of the State of Nevada Grateful to **Almighty God** for our freedom in order to secure its blessings, insure domestic tranquility, and form a more perfect Government, do establish this Constitution."*

New Hampshire

New Hampshire does not have a Preamble to their State Constitution but three of the articles in their Constitution do mention natural rights and God.

Article 4 Rights of Conscience Unalienable *"Among the **natural rights,** some are, in their very nature unalienable, because no equivalent can be given or received for them. Of this kind are the Rights of Conscience."* June 2, 1784

Article 5 Religious Freedom Recognized. *"Every individual has a natural and unalienable right to worship God according to the dictates of his own conscience, and reason; and no subject shall be hurt, molested, or restrained, in his peers on, liberty, or estate, for worshipping God in the manner and season most agreeable to the dictates of his own conscience; or for his religious profession, sentiments, or persuasion; provided he doth not disturb the public peace or disturb others in their religious worship."* June 2, 1784

Article 6 Morality and Piety *"**As morality and piety, rightly grounded on high principles, will give the best and greatest security to government, and will lay, in the hearts of men, the strongest obligations to due subjection; and as the knowledge of these is most likely to be propagated through a society, therefore, the several parishes, bodies, corporate, or religious societies shall at all times have the right of electing their own teachers, and of contracting with them for their support or maintenance, or both. But no person shall ever be compelled to pay towards the support of the schools of any sect or denomination. And every person, denomination or sect shall be equally under the protection of the law; and no subordination of any one sect, denomination or persuasion to another shall ever be established."***

June 2, 1784

New Jersey

*"We, the people of the State of New Jersey, grateful to **Almighty God** for the civil and religious liberty which **He** hath so long permitted us to enjoy, and looking to **Him** for a blessing upon our endeavors to secure and transmit the same unimpaired to succeeding generations, do ordain and establish this Constitution."*

New Mexico

*"We, the people of New Mexico, grateful to **Almighty God** for the blessings of liberty, in order to secure the advantages of a state government, do ordain and establish this constitution."*

New York

*"We The People of the State of New York, grateful to **Almighty God** for our Freedom, in order to secure its blessings, DO ESTABLISH THIS CONSTITUTION."*

North Carolina

*"We, the people of the State of North Carolina, grateful to **Almighty God, the Sovereign Ruler of Nations**, for the preservation of the American Union and the existence of our civil, political and religious liberties, and acknowledging our dependence upon **Him** for the continuance of those blessings to us and our posterity, do, for the more certain security thereof and for the better government of this State, ordain and establish this Constitution."*

North Dakota

*"We, the people of North Dakota, grateful to **Almighty God** for the blessings of civil and religious liberty, do ordain and establish this constitution."*

Ohio

*"We, the people of the State of Ohio, grateful to **Almighty God** for our freedom, to secure its blessings and promote our common welfare, do establish this Constitution."*

Oklahoma

*"Invoking the guidance of **Almighty God**, in order to secure and perpetuate the blessing of liberty; to secure just and rightful government; to promote our*

mutual welfare and happiness, we, the people of the State of Oklahoma, do ordain and establish this Constitution."

Oregon

Oregon does not specifically mention God in their Preamble. The Bill of Rights within their Constitution does guarantee this protection:

Section 2 *"Freedom of worship"* All men shall be secure in the Natural right, to worship **Almighty God** according to the dictates of their own consciences."

Pennsylvania

*"WE, the people of the Commonwealth of Pennsylvania, grateful to **Almighty God** for the blessings of civil and religious liberty, and humbly invoking **His** guidance, do ordain and establish this Constitution."*

Rhode Island

*"We, the people of the State of Rhode Island and Providence Plantations, grateful to **Almighty God** for the civil and religious liberty which He hath so long permitted us to enjoy, and looking to **Him** for a blessing upon our endeavors to secure and to transmit the same, unimpaired, to succeeding generations, do ordain and establish this Constitution of government."*

South Carolina

*"We, the people of the State of South Carolina, in Convention assembled, grateful to **God** for our liberties, do ordain and establish this Constitution for the preservation and perpetuation of the same."*

South Dakota

*"We, the people of South Dakota, grateful to **Almighty God** for our civil and religious liberties, in order to form a more perfect and independent government, establish justice, insure tranquility, provide for the common defense, promote the general welfare and preserve to ourselves and to our*

posterity the blessings of liberty, do ordain and establish this Constitution for the state of South Dakota."

Tennessee

In the same fashion of the US Constitution, God is acknowledged by using the phrase, *"in the year of our Lord"*.

*"Whereas, The people of the territory of the United States south of the river Ohio, having the right of admission into the general government as a member state thereof, consistent with the Constitution of the United States, and the act of cession of the state of North Carolina, recognizing the ordinance for the government of the territory – of the United States north west of the Ohio River, by their delegates and representatives in convention assembled, did on the sixth day of February, in the **year of our Lord** one thousand seven hundred and ninety-six, ordain and establish a Constitution, or form of government, and mutually agreed with each other to form themselves into a free and independent state by the name of the state of Tennessee, and,*

*Whereas, The General Assembly of the said state of Tennessee, (pursuant to the third section of the tenth article of the Constitution,) by an act passed on the Twenty-seventh day of November, in the **year of our Lord** one thousand eight hundred and thirty-three, entitled, "An Act" to provide for the calling of a convention, passed in obedience to the declared will of the voters of the state, as expressed at the general election of August, in the **year of our Lord** one thousand eight hundred and thirty-three, did authorize and provide for the election by the people of delegates and representatives, to meet at Nashville, in Davidson County, on the third Monday in May, in the year of our Lord one thousand eight hundred and thirty-four, for the purpose of revising and amending, or changing, the Constitution, and said convention did accordingly meet and form a Constitution which was submitted to the people, and was ratified by them, on the first Friday in March, in the **year of our Lord** one thousand eight hundred and thirty-five, and,*

Whereas, The General Assembly of said state of Tennessee, under and in virtue of the first section of the first article of the Declaration of Rights, contained in and forming a part of the existing Constitution of the state, by an act passed on the fifteenth day of November, in the **year of our Lord** one thousand eight hundred and sixty-nine, did provide for the calling of a convention by the people of the state, to meet at Nashville, on the second Monday in January, in the **year of our Lord** one thousand eight hundred and seventy, and for the election of delegates for the purpose of amending or revising the present Constitution, or forming and making a new Constitution; and,

Whereas, The people of the state, in the mode provided by said Act, have called said convention, and elected delegates to represent them therein; now therefore, We, the delegates and representatives of the people of the state of Tennessee, duly elected, and in convention assembled, in pursuance of said act of Assembly have ordained and established the following Constitution and form of government for this state, which we recommend to the people of Tennessee for their ratification: That is to say –"

The Tennessee State Constitution does mention God and religion. Article 1, Section 3 under the declaration of rights, the freedom to worship and the freedom to choose not to worship is guaranteed to be protected.

ARTICLE I Declaration of Rights

Section 3. "That all men have a natural and indefeasible right to worship **Almighty God** according to the dictates of their own conscience; that no man can of right be compelled to attend, erect, or support any place of worship, or to maintain any minister against his consent; that no human authority can, in any case whatever, control or interfere with the rights of conscience; and that no preference shall ever be given, by law, to any religious establishment or mode of worship."

ARTICLE IX Disqualifications

Section 1 **"Whereas ministers of the Gospel are by their profession, dedicated to God and the care of souls, and ought not to be diverted from the great duties of their functions; therefore, no minister of the**

Gospel, or priest of any denomination whatever, shall be eligible to a seat in either House of the Legislature."

Section 2 *"No person who denies the being of God, or a future state of rewards and punishments, shall hold any office in the civil department of this state."*

Article 9, Section 1 is very interesting because the State Constitution forbids active clergy from holding public office NOT because government and religion should be kept separate or because of any separation clause but so that an active member of the clergy can devote his/her time to the duties and functions of the clergy.

Article 9, Section 2 is also very interesting because it denies atheists and deniers of God and His promises a position in civil duty.

Clearly the authors of the Constitution of the State of Tennessee believed that men and women of God were suited for public service but not those who deny the existence of God.

The oath of those elected to office is clearly established in the State Constitution that every legislator must protect this Constitution and follow its wording.

ARTICLE X. Section 2.

Each member of the Senate and House of Representatives, shall before they proceed to business take an oath or affirmation to support the Constitution of this state, and of the United States and also the following oath: *"I (person's name), do solemnly swear (or affirm) that as a member of this General Assembly, I will, in all appointments, vote without favor, affection, partiality, or prejudice; and that I will not propose or assent to any bill, vote or resolution, which shall appear to me injurious to the people, or consent to any act or thing, whatever, that shall have a tendency to lessen or abridge their rights and privileges, as declared by the Constitution of this state."*

ARTICLE XI Miscellaneous Provisions

Section 15 *"No person shall in time of peace be required to perform any service to the public on any day set apart by his religion as a day of rest."*

Texas

*"Humbly invoking the blessings of **Almighty God**, the people of the State of Texas, do ordain and establish this Constitution."*

Utah

*"Grateful to **Almighty God** for life and liberty, we, the people of Utah, in order to secure and perpetuate the principles of free government, do ordain and establish this CONSTITUTION."*

Vermont

The Preamble to the 1786 Vermont State Constitution

*"Whereas, all government ought to be instituted and supported for the security and protection of the community as such and to enable the individuals who compose it, to enjoy their natural rights, and the other blessings which the **Author of existence** has bestowed upon man; and whenever those great ends of government are not obtained, the people have a right, by common consent, to change it, and take such measures as to them may appear necessary to promote their safety and happiness."*

1793 Vermont State Constitution

Article 3 Freedom in religion; right and duty of religious worship

*"That all persons have a natural and unalienable right, to worship **Almighty God**, according to the dictates of their own consciences and understandings, as in their opinion shall be regulated by **the word of God**; and that no person ought to, or of right can be compelled to attend any religious worship, or erect or support any place of worship, or maintain any minister, contrary to the dictates of conscience, nor can any person be justly deprived or abridged of*

*any civil right as a citizen, on account of religious sentiments, or peculiar mode of religious worship; and that no authority can, or ought to be vested in, or assumed by, any power whatever, that shall in any case interfere with, or in any manner control the rights of conscience, in the free exercise of religious worship. Nevertheless, **every sect or denomination of Christians ought to observe the Sabbath or Lord's day, and keep up some sort of religious worship, which to them shall seem most agreeable to the revealed will of God.**"*

Chapter II

Plan or Frame of Government

SECTION 29th

"Every officer, whether judicial, executive or military, in authority under this State, before he enters upon the execution of his office, shall take and subscribe the following oath or affirmation of allegiance to this State, (unless he shall produce evidence that he has before taken the same) and also the following oath or affirmation of office, except military officers, and such as shall be exempted by the Legislature."

The oath or affirmation of allegiance

*"You do solemnly swear (or affirm) that you will be true and faithful to the State of Vermont, and that you will not, directly or indirectly, do any act or thing injurious to the Constitution or Government thereof, as established by Convention. (If an oath) So help you **God**. (If an affirmation) under the pains and penalties of perjury."*

The oath or affirmation of office

*"You do solemnly swear (or affirm) that you will faithfully execute the office of for the of ; and will therein do equal right and justice to all men, to the best of your judgment and abilities, according to law. (If an oath) So help you **God**. (If an affirmation) under the pains and penalties of perjury."*

All oaths and affirmations in the Vermont State Constitution use the phrase *"So help you God"*.

October 20, 1790, Governor Thomas Chittenden in an Executive Speech delivered to the council and assembly of the State of Vermont.

This is an excerpt from that speech,

"Therefore with a firm reliance on receiving that kind aid and support from the Council and House of Representatives that the nature of my office requires, I shall accept the office to which I am elected, and am ready to take the qualifications pointed out by the constitution; and **I pray God to grant me wisdom to conduct agreeable to His will, and then I trust it will be for the best good of His and my people."**

Moses Robinson, Governor of the State of Vermont, farewell speech

October 14, 1790

Gentlemen of the Council and House of Representatives

"At the last annual election of the officers of this government, there was no choice made by the freemen of the supreme magistrate of the state; it was therefore the duty of the council and house of representatives, by their joint ballot, to elect some person to that office; it was the pleasure of the two houses to honor me with the appointment, of which I cheerfully accepted, and am conscious to myself that I have faithfully discharged my duty in the execution of that trust.

It appears from the present election, that the freemen have given their suffrages in favor of his Excellency governor CHITTENDEN. I heartily acquiesce in the choice, and shall, with the greatest satisfaction, retire to private life, where I expect to enjoy that peace which naturally results from a consciousness of having done my duty.

The freemen have an undoubted right, when they see it for the benefit of the community, to call forth their citizens from behind the curtain of private life, and make them their rulers, and for the same reason to dismiss them at pleasure and elect others in their place. This privilege is essential to all free, and to republican governments. As a citizen I trust I shall ever feel for the interest of the state: the confidence the freemen have repeatedly placed in me ever since the first formation of government, lays me under additional obligation to promote their true interest."

Fellow citizens of the legislature, **I wish you the benediction of Heaven in the prosecution of the important business of the present session; that all your consultations may terminate for the glory of God the interest of the citizens of this state, and that both those in public and private life may so conduct, in the several spheres in which God in his providence shall call them to act, as that, when death shall close the scene of life, we may each of us have the satisfaction of a good conscience and the approbation of our JUDGE."**

The following is the exit speech given by the first Governor of Vermont, Thomas Chittenden.

Executive Speech of Thomas Chittenden

Tuesday, October 18, 1796.

"Gentlemen of the Council and Assembly – You are so well knowing to the manifold favours and blessings bestowed on us, as a people, by the great ruler of the universe, that it would be unnecessary for me to recapitulate them. I would therefore only observe, that but a few years since we were without constitution, law or government, in a state of anarchy and confusion, at war with a potent foreign power, opposed by a powerful neighbouring state, discountenanced by the congress, distressed by internal dissentions, all our landed property in imminent danger, and without the means of defence.

Now your eyes behold the happy day, when we are in the full and uninterrupted enjoyment of a well-regulated government, suited to the situation and genius of the people, acknowledged by all the powers of the earth, supported by the congress, at peace with our sister states, among ourselves and all the world.

From whence did these great blessings come? From God. Are they not worth enjoying? They surely are. Does it not become us as a people, to improve them, that we may have reason to hope they may be continued to us, and transmitted to posterity? It certainly does.

What are the most likely measures to be taken by us, as a people, to obtain this great end? To be a faithful, virtuous, industrious, and a moral people.

Does it not become us as the legislature, to take every method in our power to encourage virtue, industry, morality, religion, and learning? I think it does.

Is there any better method that can be taken by us, to answer this purpose, than by our own example, and having a sacred regard to virtue, industry, integrity, and morality, in all our appointments of executive and judicial offices? This is the day we have appointed to nominate all our subordinate, executive, and judicial officers, through the state, for the present year.

The people by their free suffrages, have given us the power, and in us they have placed their confidence, and to God, to them, and our own consciences we are accountable.

Suffer me, Sir, as a leader, as a father, as a friend and a lover of this people, and as one whose voice cannot be much longer heard here, to instruct you in all your appointments, to have regard to none, but those who maintain a good moral character, men of integrity, and distinguished for wisdom and abilities; in doing this you will encourage virtue which is the glory of a people, and discountenance and discourage vice and profaneness, which is a reproach to any people."

Governor Thomas Chittenden, 1796

Virginia

The Virginia State Constitution does not have an actual preamble. Just as with the US Constitution inherent rights are granted by God, not men.

Virginia has amended their Constitution several times since 1776 mostly due to the rights of landowners and to reflect the growing dissention between southern States and the Federal government concerning States' rights and the movement among abolitionists to make slavery illegal in every US State.

The first Constitution for the State of Virginia was authored by George Mason and James Madison. This document declared that Great Britain no longer ruled Virginia and it accused King George III of establishing tyranny. In June of 1776 this document became the first Constitution of the State of Virginia.

Virginia Bill of Rights (Unanimously adopted, June 12th, 1776.)

A declaration of rights made by the representatives of the good people of Virginia, assembled in full and free convention; which rights do pertain to them and their posterity, as the basis and foundation of government.

Section 1 Equality and rights of men

1. *"That all men are by nature equally free and independent, and have certain inherent rights, of which, when they enter into a state of society, they cannot, by any compact, deprive or divest their posterity; namely, the enjoyment of life and liberty, with the means of acquiring and possessing property, and pursuing and obtaining happiness and safety."*

Section 16 Free exercise of religion; no establishment of religion

*"That religion or the duty which we owe to our **Creator**, and the manner of discharging it, can be directed only by reason and conviction, not by force or violence; and, therefore, all men are equally entitled to the free exercise of religion, according to the dictates of conscience; and that **it is the mutual duty of all to practice Christian forbearance, love, and charity towards each other.***

No man shall be compelled to frequent or support any religious worship, place, or ministry whatsoever, nor shall be enforced, restrained, molested, or burthened in his body or goods, nor shall otherwise suffer on account of his religious opinions or belief; but all men shall be free to profess and by argument to maintain their opinions in matters of religion, and the same shall in nowise diminish, enlarge, or affect their civil capacities.

And the General Assembly shall not prescribe any religious test whatever, or confer any peculiar privileges or advantages on any sect or denomination, or pass any law requiring or authorizing any religious society, or the people of any district within this Commonwealth, to levy on themselves or others, any tax for the erection or repair of any house of public worship, or for the support of any church or ministry; but it shall be left free to every person to select his religious instructor, and to make for his support such private contract as he shall please."

Article 2, Section 7 Oath or affirmation

*"I do solemnly swear (or affirm) that I will support the Constitution of the United States, and the Constitution of the Commonwealth of Virginia, and that I will faithfully and impartially discharge all the duties incumbent upon me as ...., according to the best of my ability (so help me **God**)."*

Washington State

*"We, the people of the State of Washington, grateful to the **Supreme Ruler of the Universe** for our liberties, do ordain this constitution."*

West Virginia

*"Since through **Divine Providence** we enjoy the blessings of civil, political and religious liberty, we, the people of West Virginia, in and through the provisions of this Constitution, reaffirm our faith in and constant reliance upon **God** and seek diligently to promote, preserve and perpetuate good government in the state of West Virginia for the common welfare, freedom and security of ourselves and our posterity."*

Wisconsin

*"We, the people of Wisconsin, grateful to **Almighty God** for our freedom, in order to secure its blessings, form a more perfect government, insure domestic tranquility and promote the general welfare, do establish this constitution."*

Wyoming

*"We, the people of the State of Wyoming, grateful to **God** for our civil, political and religious liberties, and desiring to secure them to ourselves and perpetuate them to our posterity, do ordain and establish this Constitution."*

The individual States created and worded their Constitution based on the words of the Founders' and the words in our founding documents.

The intent, the design and the founding principles of the Founders are the basis for US and State laws. The Founding Fathers made it very clear that this nation is a gift from God and that in order to govern this nation properly that everyone should look to the wisdom and the laws of God the Creator for direction in proper governance.

"The happiness of a people, and the good order and preservation of civil government, essentially depend on piety, religion and morality." The Massachusetts Constitution of 1780

*"The belief in **God** all powerful wise and good, is so essential to the moral order of the world and to the happiness of man, that arguments which enforce it cannot be drawn from too many sources nor adapted with too much*

solicitude to the different characters and capacities to be impressed with it."
James Madison, 1788

Part Seven

In God We Trust

During the War of 1812, Francis Scott Key, a lawyer from Baltimore was brought aboard a British warship to negotiate the release of British-held US prisoners of war.

This event in history occurred on September 13-14, 1814. Key was there with two other gentlemen as part of this negotiating team but they were not allowed to leave the British warship because the British feared that the negotiators had become too familiar with the strength of the British fleet about to attack Fort McHenry in the Baltimore harbor.

Key and the other men were witnesses to the British attack on Fort McHenry and on the morning after the final bombardment he saw that the US flag was still waving over the fort which meant that the British attack had failed.

Francis Scott Key wrote a poem entitled *"The Defense of Fort McHenry"* which later became known as a song titled *"The Star-Spangled Banner"* and in 1931 became our national anthem.

In this poem from 1814 Francis Scott Key included these words toward the end of his poem, *"And this be our motto: "In **God** is our trust."*

In April of 1864 Congress approved adding the motto **In God We Trust** to US currency in response to a directive from Salmon P. Chase to add the motto to our currency.

 In a letter to James Pollack, Director of the Philadelphia Mint in November 1861 stated,

"No nation can be strong except in the strength of God, or safe except in His defense. The trust of our people in God should be declared on all

of our national coins. You will cause a device to be prepared without unnecessary delay with a motto expressing in the fewest and tersest words possible this national recognition."

In 1864 the United States was embroiled in a Civil War, a War Between the States which came about because of slavery, prejudice, economics, States' rights and several other reasons which are debated even to this day.

President Abraham Lincoln and the US government were painfully aware of the hate and division among the North and the South and their respective supporters caused by this war. The belief was that in order for the US to survive this war and heal the wounds it caused was to come to **God**, to make sure that the nation was on God's side in the matter and place the nation's **FAITH &** *TRUST IN GOD*.

*"**God** who gave us life gave us liberty. Can the liberties of a nation be secure when we have removed a conviction that these liberties are the gift of **God**? Indeed I tremble for my country when I reflect that **God** is just, that his justice cannot sleep forever. Commerce between master and slave is despotism. Nothing is more certainly written in the book of fate than that these people are to be free. Establish a law for educating the common people. This it is the business of the state and on a general plan."* **Thomas Jefferson Memorial, Third panel of the Memorial dome**

President Lincoln knew that slavery was wrong and that slavery goes against the law of God; he wanted slavery to end and he wanted the war to end but the US had suffered a multitude of lost battles and families on both sides had lost sons, husbands and fathers. President Lincoln and the US government were sure that the nation had to "get right with **God**" because if they did not, they believed that the country would be lost and the South would win the war.

The motto *"In God We Trust"* was placed on US coins as a way to begin the nation's reconciliation with God and to bring the nation together through its shared belief in God which was through the motto as a unified expression of faith and trust in God.

Those who are revising US history have chosen to erase our heritage from the history books. Many of these same revisionists of history are school teachers and college professors whose goal is to change US history and teach their lies and intentional misrepresentations to young minds which absorb like a sponge the lies taught to them.

Now I am not accusing every teacher and professor in the US of willfully teaching lies to their students because these same lies were taught to them when they were young students.

The time is now that we hold these teachers responsible for perpetuating these outrageous lies which lead students away from the truth. So many people have bought into the lies taught by these atheist professors and teachers and it is our responsibility to educate people in the truth about this nation.

I cannot begin to relate the numerous discussions that I have had with people who only know the lies taught by the atheists in our schools and institutions of higher learning. All these people know are lies, they do not know the truth and quite honestly so many of these people I talk with have absolutely NO DESIRE to unlearn these lies and know the truth.

The United States of America has never been perfect and it can never be perfect. Our nation carries the memories of the injustices perpetrated on ethnic groups, other races of human beings and on foreign nationals. Some of the people in these groups were brought here against their will and some came here to escape prejudice and injustice only to find it here in the US.

Those things are in our past and that is where it should forever remain. Ordinary people and soldiers have already fought and died to end those injustices and to dredge up and give rebirth to old wounds will prevent this nation from healing and coming together.

But as the Founders placed their faith and trust in God to bring this nation into His light so that God could bless this nation and her people.

Yes it is absolutely true that the Founders did not want every US citizen to be forced into the same group and they worded our founding documents in such a way so that every one of us shall live freely and not under the yoke of government. Those men knew that the only government that would be incorruptible would be the government of God...the one and only God the Creator of all creation.

The Founding Fathers placed their trust in God and their hope was that future generations would embody and reflect the same faith and trust.

Our States remembered the Founding Fathers when they drafted their state constitutions by invoking God and by remembering God in their Constitution.

Part Eight

God in US Code

Prayer has always opened a session of Congress and the Senate, *Marsh v. Chambers, 463 U.S. 783, 787, 792 (1983)*.

The founders repeatedly refer to God and His guidance on this country.

God is on our coins and paper money. *31 USC Sec. 5112, 31 USC Sec. 5114*

God is in OUR pledge. *36 USC Sec. 302, 4 USC Sec. 4*

God is included in our national anthem.

God is engraved in marble and stone in our government buildings and national monuments.

God is in our courts. *10 USC Append, 28 USC Append. 28 USC Sec. 453, 28 USC Sec. 951*

God is in our National Observances. *36 USC Sec. 119*

God is in our oaths to this nation. *28 USC Append. 32 USC Sec. 304*

God is in our motto. *36 USC Sec. 302*

God is in our military code. *10 USC Sec. 802*

In all, there are 68 references to God in US Code.

Part Nine

Is the United States of America a Christian Nation?

The Holy Trinity Church vs. The US is a SCOTUS case from 1892.

This 1892 SCOTUS decision contains this sentence in their ruling, *"There is no dissonance in these declarations. There is a universal language pervading them all, having one meaning. They affirm and reaffirm that this is a **Christian nation**. They are organic utterances. They speak the voice of the entire people."*

It is said that the Declaration of Independence was the promise; the Constitution was the fulfillment of that promise.

Article 7 of the US Constitution

"The Ratification of the Conventions of nine States shall be sufficient for the Establishment of this Constitution between the States so ratifying the Same."

"The Word, "the," being interlined between the seventh and eighth Lines of the first Page, the Word "Thirty" being partly written on an Erazure in the fifteenth Line of the first Page, The Words "is tried" being interlined between the thirty second and thirty third Lines of the first Page and the Word "the" being interlined between the forty third and forty fourth Lines of the second Page."

Attest William Jackson Secretary

"done in Convention by the Unanimous Consent of the States present the Seventeenth Day of September in the Year of our Lord one thousand seven hundred and Eighty seven and of the Independence of

262

the United States of America the Twelfth In witness whereof We have hereunto subscribed our Names,"

In 1897 the Supreme Court of the United States declared that… "the Constitution is the body and letter of which the Declaration of Independence is the thought and the spirit, and it is always safe to read the letter of the Constitution in the spirit of the Declaration of Independence."

In the book, **"Jubilee of the Constitution"** by John Quincy Adams, son of John Adams and the Sixth President of the United States of America, Adams explained that the US Constitution is dependent upon the virtues stated in the Declaration of Independence.

"The motive for the Declaration of Independence was on its face an, owed to be "a decent respect for the opinions of mankind." Its purpose to declare the causes which impelled the people of the English colonies on the continent of North America, to separate themselves from the political community of the British nation. They declare only, the causes of their separation, but they announce at the same time their assumption of the separate and equal station to which the laws of nature and of nature's God entitle them, among the powers of the earth."

"Thus their first movement is to recognize and appeal to the laws of nature and to nature's God, for their right to assume the attributes of sovereign power as an independent nation."

"The causes of their necessary separation, for they begin and end by declaring it necessary, alleged in the Declaration, are all founded on the same laws of nature and of nature's God – and hence as preliminary to the enumeration of the causes of separation, they set forth as self-evident truths, the rights of individual man, by the laws of nature and of nature's God, to life, to liberty, to the pursuit of happiness. That all men are created equal. That to secure the rights of life, liberty and the pursuits of happiness, governments are instituted among men, deriving their just powers from the consent of the governed. This is by the laws of nature and of nature's God, and of course presupposes the

existence of a **God**, *the moral ruler of the universe, and a rule of right and wrong, of just and unjust, binding upon man, preceding all institutions of human society and of government. It avers, also, that governments are instituted to secure these rights of nature and of nature's* **God***, and that whenever any form of government becomes destructive of those ends, it is the right of THE PEOPLE to alter, or to abolish it, and to institute a new government – to throw off a government degenerating into despotism, and to provide new guards for their future security."*

"In conclusion, the Representatives of the United States of America, in general Congress assembled, appealing to the **Supreme judge of the world** *for the rectitude of their intentions, do, in the name and by the authority of the good people of these Colonies, solemnly publish and declare that these United Colonies, are, and of right ought to be, free and independent States; that they are absolved from all allegiance to the British crown; and that all political connection between them and the state of Great Britain, is, and ought to be totally dissolved; and that as free and independent States, they have full power to levy war, conclude peace, contract alliances, establish commerce, and to do all other acts and things which independent States may of right do. The appeal to the Supreme judge of the world, and the rule of right and wrong as paramount events to the power of independent States, are here again repeated in the very act of constituting a new sovereign community."*

"The Declaration of Independence and the Constitution of the United States, are parts of one consistent whole, founded upon one and the same theory of government, then new, not as a theory, for it had been working itself into the mind of man for many ages, and been especially expounded in the writings of Locke, but had never before been adopted by a great nation in practice." John Quincy Adams, The Jubilee of the Constitution: A Discourse, 1839

The Ten Commandments are inscribed in stone on the Supreme Court building and on US national monuments. Stone is used because of its strength and durability; stone inscriptions will endure for centuries. When the United States government commissioned for these buildings and monuments to be built out of stone and marble the intention was that these structures endure and last for centuries, that includes those inscriptions.

What this naturally means is that the Founders wrote the US Constitution as a link to all founding documents because the US Constitution is the continuation of the Declaration of Independence.

This part of the US Constitution makes that connection to the Declaration of Independence, *"in the Year of our Lord one thousand seven hundred and Eighty seven and of the Independence of the United States of America the Twelfth"*.

John Quincy Adams confirms this fact when he wrote in 1839 *"The Declaration of independence and the Constitution of the United States, are parts of one consistent whole, founded upon one and the same theory of government, then new, not as a theory, for it had been working itself into the mind of man for many ages, and been especially expounded in the writings of Locke, but had never before been adopted by a great nation in practice."*

John Quincy Adams concludes his book this way,

*"Fellow-citizens, the ark of your covenant is the Declaration of Independence. Your Mount Ebal is the confederacy of separate state sovereignties, and your Mount Gerizim is the Constitution of the United States. In that scene of tremendous and awful solemnity, narrated in the **Holy Scriptures**, there is not a curse pronounced against the people, upon Mount Ebal, not a blessing promised them upon Mount Gerizim, which your posterity may not suffer or enjoy, from your and their adherence to, or departure from, the principles of the Declaration of Independence, practically interwoven in the Constitution of the United States."*

"Lay up these principles, then, in your hearts, and in your souls – bind them for signs upon your hands, that they may be as frontlets between your eyes – teach them to your children, speaking of them when sitting in your houses, when walking by the way, when lying down and when rising up – write them upon the doorplates of your houses, and upon your gates – cling to them as to

the issues of life – adhere to them as to the cords of your eternal salvation. So may your children's children at the next return of this day of jubilee, after a full century of experience under your national Constitution, celebrate it again in the full enjoyment of all the blessings recognized by you in the commemoration of this day, and of all the blessings promised to the **children of Israel** upon Mount Gerizim, as the reward of obedience to the law of **God**."

There are surely more links connecting these two important founding documents proving that the US Constitution is the continuation of our Declaration of Independence but the debate ends with the points of the facts in this chapter.

The Founders said so...in 1776.

IN CONGRESS, July 4, 1776

The unanimous Declaration of the thirteen united States of America,

*"When in the Course of human events, it becomes necessary for one people to dissolve the political bands which have connected them with another, and to assume among the powers of the earth, the separate and equal station to which the **Laws of Nature and of Nature's God** entitle them, a decent respect to the opinions of mankind requires that they should declare the causes which impel them to the separation."*

*"We hold these truths to be self-evident, that all men are created equal, that they are endowed by their **Creator** with certain unalienable Rights, that among these are Life, Liberty and the pursuit of Happiness.--That to secure these rights, Governments are instituted among Men, deriving their just powers from the consent of the governed,"*

"The virtue which had been infused into the Constitution of the United States ... was no other than the concretion of those abstract principles which had been first proclaimed in the Declaration of Independence. ... This was the platform upon which the Constitution of the United States had been erected. Its virtues, its republican character, consisted in its conformity to the

principles proclaimed in the Declaration of Independence and as its administration ... was to depend upon the ... virtue, or in other words, of those principles proclaimed in the Declaration of Independence and embodied in the Constitution of the United States." **John Quincy Adams**, United States Founding Father, Foreign Ambassador under Washington, Adams, and Madison, Secretary of State under Monroe, Member Massachusetts Legislature, United States Senator, United States House of Representatives, Sixth President of the United States under the Constitution

"The Jubilee of the Constitution: A Discourse, Delivered at the Request of the New York Historical Society, in the City of New York, on Tuesday, the 30th of April 1839; Being the Fiftieth Anniversary of the Inauguration of George Washington as President of the United States, on Thursday, the 30th of April, 1789"

Proclamation – America Seeks God in a Time of War – 1777

IN CONGRESS

November 1, 1777

*FORASMUCH as it is the indispensable Duty of all Men to adore the superintending Providence of **Almighty God**; to acknowledge with Gratitude their Obligation to **him** for benefits received, and to implore such farther Blessings as they stand in Need of; And it having pleased him in **his abundant Mercy** not only to continue to us the innumerable Bounties of **his** common Providence, but also to smile upon us in the Prosecution of a just and necessary War, for the Defence and Establishment of our unalienable Rights and Liberties; particularly in that **he** hath been pleased in so great a Measure to prosper the Means used for the Support of our Troops and to crown our Arms with most signal success:*

It is therefore recommended to the legislative or executive powers of these United States, to set apart THURSDAY, the eighteenth Day of December next, for Solemn Thanksgiving and Praise; That with one Heart

and one Voice the good People may express the grateful Feelings of their Hearts, and consecrate themselves to the Service of their **Divine Benefactor**; and that together with their sincere Acknowledgments and Offerings, they may join the penitent Confession of their manifold Sins, whereby they had forfeited
every Favour, and their humble and earnest Supplication that it may please **GOD**, through the Merits of **Jesus Christ**, mercifully to forgive and blot them out of Remembrance; That it may please **him** graciously to afford **his** Blessing on the Governments of these States respectively, and prosper the public Council of the whole; to inspire our Commanders both by Land and Sea, and all under them, with that Wisdom and Fortitude which may render them fit Instruments, under the Providence of **Almighty GOD**, to secure for these United States the greatest of all human blessings, INDEPENDENCE and PEACE; That it may please **him** to prosper the Trade and Manufactures of the People and the Labour of the Husbandman, that our Land may yet yield its Increase; To take Schools and Seminaries of Education, so necessary for cultivating the Principles of true Liberty, Virtue and Piety, under **his** nurturing Hand, and to prosper the Means of Religion for the promotion and enlargement of that Kingdom which consisteth "in Righteousness, Peace and Joy in the Holy Ghost."

And it is further recommended, that servile Labour, and such Recreation as, though at other Times innocent, may be unbecoming the Purpose of this Appointment, be omitted on so solemn an Occasion.

Extract from the Minutes,

Charles Thomson, Secr.

The conclusion is that this nation, the United States of America was founded upon Christian principles and this nation was to be a reflection of those Godly principles, this fact is absolutely clear.

Although not one of the Founding Fathers of this nation, President Abraham Lincoln expressed the sentiment of the Founding Fathers in his speech, *The Gettysburg Address* in 1863.

"Four score and seven years ago our fathers brought forth on this continent a new nation, conceived in Liberty, and dedicated to the proposition that all men are created equal.

Now we are engaged in a great civil war, testing whether that nation or any nation so conceived and so dedicated, can long endure. We are met on a great battle-field of that war. We have come to dedicate a portion of that field, as a final resting place for those who here gave their lives that that nation might live. It is altogether fitting and proper that we should do this.

*But, in a larger sense, we cannot dedicate – we cannot consecrate – we cannot hallow – this ground. The brave men, living and dead, who struggled here, have consecrated it, far above our poor power to add or detract. The world will little note, nor long remember what we say here, but it can never forget what they did here. It is for us the living, rather, to be dedicated here to the unfinished work which they who fought here have thus far so nobly advanced. It is rather for us to be here dedicated to the great task remaining before us – that from these honored dead we take increased devotion to that cause for which they gave the last full measure of devotion – that we here highly resolve that these dead shall not have died in vain – that **this nation, under God,** shall have a new birth of freedom – and that government of the people, by the people, for the people, shall not perish from the earth."*

Abraham Lincoln, Gettysburg, Pennsylvania, 1863

President Lincoln said, *"**this nation, under God**".*

The year 1863 was not that far removed from the days of George Washington, Thomas Jefferson, John Adams, James Madison, Benjamin Franklin, James Wilson and the remainder of our nation's founders.

When President Lincoln delivered the *Gettysburg Address* in 1863 it had been less than 100 years since 1787 & 1788 when the Constitutional Convention produced our foundation of law and its protections for all US citizens- *The US Constitution* was ratified into existence.

The faith of the Founding Fathers was still felt in 1863 and their belief in our founding principles did not change even during one of this nation's darkest periods, *The War Between the States/The American Civil War.*

President Lincoln who is still to this day, revered as one of our greatest presidents was fully aware of this nation's founding principles; he understood that the United States of America was founded as a **nation under God**.

Evidence of the Christian faith of the Founding Fathers

George Washington

Commander-in-Chief of the US Continental Army, US Statesman, First US President, Father of Our Country

WASHINGTON'S INAUGURAL ADDRESS OF 1789

April 30, 1789

Fellow Citizens of the Senate and the House of Representatives

"Among the vicissitudes incident to life, no event could have filled me with greater anxieties than that of which the notification was transmitted by your order, and received on the fourteenth day of the present month."

"On the one hand, I was summoned by my Country, whose voice I can never hear but with veneration and love, from a retreat which I had chosen with the fondest predilection, and, in my flattering hopes, with an immutable decision, as the asylum of my declining years: a retreat which was rendered every day more necessary as well as more dear to me, by the addition of habit to inclination, and of frequent interruptions in my health to the gradual waste committed on it by time."

"On the other hand, the magnitude and difficulty of the trust to which the voice of my Country called me, being sufficient to awaken in the wisest and most experienced of her citizens, a distrustful scrutiny into his qualifications, could not but overwhelm with despondence, one, who, inheriting inferior endowments from nature and unpracticed in the duties of civil administration, ought to be peculiarly conscious of his own deficiencies."

"In this conflict of emotions, all I dare aver, is, that it has been my faithful study to collect my duty from a just appreciation of every circumstance, by

which it might be affected. All I dare hope, is, that, if in executing this task I have been too much swayed by a grateful remembrance of former instances, or by an affectionate sensibility to this transcendent proof, of the confidence of my fellow-citizens; and have thence too little consulted my incapacity as well as disinclination for the weighty and untried cares before me; my error will be palliated by the motives which misled me, and its consequences be judged by my Country, with some share of the partiality in which they originated."

"Such being the impressions under which I have, in obedience to the public summons, repaired to the present station; it would be peculiarly improper to omit in this first official Act, my fervent supplications to that **Almighty Being who rules over the Universe**, who presides in the Councils of Nations, and whose providential aids can supply every human defect, that his benediction may consecrate to the liberties and happiness of the People of the United States, a Government instituted by themselves for these essential purposes: and may enable every instrument employed in its administration to execute with success, the functions allotted to his charge. In tendering this homage to the **Great Author** of every public and private good I assure myself that it expresses your sentiments not less than my own; nor those of my fellow-citizens at large, less than either."

"No People can be bound to acknowledge and adore the invisible hand, which conducts the Affairs of men more than the People of the United States. Every step, by which they have advanced to the character of an independent nation, seems to have been distinguished by some token of providential agency. And in the important revolution just accomplished in the system of their United Government, the tranquil deliberations and voluntary consent of so many distinct communities, from which the event has resulted, cannot be compared with the means by which most Governments have been established, without some return of pious gratitude along with an humble anticipation of the future blessings which the past seem to presage. These reflections, arising out of the present crisis, have forced themselves too strongly on my mind to be suppressed."

"You will join with me I trust in thinking, that there are none under the influence of which, the proceedings of a new and free Government can more auspiciously commence. By the article establishing the Executive Department, it is made the duty of the President "to recommend to your consideration, such measures as he shall judge necessary and expedient."

"The circumstances under which I now meet you, will acquit me from entering into that subject, farther than to refer to the Great Constitutional Charter under which you are assembled; and which, in defining your powers, designates the objects to which your attention is to be given. It will be more consistent with those circumstances and far more congenial with the feelings which actuate me, to substitute, in place of a recommendation of particular measures, the tribute that is due to the talents, the rectitude, and the patriotism which adorn the characters selected to devise and adopt them. In these honorable qualifications, I behold the surest pledges, that as on one side, no local prejudices, or attachments; no separate views, nor party animosities, will misdirect the comprehensive and equal eye which ought to watch over this great assemblage of communities and interests: so, on another, that the foundations of our National policy will be laid in the pure and immutable principles of private morality; and the pre-eminence of a free Government, be exemplified by all the attributes which can win the affections of its Citizens, and command the respect of the world."

"I dwell on this prospect with every satisfaction which an ardent love for my Country can inspire: since there is no truth more thoroughly established, than that there exists in the economy and course of nature, an indissoluble union between virtue and happiness, between duty and advantage, between the genuine maxims of an honest and magnanimous policy, and the solid rewards of public prosperity and felicity: Since we ought to be no less persuaded that the propitious smiles of Heaven, can never be expected on a nation that disregards the eternal rules of order and right, which Heaven itself has ordained: And since the preservation of the sacred fire of liberty, and the destiny of the Republican model of Government, are justly considered as deeply, perhaps as finally staked, on the experiment entrusted to the hands of the American people."

"Besides the ordinary objects submitted to your care, it will remain with your judgment to decide, how far an exercise of the occasional power delegated by the Fifth article of the Constitution is rendered expedient at the present juncture by the nature of objections which have been urged against the System, or by the degree of inquietude which has given birth to them. Instead of undertaking particular recommendations on this subject, in which I could be guided by no lights derived from official opportunities, I shall again give way to my entire confidence in your discernment and pursuit of the public good: For I assure myself that whilst you carefully avoid every alteration which might endanger the benefits of an United and effective Government, or which ought to await the future lessons of experience; a reverence for the characteristic rights of freemen, and a regard for the public harmony, will sufficiently influence your deliberations on the question how far the former can be more impregnably fortified, or the latter be safely and advantageously promoted."

"To the preceding observations I have one to add, which will be most properly addressed to the House of Representatives. It concerns myself, and will therefore be as brief as possible. When I was first honoured with a call into the Service of my Country, then on the eve of an arduous struggle for its liberties, the light in which I contemplated my duty required that I should renounce every pecuniary compensation. From this resolution I have in no instance departed. And being still under the impressions which produced it, I must decline as inapplicable to myself, any share in the personal emoluments, which may be indispensably included in a permanent provision for the Executive Department; and must accordingly pray that the pecuniary estimates for the Station in which I am placed, may, during my continuance in it, be limited to such actual expenditures as the public good may be thought to require."

"Having thus imported to you my sentiments, as they have been awakened by the occasion which brings us together, I shall take my present leave; but not without resorting once more to the benign parent of the human race, in humble supplication that since he has been pleased to favour the American people, with opportunities for deliberating in perfect tranquility, and dispositions for deciding with unparalleled unanimity on a form of Government, for the security of their Union, and the advancement of their happiness; so his divine blessing may be equally conspicuous in the enlarged views, the temperate consultations, and the wise measures on which the success of this Government must depend." **George Washington, President of the United States, 1789**

"*Almighty and eternal Lord God, the great creator of heaven & earth, and the God and Father of our Lord Jesus Christ; look down from heaven, in pity and compassion upon me thy servant, who humbly prostrate myself before thee, sensible of thy mercy and my own misery; there is an infinite distance between thy glorious majesty and me, thy poor creature, the work of thy hand, between thy infinite power, and my weakness, thy wisdom, and my folly> thy eternal Being, and my mortal frame, but, O Lord, I have set myself at a greater distance from thee by my sin and wickedness, and humbly acknowledge the corruption of my nature and the many rebellions of my life. I have sinned against heaven and before thee, in thought, word & deed; I have contemned thy majesty and holy laws. I have likewise sinned by omitting what I ought to have done, and committing what I ought not. I have rebelled against light, despised thy mercies and judgments, and broken my vows and promises; I have neglected the means of Grace, and opportunities of becoming better; my iniquities are multiplied, and my sins are very great. I confess them, O Lord, with shame and sorrow, detestation and loathing, and desire to be vile in my own eyes, as I have rendered myself vile in thine. I humbly beseech thee to be merciful to me in the free pardon of my sins, for the sake of thy dear Son, my only Saviour, J. C., who came not to call the righteous, but sinners to repentance; be pleased to renew my nature and write thy laws upon my heart, and help me to live, righteously, soberly and godly in this evil world; make me humble, meek, patient and contented, and work in me the grace of thy holy spirit, prepare me for death and judgment, and let the thoughts thereof awaken me to a greater care and study to approve myself unto thee in well doing, bless our rulers in church & state. Help all in affliction or adversity – give them patience and a sanctified use of their affliction, and in thy good time deliverance from them; forgive my enemies, take me unto thy protection this day, keep me in perfect peace, which I ask in the name & for the sake of Jesus. Amen.*" **George Washington,**

Wednesday Morning Prayer recorded in the Prayer Journal, dated April 21-23, 1752

*"While we are contending for our own Liberty, we should be very cautious of violating the Rights of Conscience in others, ever considering that **God** alone is the Judge of the Hearts of Men, and to him only in this Case, they are answerable"* **George Washington, letter to Benedict Arnold, September 14, 1775**

General George Washington's instructions to Colonel Benedict Arnold

By his Excellency George Washington, Esqr.

Commander in Chief of the Army of the United Colonies of North America.

*1. You are immediately on their March from Cambridge to take the Command of the Detachment from the Continental Army against Quebec, & use all possible Expedition as the Winter Season is now Advancing, and the Success of this Enterprise (**under God**) depends wholly upon the Spirit with which it is pushed, & the favourable Disposition of the Canadians & Indians.* **George Washington, Cambridge, 14 September 1775**

*"The fate of unborn millions will now depend, under **God**, on the courage and conduct of this army. Our cruel and unrelenting enemy leaves us only the choice of brave resistance, or the most abject submission. We have, therefore, to resolve to conquer or die."* **Address to the Continental Army before the Battle of Long Island August 27, 1776**

*"It having pleased the **Almighty Ruler of the universe** propitiously to defend the cause of the United American States...by raising up a powerful Friend among the Princes of the Earth to establish our liberty and Independence upon lasting foundations, it becomes us to set apart a day for gratefully acknowledging the divine Goodness, and celebrating the important Event which we owe to his benign interposition.* **George Washington,**

General Orders, May 5, 1778, Head-Quarters V. Forge Tuesday May 5th 1778

*"You do well to wish to learn our arts and ways of life, and above all, the religion of **Jesus Christ**. These will make you a greater and happier people than you are. Congress will do everything they can to assist you in this wise intention; and to tie the knot of friendship and union so fast, that nothing shall ever be able to lose it. Brothers: I pray **God** he may make your Nation wise and Strong, that they may always see their own, true interest and have courage to walk in the right path; and that they never may be deceived by lies to do anything against the people of these States, who are their Brothers and ought always to be one people with them."* **George Washington's Address to the Delaware Nation, May 12, 1779**

Gentlemen,

While I receive, with much satisfaction, your Address replete with expressions of affection and esteem; I rejoice in the opportunity of assuring you, that I shall always retain a grateful remembrance of the cordial welcome I experienced in my visit to Newport, from all classes of Citizens.

The reflection on the days of difficulty and danger which are past is rendered the more sweet, from a consciousness that they are succeeded by days of uncommon prosperity and security. If we have wisdom to make the best use of the advantages with which we are now favored, we cannot fail, under the just administration of a good Government, to become a great and a happy people.

The Citizens of the United States of America have a right to applaud themselves for having given to mankind examples of an enlarged and liberal policy: a policy worthy of imitation. All possess alike liberty of conscience and immunities of citizenship. It is now no more that toleration is spoken of, as if it was by the indulgence of one class of people, that another enjoyed the exercise of their inherent natural rights. For happily the Government of the United States, which gives to bigotry no sanction, to persecution no assistance requires only that they who live under its protection should demean themselves as good citizens, in giving it on all occasions their effectual support.

*It would be inconsistent with the frankness of my character not to avow that I am pleased with your favorable opinion of my Administration, and fervent wishes for my felicity. May the Children of the Stock of Abraham, who dwell in this land, continue to merit and enjoy the good will of the other Inhabitants; while everyone shall sit in safety under his own vine and fig tree, and there shall be none to make him afraid. May **the father of all mercies** scatter light and not darkness in our paths, and make us all in our several vocations useful here, and in his own due time and way everlastingly happy.* **George Washington letter to the Hebrew Congregation of Newport, Rhode Island, August 18, 1790**

*"While we are zealously performing the duties of good citizens and soldiers, we certainly ought not to be inattentive to the higher duties of religion. To the distinguished character of Patriot, it should be our highest glory to add the more distinguished character of **Christian**.*

*The blessing and protection of Heaven are at all times necessary but especially so in times of public distress and danger. The General hopes and trusts that every officer and man will endeavor to live and act as becomes a **Christian soldier**, defending the dearest rights and liberties of his country."*

*"I am sure there never was a people, who had more reason to acknowledge a interposition in their affairs, than those of the United States; and I should be pained to believe that they have forgotten that agency, which was so often manifested during our Revolution, or that they failed to consider the omnipotence of that **God** who is alone able to protect them."* **George Washington letter to John Armstrong, Philadelphia, March 11, 1792**

"Your love of liberty, your respect for the laws, your habits of industry, and your practice of the moral and religious obligations, are the strongest claims to national and individual happiness, and they will, I trust, be firmly and lastingly established." **George Washington, letter to the Residents of Boston, October 27, 1789**

*"I now make it my earnest prayer, that **God** would have you, and the State over which you preside, in **his** holy protection, that he would incline the hearts of the Citizens to cultivate a spirit of subordination and obedience to Government, to entertain a brotherly affection and love for one another, for their fellow Citizens of the United States at large, and particularly for their brethren who have served in the Field, and finally, that he would most graciously be pleased to dispose us all, to do Justice, to love mercy, and to demean ourselves with that Charity, humility and pacific temper of mind, which were the Characteristicks of the **Divine Author of our blessed Religion**, and without an humble imitation of whose example in these things, we can never hope to be a happy Nation."* **George Washington, Circular Letter Addressed to the Governors of all the States on the Disbanding of the Army, Head Quarters, Newburgh, June 8, 1783**

To the United Baptist Churches of Virginia

New York, May 1789

Gentlemen,

"I request that you will accept my best acknowledgments for your congratulation on my appointment to the first office in the nation. The kind manner in which you mention my past conduct equally claims the expression of my gratitude.

After we had, by the smiles of Heaven on our exertions, obtained the object for which we contended, I retired at the conclusion of the war, with an idea that my country could have no farther occasion for my services, and with the intention of never entering again into public life: But when the exigence of my country seemed to require me once more to engage in public affairs, an honest conviction of duty superseded my former resolution, and became my apology for deviating from the happy plan which I had adopted.

If I could have entertained the slightest apprehension that the Constitution framed in the Convention, where I had the honor to preside, might possibly endanger the religious rights of any ecclesiastical Society, certainly I would never have placed my signature to it; and if I could now conceive that the *general Government might ever be so administered as to render the liberty of conscience insecure, I beg you will be persuaded that no one would be more zealous than myself to establish effectual barriers against the horrors of spiritual tyranny, and every species of religious persecution – For you, doubtless, remember that I have often expressed my sentiment, that every man, conducting himself as a good citizen, and being accountable to **God** alone for his religious opinions, ought to be protected in worshipping **God** according to the dictates of his own conscience.*

While I recollect with satisfaction that the religious Society of which you are Members, have been, throughout America, uniformly, and almost unanimously, the firm friends to civil liberty, and the persevering Promoters of our glorious revolution; I cannot hesitate to believe that they will be the faithful Supporters of a free, yet efficient general Government. Under this pleasing expectation I rejoice to assure them that they may rely on my best wishes and endeavors to advance their prosperity."

"In the meantime be assured, Gentlemen, that I entertain a proper sense of your fervent supplications to God for my temporal and eternal happiness."

G. Washington

John Adams

Second US President

"Let the pulpit resound with the doctrine and sentiments of religious liberty. Let us hear of the dignity of man's nature, and the noble rank he holds among the works of **God***... Let it be known that British liberties are not the grants of princes and parliaments."*

"Liberty cannot be preserved without a general knowledge among the people, who have a right, from the frame of their nature, to knowledge, as their great **Creator***, who does nothing in vain, has given them understandings, and a desire to know; but besides this, they have a right, an indisputable, unalienable, indefeasible, divine right to that most dreaded and envied kind of knowledge; I mean, of the characters and conduct of their rulers."* **John Adams, Dissertation on the Canon and Feudal Law, 1765**

"I am apt to believe that it will be celebrated, by succeeding Generations, as the great anniversary Festival. It ought to be commemorated, as the Day of Deliverance by solemn Acts of Devotion to **God Almighty***. It ought to be solemnized with Pomp and Parade, with Shews, Games, Sports, Guns, Bells, Bonfires and Illuminations from one End of this Continent to the other from this Time forward forever more. You will think me transported with Enthusiasm but I am not. -- I am well aware of the Toil and Blood and Treasure, that it will cost us to maintain this Declaration; and support and defend these States. -- Yet through all the Gloom I can see the Rays of ravishing Light and Glory. I can see that the End is more than worth all the Means. And that Posterity will tryumph in that Days Transaction, even altho. We should rue it, which* **I trust in God** *we shall not."* **John Adams letter to his wife Abigail, July 3, 1776**

"It is the duty of all men in society, publicly, and at stated seasons, to worship the **SUPREME BEING, the great Creator and Preserver of the universe.** *And no subject shall be hurt, molested, or restrained, in his person, liberty, or estate, for worshipping* **GOD** *in the manner most agreeable to the dictates of his own conscience; or for his religious profession or sentiments; provided he*

doth not disturb the public peace, or obstruct others in their religious worship." **John Adams, Thoughts on Government, 1776**

"The foundation of national morality must be laid in private families... How is it possible that Children can have any just Sense of the sacred Obligations of Morality or Religion if, from their earliest Infancy, they learn their Mothers live in habitual Infidelity to their fathers, and their fathers in as constant Infidelity to their Mothers?" **John Adams' diary, 1778**

"The moment the idea is admitted into society, that property is not as sacred as the laws of **God**, and that there is not a force of law and public justice to protect it, anarchy and tyranny commence. If "Thou shalt not covet," and "Thou shalt not steal," were not commandments of Heaven, they must be made inviolable precepts in every society, before it can be civilized or made free." **John Adams, Defence of the Constitutions of Government of the United States, 1787**

"The Christian Religion is, above all the Religions that ever prevailed or existed in ancient or modern Times, The Religion of Wisdom, Virtue, Equity and Humanity, let the Blackguard Paine say what he will. It is Resignation to **God** -- it is Goodness itself to Man." **John Adams' diary, July, 26 1796**

John Adams - Special Message to the Senate and the House; May 16 1797

SPECIAL SESSION MESSAGE

UNITED STATES, May 16, 1797

Gentlemen of the Senate arid Gentlemen of the House of Representatives:

The personal inconveniences to the members of the Senate and of the House of Representatives in leaving their families and private affairs at this season of the year are so obvious that I the more regret the extraordinary occasion which has rendered the convention of Congress indispensable.

It would have afforded me the highest satisfaction to have been able to congratulate you on a restoration of peace to the nations of Europe whose *animosities have endangered our tranquility; but we have still abundant cause of gratitude to the Supreme Dispenser of National Blessings for general health and promising seasons, for domestic and social happiness, for the rapid progress and ample acquisitions of industry through extensive territories, for civil, political, and religious liberty.*

Convinced that the conduct of the Government has been just and impartial to foreign nations, that those internal regulations which have been established by law for the preservation of peace are in their nature proper, and that they have been fairly executed, nothing will ever be done by me to impair the national engagements, to innovate upon principles which have been so deliberately and uprightly established, or to surrender in any manner the rights of the Government.

To enable me to maintain this declaration I rely, under God, with entire confidence on the firm and enlightened support of the National Legislature and upon the virtue and patriotism of my fellow-citizens.

JOHN ADAMS, May 16 1797

John Adams - Reply to the Senate of May 24, 1797

Reply of the President

Mr. Vice-President and Gentlemen of the Senate:

It would be an affectation in me to dissemble the pleasure I feel on receiving this kind address.

My long experience of the wisdom, fortitude, and patriotism of the Senate of the United States enhances in my estimation the value of those obliging expressions of your approbation of my conduct, which are a generous reward for the past and an affecting encouragement to constancy and perseverance in future.

Our sentiments appear to be so entirely in unison that I cannot but believe them to be the rational result of the understandings and the natural feelings of the hearts of Americans in general on contemplating the present state of the nation.

While such principles and affections prevail they will form an indissoluble bond of union and a sure pledge that our country has no essential injury to apprehend from any portentous appearances abroad. In a humble reliance on **Divine Providence** *we may rest assured that while we reiterate with sincerity our endeavors to accommodate all our differences with France, the independence of our country cannot be diminished, its dignity degraded, or its glory tarnished by any nation or combination of nations, whether friends or enemies,*

JOHN ADAMS, MAY 24, 1797

"Our Constitution was made only for a moral and religious people. It is wholly inadequate to the government of any other." **John Adams to the Massachusetts Militia, October 11, 1798**

"I pray Heaven to bestow the best of blessings on this house and all that shall hereafter inhabit it. May none but honest and wise men ever rule under this roof." **John Adams, Statement on the White House, in a letter to Abigail Adams, November 2, 1800**

"The general Principles, on which the Fathers Achieved Independence, were the only Principles in which, that beautiful Assembly of young Gentlemen could Unite, and these Principles only could be intended by them in their Address, or by me in my Answer. And what were these general Principles? I answer, the general Principles of Christianity, in which all those Sects were United: And the general Principles of English and American Liberty, in which all those young Men United, and which had United all Parties in America, in Majorities Sufficient to assert and maintain her Independence."

"Now I will avow, that I then believed, and now believe, that those general Principles of Christianity, are as eternal and immutable, as the Existence and Attributes of **God***: and that those Principles of Liberty, are as unalterable as human Nature and our terrestrial, mundane System."* **John Adams letter to Thomas Jefferson, June 28, 1813**

John Quincy Adams

Foreign Ambassador, Secretary of State, Senator, President

*"Why is it that next to the birthday of the **Savior of the World**, your most joyous and most venerated festival returns on this day, the 4th of July? Is it not that, in the chain of human events, the birthday of the nation is indissolubly linked with the birthday of the Savior? That it forms a leading event in the progress of the gospel dispensation? Is it not that the Declaration of Independence first organized the social compact on the foundation of the **Redeemer's** mission upon earth? That is laid the cornerstone of human government upon the first precepts of **Christianity?**"*

*"Is it not that, in the chain of human events, the birthday of the nation is indissolubly linked with the birthday of the **Savior**? That it forms a leading event in the progress of the gospel dispensation? Is it not that the Declaration of Independence first organized the social compact on the foundation of the **Redeemer's** mission upon the earth?"*

*"That it laid the cornerstone of human government upon the first precepts of **Christianity**, and gave to the world the first irrevocable pledge of the fulfilment of the prophecies, announced directly from Heaven at the birth of the **Savior** and predicted by the greatest of the Hebrew prophets six hundred years before?* **"An Oration Delivered Before the Inhabitants of the Town of Newburyport at their Request on the Sixty-First Anniversary of the Declaration of Independence, July 4, 1837**

*"The Declaration of Independence cast off all the shackles of this dependency. The United States of America were no longer Colonies. They were an independent nation of **Christians**."* **John Quincy Adams, An Oration Delivered Before the Inhabitants of the Town of Newburyport at Their Request on the Sixty-First Anniversary of the Declaration of Independence, July 4, 1837**

*"My hopes of a future life are all founded upon the **Gospel of Christ** and I cannot cavil or quibble away evade or object to. . . . the whole tenor of **His***

*conduct by which **He** sometimes positively asserted and at others countenances, permits **His** disciples in asserting that **He** was **God**.*

*The hope of a Christian is inseparable from his faith. Whoever believes in the **Divine inspiration of the Holy Scriptures** must hope that the religion of **Jesus** shall prevail throughout the earth. Never since the foundation of the world have the prospects of mankind been more encouraging to that hope than they appear to be at the present time. And may the associated distribution of the Bible proceed and prosper till the **Lord** shall have made "bare **His holy arm** in the eyes of all the nations, and all the ends of the earth shall see the salvation of our **God**" Isaiah 52:10.*

"To a man of liberal education, the study of history is not only useful, and important, but altogether indispensable, and with regard to the history contained in the Bible, the observation which Cicero makes respecting that of his own country is much more emphatically applicable, that 'it is not so much praiseworthy to be acquainted with as it is shameful to be ignorant of it."
John Quincy Adams, letters to his son

Samuel Adams

Father of the American Revolution, Signer of the Declaration of Independence, Ratifier of the U. S. Constitution, Governor of Massachusetts

"The right to freedom being the gift of **God Almighty***, it is not in the power of man to alienate this gift and voluntarily become a slave… These may be best understood by reading and carefully studying the institutes of the great* **Law Giver and Head of the Christian Church***, which are to be found clearly written and promulgated in the New Testament."* **Samuel Adams, The Rights of the Colonists, 1772**

"It is the greatest absurdity to suppose it in the power of one, or any number of men, at the entering into society, to renounce their essential natural rights, or the means of preserving those rights; when the grand end of civil government, from the very nature of its institution, is for the support, protection, and defence of those very rights; the principal of which, as is before observed, are Life, Liberty, and Property. If men, through fear, fraud, or mistake, should in terms renounce or give up any essential natural right, the eternal law of reason and the grand end of society would absolutely vacate such renunciation. The right to freedom being the gift of **God Almighty***, it is not in the power of man to alienate this gift and voluntarily become a slave."* **Samuel Adams, The Rights of the Colonists, 1772**

"The Opinion of others I very little regard, & have a thorough Contempt for all men, be their Names Characters & Stations what they may, who appear to be the irreclaimable Enemies of Religion & Liberty." **Samuel Adams letter to William Checkley, 1772**

"In regard to religion, mutual toleration in the different professions thereof is what all good and candid minds in all ages have ever practiced, and, both by precept and example, inculcated on mankind." **Samuel Adams, The Rights of the Colonists, 1772**

"Nothing is more essential to the establishment of manners in a State than that all persons employed in places of power and trust be men of unexceptionable characters. The public cannot be too curious concerning the character of public men." **Samuel Adams letter to James Warren, 1775**

"You have seen the MOST GRACIOUS Speech–Most Gracious! How strangely will the Tools of a Tyrant pervert the plain Meaning of Words! It discovers, to be sure, the most BENEVOLENT & HUMANE Feelings of its Author. I have heard that he is his own Minister –that he follows the Dictates of his own Heart. If so, why should we cast the odium of distressing Mankind upon his Minions & Flatterers only. Guilt must lie at his Door. Divine Vengeance will fall on his head; for all-gracious Heaven cannot be an indifferent Spectator of the virtuous Struggles of this people." **Samuel Adams letter to John Pitts, 1776**

"Courage, then, my countrymen, our contest is not only whether we ourselves shall be free, but whether there shall be left to mankind an asylum on earth for civil and religious liberty." **Samuel Adams, Speech at the State House, Philadelphia, 1776**

"Our unalterable resolution would be to be free. They have attempted to subdue us by force, but **God** be praised! In vain their arts may be more dangerous than their arms. Let us then renounce all treaty with them upon any score but that of total separation, and under God trust our cause to our swords." **Samuel Adams letter to James Warren, 1776**

"Religion and good morals are the only solid foundation of public liberty and happiness." **Samuel Adams letter to John Trumbull, 1778**

"The importance of piety and religion; of industry and frugality; of prudence, economy, regularity and an even government; all … are essential to the well-being of a family." **Samuel Adams letter to Thomas Wells, 1780**

"Let each citizen remember at the moment he is offering his vote that he is not making a present or a compliment to please an individual — or at least that he ought not so to do; but that he is executing one of the most solemn trusts in human society for which he is accountable to **God** and his country." **Samuel Adams, Boston Gazette, 1781**

"In the supposed state of nature, all men are equally bound by the laws of nature, or to speak more properly, the laws of the **Creator**." **Samuel Adams letter to the Legislature of Massachusetts, 1794**

A Proclamation

For a Day of PUBLIC FASTING, HUMILIATION and PRAYER

THE **supreme Ruler of the Universe**, having been pleased, in the course of **his** Providence, to establish the Independence of the United States of America, and to cause them to assume their rank, amount the nations of the Earth, and bless them with Liberty, Peace and Plenty; we ought to be led by Religious feelings of Gratitude; and to walk before **Him**, in all Humility, according to **his most Holy Law**.

But, as the depravity of our Hearts has, in so many instances drawn us aside from the path of duty, so that we have frequently offended our **Divine and Merciful Benefactor**; it is therefore highly incumbent on us, according to the ancient and laudable practice of our pious Ancestors, to open the year by a public and solemn Fast.

That with true repentance and contrition of Heart, we may unitedly implore the forgiveness of our Sins, through the merits of **Jesus Christ**, and humbly supplicate our **Heavenly Father**, to grant us the aids of **his Grace**, for the amendment of our Hearts and Lives, and vouchsafe his smiles upon our temporal concerns:

I HAVE therefore thought fit to appoint, and with the advice and consent of the Council, I do hereby appoint Thursday, the Second Day of April next, to be observed as a Day of Public Fasting, Humiliation and Prayer throughout this Commonwealth:

Calling upon the Ministers of the Gospel, of every Denomination, with their respective Congregations, to assemble on that Day, and devoutly implore the **Divine** *forgiveness of our Sins,*

To pray that the **Light of the Gospel**, *and the rights of Conscience, may be continued to the people of United America; and that* **his Holy Word** *may be improved by them, so that the name of* **God** *may be exalted, and their own Liberty and Happiness secured.*

That **he** *would be graciously pleased to bless our Federal Government; that by a wise administration, it may be a sure guide and safe protection in national concerns, for the people who have established, and who support it-*

That **He** *would continue to us the invaluable Blessings of Civil Liberty; guarding us against intestine commotions; and enabling the United States, in the exercise of such Governmental powers, as are devolved upon them, so that the honor and dignity of our Nation, upon the Sea and the Land, may be supported, and Peace with the other Powers of the World, upon safe and honorable terms, may be maintained.*

That **he** *would direct the administration of our Federal and State Governments, so that the lives, liberties and property of all the Citizens, and the just rights of the People, as Men and Citizens, may be forever acknowledged, and at all times defended, by Constitutions, founded upon equal rights; and by good and wholesome Laws, wisely and judiciously administered and duly executed.*

That **he** *would enable Legislators and Magistrates of this Commonwealth, to discharge the important duties incumbent on them, that the People may have good reason to feel themselves happy and safe, and lead quiet and peaceable lives in all* **Godliness** *and Honesty.*

That **he** *would incline the Natives of the Wilderness, to listen to reasonable offers of Peace, that tranquility and security may be established on the Frontiers Of our Country;*

That *he* would graciously regard the Lives and Health of the People of this and our sister States, and preserve them from contagious and wasting diseases:

To crown the ensuing Year with Plenty and Prosperity, by *his* blessing on our Husbandry, our Fisheries, our Commerce, and all the labor of our Hands- to affect our minds with a sense of our entire dependence upon **Him**, and of *his* great goodness towards us, that when we may present ourselves before **Him**, at the close of the Year, with our thank-offerings, our Hearts may by *his* grace, be prepared to do it in a manner acceptable to **Him**.

That **He** would be graciously pleased to establish the French Republic, and prosper others who are contending for the Rights of Men, and dispose all Nations to favor the same principles, and return to Peace and Friendship.

That **He** would in *his* great Mercy, remember the unhappy state of our Fellow-Citizens and others, who are groaning under bondage, in a foreign Land.

That **He** would soften the Hearts of those who have led them captive, inclining that People to show them favor during their Captivity, and in **His** own due time open a door for their relief:

And finally, that **He** would over-rule all the confusions that are in the Earth, of the speedy establishment of the **Redeemer's Kingdom**, which consisteth in Righteousness and Peace.

And I do recommend to the People of this Commonwealth, to abstain from all unnecessary Labor and Recreation on the said Day.

GIVEN at the Council-Chamber, in Boston, this Twenty-eighth Day of February, in the **Year of our Lord**, One Thousand Seven Hundred and Ninety-five, and in the Nineteenth Year of the Independence of the United States of America.

SAMUEL ADAMS Attest: John Avery, jun. Secretary

Commonwealth of Massachusetts **GOD** *Save the COMMONWEALTH of MASSACHUSETTS!*

Elias Boudinot

President of Congress, First Attorney, Supreme Court Bar, Bill of Rights Framer, Director of the US Mint

"Let us enter on this important business under the idea that we are **Christians** *on whom the eyes of the world are now turned… Let us earnestly call and beseech* **Him,** *for Christ's sake, to preside in our councils. . . . We can only depend on the all-powerful influence of the* **Spirit of God,** *Whose* **Divine** *aid and assistance it becomes us as a* **Christian** *people most devoutly to implore. Therefore I move that some minister of the Gospel be requested to attend this Congress every morning . . . in order to open the meeting with prayer."* **Speech in the First Provincial Congress of New Jersey**

"For nearly half a century have I anxiously and critically studied that invaluable treasure **[the Bible]***; and I still scarcely ever take it up that I do not find something new – that I do not receive some valuable addition to my stock of knowledge or perceive some instructive fact never observed before. In short, were you to ask me to recommend the most valuable book in the world, I should fix on the* **Bible** *as the most instructive both to the wise and ignorant. Were you to ask me for one affording the most rational and pleasing entertainment to the inquiring mind, I should repeat, it is the* **Bible***; and should you renew the inquiry for the best philosophy or the most interesting history, I should still urge you to look into your* **Bible***. I would make it, in short, the Alpha and Omega of knowledge."* **Letter to his daughter Susan, October 30, 1782**

Jacob Broom

Signer of the US Constitution

"I flatter myself you will be what I wish, but don't be so much flatterer as to relax of your application – don't forget to be a Christian. I have said much to you on this head, and I hope an indelible impression is made." **Jacob Broom letter to his son James, February 24, 1794**

Charles Carroll

Signer of the Declaration of Independence, Delegate to the Constitutional Convention, Framer of the Bill of Rights

"Without morals a republic cannot subsist any length of time; they therefore who are decrying the **Christian religion**, *whose morality is so sublime & pure, [and] which denounces against the wicked eternal misery, and [which] insured to the good eternal happiness, are undermining the solid foundation of morals, the best security for the duration of free governments."* **Charles Carroll letter to John McHenry on November 4, 1800**

John Dickinson

Signer of the US Constitution

"Kings or parliaments could not give the rights essential to happiness. ... We claim them from a higher source--from the King of kings, and **Lord of all the earth**. *They are not annexed to us by parchments and seals. They are created in us by the decrees of Providence ... It would be an insult on the* **divine Majesty** *to say, that* **he** *has given or allowed any man or body of men a right to make me miserable. If no man or body of men has such a right, I have a right to be happy. If there can be no happiness without freedom, I have a right to be free. If I cannot enjoy freedom without security of property, I have a right to be thus secured."* **Reply to a Committee in Barbados, 1766**

"The all wise **Creator of man** *imprest certain laws on his nature. A desire of happiness, and of society, are two of those laws. They were not intended to destroy, but to support each other. Man has therefore a right to promote the best union of both, in order to enjoy both in the highest degree. Thus, while this right is properly exercised, desires, that seem selfish, by a happy combination, produce the welfare of others."* **Political Writings, 1774**

Declaration of taking up arms, Resolutions of the Second Continental Congress, John Dickinson and Thomas Jefferson July 6, 1775

"With hearts fortified with these animating reflections, we most solemnly, before **God** *and the world, declare that, exerting the utmost energy of those powers which our beneficent* **Creator** *hath graciously bestowed upon us, the arms we have been compelled by our enemies to assume we will, in defiance of every hazard, with unabating firmness and perseverance, employ for the preservation of our liberties; being with our one mind resolved to die free men rather than live slaves."*

"Governments could not give the rights essential to happiness... We claim them from a higher source: from the **King of kings**, *and* **Lord of all the**

earth." **John Dickinson, The Political Writings of John Dickinson, 1801**

*"Rendering thanks to my **Creator** for my existence and station among **His** works, for my birth in a country enlightened by the **Gospel** and enjoying freedom, and for all **His** other kindnesses, to **Him** I resign myself, humbly confiding in **His** goodness and in **His** mercy through **Jesus Christ** for the events of eternity."* **From the Last Will & Testament of John Dickinson, attested March 25, 1808**

Benjamin Franklin

Signer of the Declaration of Independence, Foreign Diplomat, Signer of the US Constitution

"Talking against religion is unchaining a tiger; the beast let loose may worry his deliverer." **Poor Richard's Almanack, 1751**

Benjamin Franklin letter to Joseph Huey, 1753

Philada. June 6. 1753

Sir,

"I received your kind Letter of the 2d Inst. and am glad to hear that you increase in Strength; I hope you will continue mending till you recover your former Health and Firmness. Let me know whether you still use the cold Bath, and what Effect it has.

As to the Kindness you mention, I wish it could have been of more Service to you. But if it had, the only Thanks I should desire is, that you would always be equally ready to serve any other Person that may need your Assistance, and so let good Offices go round, for Mankind are all of a Family.

*For my own Part, when I am employed in serving others, I do not look upon myself as conferring Favours, but as paying Debts. In my Travels and since my Settlement I have received much Kindness from Men, to whom I shall never have any Opportunity of making the least direct Return. And numberless Mercies from **God**, who is infinitely above being benefited by our Services. These Kindnesses from Men I can therefore only return on their Fellow-Men; and I can only show my Gratitude for those Mercies from **God**, by a Readiness to help his other Children and my Brethren. For I do not think that Thanks, and Compliments, tho' repeated Weekly, can discharge our real Obligations to each other, and much less those to our **Creator**.*

*You will see in this my Notion of Good Works, that I am far from expecting (as you suppose) that I shall merit **Heaven** by them.*

*By **Heaven** we understand, a State of Happiness, infinite in Degree, and eternal in Duration: I can do nothing to deserve such Reward: He that for giving a Draught of Water to a thirsty Person should expect to be paid with a good Plantation, would be modest in his Demands, compar'd with those who think they deserve Heaven for the little Good they do on Earth. Even the mix'd imperfect Pleasures we enjoy in this World are rather from **God's Goodness** than our Merit; how much more such Happiness of Heaven. For my own part, I have not the Vanity to think I deserve it, the Folly to expect it, nor the Ambition to desire it; but content myself in submitting to the Will and Disposal of that **God** who made me, who has hitherto preserv'd and bless'd me, and in whose fatherly Goodness I may well confide, that he will never make me miserable, and that even the Afflictions I may at any time suffer shall tend to my Benefit.*

*The Faith you mention has doubtless its use in the World; I do not desire to see it diminished, nor would I endeavour to lessen it in any Man. But I wish it were more productive of Good Works than I have generally seen it: I mean real good Works, Works of Kindness, Charity, Mercy, and Publick Spirit; not Holiday-keeping, Sermon-Reading or Hearing, performing Church Ceremonies, or making long Prayers, fill'd with Flatteries and Compliments, despis'd even by wise Men, and much less capable of pleasing the Deity. The Worship of **God** is a Duty, the hearing and reading of Sermons may be useful; but if Men rest in Hearing and Praying, as too many do, it is as if a Tree should value itself on being water'd and putting forth Leaves, tho' it never produc'd any Fruit.*

*Your great Master tho't much less of these outward Appearances and Professions than many of his modern Disciples. He prefer'd the Doers of the Word to the meer Hearers; the Son that seemingly refus'd to obey his **Father** and yet perform'd **his** Commands, to him that profess'd his Readiness but neglected the Works; the heretical but charitable Samaritan, to the uncharitable tho' orthodox Priest and sanctified Levite: and those who gave Food to the hungry, Drink to the Thirsty, Raiment to the Naked, Entertainment to the Stranger, and Relief to the Sick, &c. tho' they never heard of **his** Name, **he** declares shall in the last Day be accepted, when those* *who cry* **Lord, Lord**; *who value themselves on their Faith tho' great enough to perform Miracles but have neglected good Works shall be rejected.* **He** *profess'd that* **he** *came not to call the Righteous but Sinners to Repentance; which imply'd* **his** *modest Opinion that there were some in* **his** *Time so good that they need not hear even* **him** *for Improvement; but now a days we have scarce a little Parson, that does not think it the Duty of every Man within his Reach to sit under his petty Ministrations, and that whoever omits them offends* **God**.

I wish to such more Humility, and to your Health and Happiness, being Your Friend and Servant."

B. Franklin

"I am fully of your opinion respecting religious tests; but, though the people of Massachusetts have not in their new Constitution kept quite clear of them, yet, if we consider what that people were 100 years ago, we must allow they have gone great lengths in liberality of sentiment on religious subjects; and we may hope for greater degrees of perfection, when their constitution, some years hence, shall be revised. If **Christian** *preachers had continued to teach as* **Christ and his Apostles** *did, without salaries, and as the Quakers now do, I imagine tests would never have existed; for I think they were invented, not so much to secure religion itself, as the emoluments of it.*

When a religion is good, I conceive that it will support itself; and, when it cannot support itself, and **God** *does not take care to support, so that its professors are obliged to call for the help of the civil power, it is a sign, I apprehend, of its being a bad one."* **Benjamin Franklin letter to Richard Price, October 9, 1780**

Mr. President

"The small Progress we have made after 4 or 5 Weeks close Attendance and continual Reasonings with each other, our different Sentiments on almost every Question, several of the last producing as many Noes as Ayes, is methinks a melancholy Proof of the Imperfection of the Human Understanding. We indeed seem to feel our own Want of political Wisdom,

since we have been running all about in search of it. We have gone back to ancient History for Models of Government, and examin'd the different Forms of those Republicks, which, having been originally form'd with the Seeds of their own Dissolution, now no longer exist. And we have view'd modern States all round Europe, but find none of their Constitutions suitable to our Circumstances.

In this Situation of this Assembly, groping, as it were, in the dark, to find Political Truth, and scarce able to distinguish it when presented to us, how has it happened, Sir, that we have not, hitherto once thought of humbly applying to the **Father of Lights** to illuminate our Understandings?

In the Beginning of the Contest with Britain, when we were sensible of Danger, we had daily Prayers in this Room for the **Divine** Protection! Our Prayers, Sir, were heard; and they were graciously answered. All of us, who were engag'd in the Struggle, must have observ'd frequent Instances of a Superintending Providence in our Favour. To that kind Providence we owe this happy Opportunity of Consulting in Peace on the Means of establishing our future national Felicity.

And have we now forgotten that powerful Friend? or do we imagine we no longer need its Assistance?

I have lived, Sir, a long time; and the longer I live, the more convincing Proofs I see of this Truth, That **GOD** governs in the Affairs of Men! And if a Sparrow cannot fall to the Ground without his Notice, is it probable that an Empire can rise without **his** Aid?

We have been assured, Sir, in the Sacred Writings, that "except the **Lord** build the House, they labor in vain that build it." I firmly believe this; and I also believe that without **his** concurring Aid, we shall succeed in this political Building no better than the Builders of Babel: We shall be divided by our little partial local Interests, our Projects will be confounded and we ourselves shall become a Reproach and a Byeword down to future Ages.

And what is worse, Mankind may hereafter, from this unfortunate Instance, despair of establishing Government by human Wisdom, and leave it to Chance, War and Conquest. I therefore beg leave to move,

That henceforth Prayers, imploring the Assistance of Heaven, and its Blessing on our Deliberations, be held in this Assembly every Morning before we proceed to Business; and that one or more of the Clergy of this City be requested to officiate in that Service." **Dr. Benjamin Franklin's Motion for Prayers in the Convention, June 28, 1787**

"The longer I live, the more convincing proofs I see of this Truth-that **God** governs in the Affairs of Men."

"I also believe, that "without his concurring Aid, we shall succeed in this political Building no better than the Builders of Babel." **Benjamin Franklin's speech to the 1787 Constitutional Convention**

"You desire to know something of my religion. It is the first time I have been questioned upon it. But I cannot take your curiosity amiss, and shall endeavor in a few words to gratify it. Here is my creed. I believe in one **God, the creator of the universe.**"

"That **he** governs by **his** providence."

"That **he** ought to be worshipped."

"That the most acceptable service we render to **him** is doing good to **his** other children."

"That the soul of man is immortal, and will be treated with justice in another life respecting its conduct in this. These I take to be the fundamental points in all sound religion and I regard them as you do in whatever sect I meet with them."

"As to **Jesus of Nazareth**, my opinion of whom you particularly desire, I think **his system of morals and his religion**, as **he** left them to us, the best the world ever saw or is likely to see; but I apprehend it has received various corrupting changes, and I have, with most of the present dissenters in

302

England, some doubts as to **his divinity**; though it is a question I do not dogmatize upon, having never studied it, and think it needless to busy myself with it now, when I expect soon an opportunity of knowing the truth with less trouble."

"I see no harm, however, in its being believed, if that belief has the good consequences, as probably it has, of making his doctrines more respected and more observed; especially as I do not perceive that the **Supreme** takes it amiss, by distinguishing the unbelievers in his government of the world with any peculiar marks of his displeasure." **Benjamin Franklin letter to Ezra Stiles, March 9, 1790**

"I beg I may not be understood to infer that our general Convention was **Divinely** inspired when it formed the new federal Constitution . . . yet I must own [admit] I have so much faith in the general government of the world by Providence that I can hardly conceive a transaction of such momentous importance . . . should be suffered to pass without being in some degree influenced, guided, and governed by that omnipotent, omnipresent, and **beneficent Ruler** in Whom all inferior spirits "live and move and have their being" Acts 17:28 **Benjamin Franklin**

Alexander Hamilton

Signer of the US Constitution

Author, The Federalist Papers, Secretary of the Treasury

"For my own part, I sincerely esteem it a system which without the finger of God, never could have been suggested and agreed upon by such a diversity of interests." **Alexander Hamilton's address to Constitutional Convention, 1787**

The Christian Constitutional Society

Alexander Hamilton and the Reverend James Bayard formed the Christian Constitutional Society to help spread over the world. Alexander Hamilton said that these two things made America great:

(1) Christianity

(2) A Constitution formed under Christianity

*"I now offer you the outline of the plan they have suggested. Let an association be formed to be denominated 'The **Christian** Constitutional Society, its object to be first: The support of the **Christian** religion. Second: The support of the United States."* **Alexander Hamilton letter to James Bayard, 1802**

Quotes by Alexander Hamilton

*"I have carefully examined the evidences of the **Christian** religion, and if I was sitting as a juror upon its authenticity I would unhesitatingly give my verdict in its favor. I can prove its truth as clearly as any proposition ever submitted to the mind of man."*

"In my opinion, the present Constitution is the standard to which we are to cling. Under its banner bona fide must we combat our political foes, reflecting all changes but through the channel itself provided for amendments. By these general views of the subject have my reflections been guided."

*"I have a tender reliance on the mercy of the **Almighty**, through the merits of the **Lord Jesus Christ**. I am a sinner. I look to **Him** for mercy; pray for me."*
Alexander Hamilton, July 12, 1804 at his death from a bullet wound

John Hancock

Signer of the Declaration of Independence, President of Congress, Governor of the State of Massachusetts

As Governor of Massachusetts, John Hancock issued proclamations for thanksgiving and prayer.

Earlier in this book these proclamations by John Hancock and our first four Presidents were provided in their context.

Proclamations issued by John Hancock

A PROCLAMATION

For a Day of Public FASTING, HUMILIATION, AND PRAYER

WHEREAS it hath been the Practice of the People inhabiting the Territory of this Commonwealth, from their first Settlement, at this Season of the Year, unitedly to acknowledge their entire Dependence on the **SUPREME BEING**, *and to humble themselves under a Sense of their utter unworthiness of his Favors, by Reason of their Transgression; and whereas the Practice appears to have a Tendency to cultivate the Fear of* **God**, *and a due Regard to* **HIS LAWS**:

I HAVE THEREFORE THOUGHT FIT, by, and with the Advice of the COUNCIL, to appoint, and I hereby do appoint, THURSDAY, the Eleventh Day of April next, to be observed throughout this Commonwealth, as Day of solemn FASTING, HUMILIATION and PRAYER:

Calling upon Ministers, and People of every Denomination, to assemble on that Day, in their respective Congregations; that with true contrition of Heart we may confess our Sins; resolve to forsake them, and implore the **Divine** *forgiveness, through the Merits and Mediation of* **JESUS CHRIST, our SAVIOUR** –

Humbly supplicate the **Supreme Ruler of the Universe** *to prosper the Administration of the Federal Government, and that of this Commonwealth,* and the other States in the Union; enduing them with Firmness, Wisdom, Unanimity and Public Spirit; and leading them in their respective public Councils, to such Determinations as shall be adapted to Promote the great end of Government: –

The Welfare and Happiness of the People: –

To restore and maintain Peace in our Borders: Continue Health among us, and give us Wisdom to improve **HIS** Blessings, for **HIS** Glory, and our own Good: –

To smile upon our Agriculture, and mercifully prevent the diminishing the Fruits of the Earth, by devouring Insects, unseasonable Weather, or other Judgments; that so our Land may abundantly yield its Increase: –

That **HE** would protect and prosper our Navigation, Trade, Fishery, and all the Works of our Hands: –

To confirm and continue our invaluable Religious and Civil Liberties: –

To prosper the University, and other Seminaries and Means of Education: –

To cause Industry, Frugality, and all Moral and Christian Virtues to prevail among us: –

To bless the Allies of the United States, and particularly to afford **his Almighty Aid** to the French Nation, and still Guide them into such Measures, as shall tend effectually to establish a Government founded upon Reason, Justice, and the Welfare of the People. –

And finally to over-rule all the Commotions in the World, to the spreading the true Religion of our **Lord JESUS CHRIST**, in its Purity and Power, among all the People of the Earth.

And I do earnestly recommend that all unnecessary Labour and Recreation may be suspended on the said Day.

GIVEN at the COUNCIL-CHAMBER, in Boston, the Fourth Day of MARCH, in the **Year of our LORD**, One Thousand Seven Hundred and

Ninety-Three, and in the Seventeenth Year of the Independence of the United States of America!

JOHN HANCOCK

By His Excellency's Command, with the Advice and Consent of the COUNCIL,

JOHN AVERY, jun. Secretary.

Commonwealth of Massachusetts

GOD Save the Commonwealth of MASSACHUSETTS!

By the Governor

John Joseph Henry

Revolutionary War soldier, Attorney, Judge

*"**God** in his great goodness grant, in the future vicissitudes of the world, that our countrymen, whenever their essential rights shall be attacked, will divest themselves of all party prejudice, and devote their lives and properties in defence of the sacred liberties of their country, without any view to emolument, but that which springs from glorious and honorable actions."*
Personal journal, 1811

Patrick Henry

Farmer, Attorney, Orator

From Patrick Henry's "Give Me Liberty Or Give Me Death Speech" before the Virginia House of Burgesses at St. John's Church on March 23, 1775

"No man thinks more highly than I do of the patriotism, as well as abilities, of the very worthy gentlemen who have just addressed the House. But different men often see the same subject in different lights; and, therefore, I hope it will not be thought disrespectful to those gentlemen if, entertaining as I do opinions of a character very opposite to theirs, I shall speak forth my sentiments freely and without reserve.

This is no time for ceremony.

The question before the House is one of awful moment to this country.

For my own part, I consider it as nothing less than a question of freedom or slavery; and in proportion to the magnitude of the subject ought to be the freedom of the debate.

*It is only in this way that we can hope to arrive at truth, and fulfill the great responsibility which we hold to **God** and our country.*

Should I keep back my opinions at such a time, through fear of giving offense, I should consider myself as guilty of treason towards my country, and of an act of disloyalty toward the Majesty of Heaven, which I revere above all earthly kings.

Mr. President, it is natural to man to indulge in the illusions of hope. We are apt to shut our eyes against a painful truth, and listen to the song of that siren till she transforms us into beasts. Is this the part of wise men, engaged in a great and arduous struggle for liberty?

Are we disposed to be of the number of those who, having eyes, see not, and, having ears, hear not, the things which so nearly concern their temporal salvation?

For my part, whatever anguish of spirit it may cost, I am willing to know the whole truth; to know the worst, and to provide for it.

I have but one lamp by which my feet are guided, and that is the lamp of experience.

I know of no way of judging of the future but by the past. And judging by the past, I wish to know what there has been in the conduct of the British ministry for the last ten years to justify those hopes with which gentlemen have been pleased to solace themselves and the House.

Is it that insidious smile with which our petition has been lately received?

Trust it not, sir; it will prove a snare to your feet. Suffer not yourselves to be betrayed with a kiss.

Ask yourselves how this gracious reception of our petition comports with those warlike preparations which cover our waters and darken our land.

Are fleets and armies necessary to a work of love and reconciliation?

Have we shown ourselves so unwilling to be reconciled that force must be called in to win back our love?

Let us not deceive ourselves, sir. These are the implements of war and subjugation; the last arguments to which kings resort.

I ask gentlemen, sir, what means this martial array, if its purpose be not to force us to submission?

Can gentlemen assign any other possible motive for it?

Has Great Britain any enemy, in this quarter of the world, to call for all this accumulation of navies and armies?

No, sir, she has none. They are meant for us: they can be meant for no other.

They are sent over to bind and rivet upon us those chains which the British ministry have been so long forging.

And what have we to oppose to them?

Shall we try argument? Sir, we have been trying that for the last ten years.

Have we anything new to offer upon the subject? Nothing. We have held the subject up in every light of which it is capable; but it has been all in vain.

Shall we resort to entreaty and humble supplication? What terms shall we find which have not been already exhausted? Let us not, I beseech you, sir, deceive ourselves. Sir, we have done everything that could be done to avert the storm which is now coming on.

We have petitioned; we have remonstrated; we have supplicated; we have prostrated ourselves before the throne, and have implored its interposition to arrest the tyrannical hands of the ministry and Parliament.

Our petitions have been slighted; our remonstrance have produced additional violence and insult; our supplications have been disregarded; and we have been spurned, with contempt, from the foot of the throne!

In vain, after these things, may we indulge the fond hope of peace and reconciliation. There is no longer any room for hope.

If we wish to be free-- if we mean to preserve inviolate those inestimable privileges for which we have been so long contending--if we mean not basely to abandon the noble struggle in which we have been so long engaged, and which we have pledged ourselves never to abandon until the glorious object of our contest shall be obtained--we must fight!

I repeat it, sir, we must fight!

*An appeal to arms and to the **God** of hosts is all that is left us!*

They tell us, sir, that we are weak; unable to cope with so formidable an adversary.

But when shall we be stronger?

Will it be the next week, or the next year?

Will it be when we are totally disarmed, and when a British guard shall be stationed in every house?

Shall we gather strength by irresolution and inaction?

Shall we acquire the means of effectual resistance by lying supinely on our backs and hugging the delusive phantom of hope, until our enemies shall have bound us hand and foot?

*Sir, we are not weak if we make a proper use of those means which the **God** of nature hath placed in our power.*

The millions of people, armed in the holy cause of liberty, and in such a country as that which we possess, are invincible by any force which our enemy can send against us. Besides, sir, we shall not fight our battles alone.

*There is a just **God** who presides over the destinies of nations, and who will raise up friends to fight our battles for us. The battle, sir, is not to the strong alone; it is to the vigilant, the active, the brave. Besides, sir, we have no election.*

If we were base enough to desire it, it is now too late to retire from the contest.

There is no retreat but in submission and slavery!

Our chains are forged!

Their clanking may be heard on the plains of Boston!

The war is inevitable--and let it come!

I repeat it, sir, let it come.

It is in vain, sir, to extenuate the matter. Gentlemen may cry, Peace, Peace-- but there is no peace.

The war is actually begun!

The next gale that sweeps from the north will bring to our ears the clash of resounding arms!

Our brethren are already in the field!

Why stand we here idle?

What is it that gentlemen wish?

What would they have?

*Is life so dear, or peace so sweet, as to be purchased at the price of chains and slavery? Forbid it, **Almighty God**! I know not what course others may take; but as for me, give me liberty or give me death!"*

Patrick Henry – "Give Me Liberty Or Give Me Death" speech, March 23, 1775

"This book (The Holy Bible) is worth all the books that ever were printed, and it has been my misfortune that I never found time to read it with the proper attention and feeling till lately. I trust in the mercy of heaven that it is not too late." **Patrick Henry in conversation with a neighbor**

*"Amongst other strange things said of me, I hear it is said by the deists that I am one of the number; and indeed, that some good people think I am no **Christian**."*

*"This thought gives me much more pain than the appellation of Tory; because I think religion of infinitely higher importance than politics; and I find much cause to reproach myself that I have lived so long, and have given no decided and public proofs of my being a **Christian**. But, indeed, my dear child, this is a character which I prize far above all this world has, or can boast."* **Letter to his daughter, August 20, 1796**

"Doctor, I wish you to observe how real and beneficial the religion of **Christ** *is to a man about to die....I am, however, much consoled by reflecting that the religion of* **Christ** *has, from its first appearance in the world, been attacked in vain by all the wits, philosophers, and wise ones, aided by every power of man, and its triumphs have been complete."* **Spoken on his deathbed**

"This is all the inheritance I give to my dear family. The religion of **Christ** *will give them one which will make them rich indeed."* **Last Will and Testament, November 20, 1798**

John Jay

President of Congress, Diplomat, author of the Federalist Papers, Chief Justice of the U. S. Supreme Court, Governor of New York

John Jay co-authored the Federalist Papers. He was elected president of the Westchester Bible Society in 1818.

In 1821, John Jay became the president of the American Bible Society.

In December, 1776, John Jay spoke before the New York Constitutional Convention following the American defeat of three battles with British soldiers.

Jay spoke to the audience about the loss of these three battles, about their doubts of victory while reminding the audience of the moral right of their fight against the Crown of England for independence.

*"The Gospel is yet to be preached to those western Regions, & we have the highest Reason to believe that the **Almighty** will not suffer Slavery & the Gospel to go Hand in Hand. It cannot, it will not be."* **John Jay, December 1776**

*"The Bible is the best of all books, for it is the **word of God** and teaches us the way to be happy in this world and in the next. Continue therefore to read it and to regulate your life by its precepts."* **John Jay letter to Peter Augustus Jay, April 8, 1784**

*"**God's will** be done; to him I resign--in **him** I confide. Do the like. Any other philosophy applicable to this occasion is delusive. Away with it."* **John Jay letter to his wife Sally April 1794**

*"I have long been of opinion that the evidence of the truth of **Christianity** requires only to be carefully examined to produce conviction in candid minds."* **John Jay Letter to Rev. Uzal Ogden, 1796**

*"Providence has given to our people the choice of their rulers, and it is the duty, as well as the privilege and interest of **our Christian nation**, to select and prefer **Christians** for their rulers. It is to be regretted, but so I believe the fact to be, that except the **Bible** there is not a true history in the world.*

Whatever may be the virtue, discernment, and industry of the writers, I am persuaded that truth and error (though in different degrees) will imperceptibly become and remain mixed and blended until they shall be separated forever by the great and last refining fire." **John Jay letter to Jedidiah Morse, 1797**

"I do not recollect to have had more than two conversations with atheists about their tenants.

*The first was this: I was at a large party, of which were several of that description. They spoke freely and contemptuously of religion. I took no part in the conversation. In the course of it, one of them asked me if I believed in **Christ**. I answered that I did, and that I thanked **God** that I did."* **John Jay letter to John Bristed, 1811**

*"Condescend, **merciful Father**! to grant as far as proper these imperfect petitions, to accept these inadequate thanksgivings, and to pardon whatever of sin hath mingled in them for the sake of **Jesus Christ**, **our blessed Lord and Savior**; unto Whom, with Thee, and the blessed Spirit, ever one **God**, be rendered all honor and glory, now and forever."* **Prayer found among John Jay's papers and in his handwriting.**

*"Mercy and grace and favor did come by **Jesus Christ**, and also that truth which verified the promises and predictions concerning **Him** and which exposed and corrected the various errors which had been imbibed respecting the **Supreme Being**, **His** attributes, laws, and dispensations."* **John Jay letter to John Murray, April 15, 1818**

"By conveying the Bible to people . . . we certainly do them a most interesting act of kindness. We thereby enable them to learn that man was originally created and placed in a state of happiness, but, becoming disobedient, was

subjected to the degradation and evils which he and his posterity have since experienced."

*"The Bible will also inform them that our gracious **Creator** has provided for us a **Redeemer** in whom all the nations of the earth should be blessed – that this **Redeemer** has made atonement "for the sins of the whole world," and thereby reconciling the **Divine justice** with the **Divine mercy**, has opened a way for our redemption and salvation; and that these inestimable benefits are of the **free gift and grace of God**, not of our deserving, nor in our power to deserve."*

*"The Bible will also encourage them with many explicit and consoling assurances of the **Divine** mercy to our fallen race, and with repeated invitations to accept the offers of pardon and reconciliation…They, therefore, who enlist in **His** service, have the highest encouragement to fulfill the duties assigned to their respective stations; for most certain it is, that those of **His** followers who [participate in] **His** conquests will also participate in the transcendent glories and blessings of **His** Triumph."* **John Jay, Address at the Annual Meeting of the American Bible Society, May 13, 1824**

*"I recommend a general and public return of praise and thanksgiving to **Him** from whose goodness these blessings descend. The most effectual means of securing the continuance of our civil and religious liberties is always to remember with reverence and gratitude the source from which they flow."* **John Jay to the Committee of the Corporation of the City of New York on June 29, 1826**

No one could argue that the first Chief Justice of the United States of America is likely to have had a better idea than any of our current Justices as to the intent of the Founding Fathers, since he was one and knew most of them.

*"Unto **Him who is the author and giver of all good**, I render sincere and humble thanks for **His** manifold and unmerited blessings and especially for our redemption and salvation by **His beloved Son**…Blessed be **His holy name**."* **John Jay, Last Will and Testament**

Thomas Jefferson

Third US President, Author of the Declaration of Independence

Proclamation Appointing a Day of Thanksgiving and Prayer

*Whereas the Honourable the General Congress, impressed with a grateful sense of the goodness of **Almighty God**, in blessing the greater part of this extensive continent with plentiful harvests, crowning our arms with repeated successes, conducting us hitherto safely through the perils with which we have been encompassed and manifesting in multiplied instances his divine care of these infant states, hath thought proper by their act of the 20th day of October last, to recommend to the several states that Thursday the 9th of December next be appointed a day of public and solemn thanksgiving and prayer, which act is in these words, to wit.*

*Whereas it becomes us humbly to approach the throne of **Almighty God**, with gratitude and praise, for the wonders which **His goodness** has wrought in conducting our forefathers to this western world; for **His** protection to them and to their posterity, amidst difficulties and dangers; for raising us their children from deep distress, to be numbered among the nations of the earth; and for arming **the hands of just and mighty Princes in our deliverance**; and especially for that **He** hath been pleased to grant us the enjoyment of health and so to order the revolving seasons, that the earth hath produced her increase in abundance, blessing the labors of the husbandman, and spreading plenty through the land; that **He** hath prospered our arms and those of our ally, been a shield to our troops in the hour of danger, pointed their swords to victory, and led them in triumph over the bulwarks of the foe; that **He** hath gone with those who went out into the wilderness against the savage tribes; that **He** hath stayed the hand of the spoiler, and turned back **His** meditated destruction; that **He** hath prospered our commerce, and given success to those who sought the enemy on the face of the deep; and above all, that **He** hath diffused the glorious light of the gospel, whereby, through the merits of **our gracious Redeemer**, we may become the heirs of His eternal glory.*

Therefore,

Resolved, that it be recommended to the several states to appoint
*THURSDAY the 9th of December next, to be a **day of public and solemn***
***THANKSGIVING to Almighty God**, for **his** mercies, and of PRAYER, for*
the continuance of his favour and protection to these United States;

*To beseech **Him** that **He** would be graciously pleased to influence our public*
Councils, and bless them with wisdom from on high, with unanimity,
*firmness and success; that **He** would go forth with our hosts and crown our*
arms with victory;

*That **He would grant to his church**, the plentiful effusions of divine grace,*
*and pour out **His holy spirit on all Ministers of the gospel**; That **He***
would bless and prosper the means of education, and spread the light
***of Christian knowledge through the remotest corners of the earth**;*

*That **He** would smile upon the labors of his people, and cause the earth to*
bring forth her fruits in abundance, that we may with gratitude and gladness
enjoy them;

*That **He would take into His holy protection**, our illustrious ally, **give***
Him victory over His enemies**, and **render Him finally great, as the
***Father of His people**, and **the protector of the rights of mankind**; that*
***He would graciously be pleased to turn the hearts of our enemies**, and*
*to **dispense the blessings of peace to contending nations.***

*That **He** would in mercy look down upon us, pardon all our sins, and receive*
*us into **his** favour; and finally, **that He would establish the independence***
of these United States upon the basis of religion and virtue, and
support and protect them in the enjoyment of peace, liberty and safety.

I do therefore by authority from the General Assembly issue this my
proclamation, hereby appointing Thursday the 9th day of December next, a
*day of public and solemn thanksgiving and prayer to **Almighty God**,*
earnestly recommending to all the good people of this commonwealth, to set
apart the said day for those purposes, and to the several Ministers of religion

to meet their respective societies thereon, to assist them in their prayers, edify them with their discourses, and generally to perform the sacred duties of their function, proper for the occasion.

Given under my hand and the seal of the commonwealth, at Williamsburg, this 11th day of November, in the **year of our Lord**, 1779, and in the fourth of the commonwealth

Signed, THOMAS JEFFERSON

Address of the Senate to John Adams, President of the United States

"A government chosen by the people for their own safety and happiness, and calculated to secure both, cannot lose their affections so long as its administration pursues the principles upon which it was erected; and your resolution to observe a conduct just and impartial to all nations, a sacred regard to our national engagements, and not to impair the rights of our Government, contains principles which cannot fail to secure to your Administration the support of the National Legislature to render abortive every attempt to excite dangerous jealousies among us, and to convince the world that our Government and your administration of it cannot be separated from the affectionate support of every good citizen."

"And the Senate cannot suffer the present occasion to pass without thus publicly and solemnly expressing their attachment to the Constitution and Government of their country; and as they hold themselves responsible to their constituents, their consciences, and their **God**, it is their determination by all their exertions to repel every attempt to alienate the affections of the people from the Government, so highly injurious to the honor, safety, and independence of the United States."

TH: JEFFERSON, Vice-President of the United States and President of the Senate

MAY 23, 1797

To Thomas Law

Poplar Forest near Lynchburg

June 13, 1814

Dear Sir,

"The copy of your Second thoughts on Instinctive impulses with the letter accompanying it, was received just as I was setting out on a journey to this place, two or three days distant from Monticello. I brought it with me, and read it with great satisfaction; and with the more, as it contained exactly my own creed on the foundation of morality in man. It is really curious that, on a question so fundamental, such a variety of opinions should have prevailed among men; and those two of the most exemplary virtue and first order of understanding."

*"It shews how necessary was the care of the **Creator** in making the moral principle so much a part of our constitution as that no errors of reasoning or of speculation might lead us astray from its observance in practice."*

"Of all the theories on this question, the most whimsical seems to have been that of Woollaston, who considers truth as the foundation of morality."

"The thief who steals your guinea does wrong only inasmuch as he acts a lie, in using your guinea as if it were his own."

*"Truth is certainly a branch of morality, and a very important one to society. But, presented as its foundation, it is as if a tree, taken up by the roots, had its stem reversed in the air, and one of its branches planted in the ground. Some have made the love of **God** the foundation of morality."*

*"This too is but a branch of our moral duties, which are generally divided into duties to **God**, and duties to man. If we did a good act merely from the love of **God**, and a belief that it is pleasing to **Him**, whence arises the morality of the Atheist?"*

"It is idle to say as some do, that no such being exists. We have the same evidence of the fact as of most of those we act on, to wit, their own affirmations, and their reasoning's in support of them. I have observed indeed generally that, while in protestant countries the defections from the Platonic Christianity of the priests is to Deism, in Catholic countries they are to Atheism. Diderot, Dalembert, D'Holbach Condorcet, are known to have been among the most virtuous of men. Their virtue then must have had some other foundation than the love of **God**."

"The το καλον (good) of others is founded in a different faculty, that of taste, which is not even a branch of morality. we have indeed an innate sense of what we call beautiful: but that is exercised chiefly on subjects addressed to the fancy, whether thro' the eye, in visible forms, as landscape, animal figure, dress, drapery, architecture, the composition of colours Etc. or to the imagination directly, as imagery, style, or measure in prose or poetry, or whatever else constitutes the domain of criticism or taste, a faculty entirely distinct from the moral one."

"Self-interest, or rather Self-love, or Egoism, has been more plausibly substituted as the basis of morality. But I consider our relations with others as constituting the boundaries of morality. With ourselves we stand on the ground of identity, not of relation; which last, requiring two subjects, excludes self-love confined to a single one."

"To ourselves, in strict language, we can owe no duties, obligation requiring also two parties. Self-love therefore is no part of morality. Indeed it is exactly its counterpart. It is the sole antagonist of virtue, leading us constantly by our propensities to self-gratification in violation of our moral duties to others."

"Accordingly it is against this enemy that are erected the batteries of moralists and religionists, as the only obstacle to the practice of morality. Take from man his selfish propensities, and he can have nothing to seduce him from the practice of virtue. Or subdue those propensities by education, instruction, or restraint, and virtue remains without a competitor. Egoism, in a broader sense, has been thus presented as the source of moral action. It has been said *that we feed the hungry, clothe the naked, bind up the wounds of the man beaten by thieves, pour oil and wine into them, set him on our own beast, and bring him to the inn, because we receive ourselves pleasure from these acts. so Helvetius, one of the best men on earth, and the most ingenious advocate of this principle, after defining 'interest' to mean, not merely that which is pecuniary, but whatever may procure us pleasure or withdraw us from pain, says 'the humane man is he to whom the sight of misfortune is insupportable and who, to rescue himself from this spectacle, is forced to succor the unfortunate object.' this indeed is true. But it is one step short of the ultimate question. These good acts give us pleasure: but how happens it that they give us pleasure?"*

*"Because nature hath implanted in our breasts a love of others, a sense of duty to them, a moral instinct in short which prompts us irresistibly to feel and to succor their distresses; and protests against the language of Helvetius 'what other motive than self-interest could determine a man to generous actions? it is as impossible for him to love what is good for the sake of good, as to love evil for the sake of evil.' the **Creator** would indeed have been a bungling artist, had he intended man for a social animal, without planting in him social dispositions. It is true they are not planted in every man; because there is no rule without exceptions: but it is false reasoning which converts exceptions into the general rule. Some men are born without the organs of sight, or of hearing, or without hands. yet it would be wrong to say that man is born without these faculties: and sight, hearing and hands may with truth enter into the general definition of Man. the want or imperfection of the moral sense in some men, like the want or imperfection of the senses of sight and hearing in others, is no proof that it is a general characteristic of the species. when it is wanting we endeavor to supply the defect by education, by appeals to reason and calculation, by presenting to the being so unhappily conformed other motives to do good, and to eschew evil; such as the love, or the hatred or rejection of those among whom he lives and whose society is necessary to his happiness, and even existence; demonstrations by sound calculation that honesty promotes interest in the long run; the rewards & penalties established by the laws; and ultimately the prospects of a future state of retribution for the evil as well as the good done while here."*

"These are the correctives which are supplied by education, and which exercise the functions of the moralist, the preacher & legislator: and they lead into a course of correct action all those whose depravity is not too profound to be eradicated."

"Some have argued against the existence of a moral sense, by saying that if nature had given us such a sense, impelling us to virtuous actions, and warning us against those which are vicious, then nature must also have designated, by some particular ear-marks, the two sets of actions which are, in themselves, the one virtuous, and the other vicious: whereas we find in fact, that the same actions are deemed virtuous in one country, and vicious in another."

"The answer is that nature has constituted utility to man the standard & test of virtue. Men living in different countries, under different circumstances, different habits, and regimens, may have different utilities. The same act therefore may be useful, and consequently virtuous, in one country, which is injurious and vicious in another differently circumstanced."

"I sincerely then believe with you in the general existence of a moral instinct. I think it the brightest gem with which the human character is studded; and the want of it as more degrading than the most hideous of the bodily deformities. I am happy in reviewing the roll of associates in this principle which you present in your 2d letter, some of which I had not before met with. to these might be added Lord Kames, one of the ablest of our advocates, who goes so far as to say, in his Principles of Natural religion, that a man owes no duty to which he is not urged by some impulsive feeling. This is correct if referred to the standard of general feeling in the given case, and not to the feeling of a single individual. Perhaps I may misquote him, it being fifty years since I read his book."

"The leisure and solitude of my situation here has led me to the indiscretion of taxing you with a long letter on a subject whereon nothing new can be offered you. I will indulge myself no further than to repeat the assurances of my continued esteem & respect." **Thomas Jefferson letter to Thomas Law, 13 June 1814**

*"...I have sworn upon the altar of **God Eternal** hostility against every form of tyranny over the mind of man."*

Thomas Jefferson letter to Dr. Benjamin Rush, September 23, 1800

*"To the corruptions of **Christianity** I am indeed, opposed; but not to the genuine precepts of **Jesus himself**. I am a **Christian**, in the only sense in which **He** wished any one to be; sincerely attached to **His** doctrines, in preference to all others; ascribing to **himself** every human excellence; and believing **He** never claimed any other."* **Thomas Jefferson letter to Benjamin Rush, April 21, 1803**

"...the subject of religion, a subject on which I have ever been most scrupulously reserved. I have considered it as a matter between every man and his maker, in which no other, & far less the public, had a right to intermeddle." **Thomas Jefferson letter to Richard Rush May 31, 1813**

*"I must ever believe that religion substantially good which produces an honest life, and we have been authorized by One whom you and I equally respect, to judge of the tree by its fruit. Our particular principles of religion are a subject of accountability to our **God** alone. I inquire after no man's, and trouble none with mine; nor is it given to us in this life to know whether your or mine, our friends or our foes, are exactly the right."* **Thomas Jefferson letter to Miles King, September 26, 1814**

*"I too have made a wee little book, from the same materials, which I call the Philosophy of **Jesus**. It is a paradigm of his doctrines, made by cutting the texts out of the book, and arranging them on the pages of a blank book, in a certain order of time or subject. a more beautiful or precious morsel of ethics I have never seen. it is a document in proof that I am a real **Christian**, that is to say, a disciple of the doctrines of **Jesus**, very different from the Platonists, who call me infidel, and themselves **Christians** and preachers of the gospel, while they draw all their characteristic dogmas from what its **Author** never said nor saw. they have compounded from the heathen mysteries a system beyond the comprehension of man, of which the great reformer of the vicious ethics and deism of the Jews, were he to return on earth, would not recognize*

one feature. if I had time I would add to my little book the Greek, Latin and French texts, in columns side by side, and I wish I could subjoin a translation of Gassendi's Syntagma of the doctrines of Epicurus, which, notwithstanding the calumnies of the Stoics, and caricatures of Cicero, is the most rational system remaining of the philosophy of the ancients, as frugal of vicious indulgence, and fruitful of virtue as the hyperbolical extravagancies of his rival sects." **Thomas Jefferson letter to Charles Thomson, January 9, 1816**

"Epictetus & Epicurus give us laws for governing ourselves, **Jesus** *a supplement of the duties & charities we owe to others."*

Thomas Jefferson letter to William Short, October 31, 1819

"No one sees with greater pleasure than myself the progress of reason in its advances towards rational **Christianity**. *when we shall have done away the incomprehensible jargon of the Trinitarian arithmetic, that three are one, and one is three; when we shall have knocked down the artificial scaffolding, reared to mask from view the simple structure of* **Jesus**, *when, in short, we shall have unlearned everything which has been taught since his day, and got back to the pure and simple doctrines he inculcated, we shall then be truly and worthily his disciples: and my opinion is that if nothing had ever been added to what flowed purely from his lips, the whole world would at this day have been* **Christian**.

I know that the case you cite, of Dr. Drake, has been a common one. the religion-builders have so distorted and deformed the doctrines of **Jesus**, *so muffled them in mysticisms, fancies and falsehoods, have caricatured them into forms so monstrous and inconceivable, as to shock reasonable thinkers, to revolt them against the whole, and drive them rashly to pronounce its founder an imposter. had there never been a Commentator, there never would have been an infidel. in the present advance of truth, which we both approve, I do not know that you and I may think alike on all points. As the* **Creator** *has made no two faces alike, so no two minds, and probably no two creeds. we well know that among Unitarians themselves there are strong shades of difference, as between Doctors Price and Priestley for example. so there may be* peculiarities in your creed and in mine. they are honestly formed without doubt. I do not wish to trouble the world with mine, nor to be troubled for them. These accounts are to be settled only with him who made us; and to him we leave it, with charity for all others, of whom also he is the only rightful and competent judge. I have little doubt that the whole of our country will soon be rallied to the Unity of the **Creator**, and, I hope, to the pure doctrines of **Jesus** also." **Thomas Jefferson letter to Timothy Pickering, February 27, 1821**

"*The truth is that the greatest enemies to the doctrines of **Jesus** are those calling themselves the expositors of them, who have perverted them for the structure of a system of fancy absolutely incomprehensible, and without any foundation in his genuine words. And the day will come when the mystical generation of **Jesus**, by the **Supreme Being** as **his father** in the womb of a virgin will be classed with the fable of the generation of Minerva in the brain of Jupiter.*"

"*But we may hope that the dawn of reason and freedom of thought in these United States will do away all this artificial scaffolding, and restore to us the primitive and genuine doctrines of this the most venerated reformer of human errors.*" **Thomas Jefferson letter to John Adams April 11, 1823**

Rufus King

Continental Congress, Signer of the US Constitution

*"The law established by the **Creator** extends over the whole globe, is everywhere and at all times binding upon mankind. This is the **law of God** by which he makes his way known to man and is paramount to all human control."* **Rufus King, letter to C. Gore on February 17, 1820**

James Madison

Fourth US President

Father of the US Constitution

Atheists paint James Madison as a man whose belief was in deism, this is obviously not true when we read the writings and the proclamations authored by James Madison.

The internet contains lies about President Madison's religious faith. Again, as we consider the definition of deism and then read the works of James Madison it is absolutely clear that James Madison was not a deist.

"A watchful eye must be kept on ourselves lest, while we are building ideal monuments of renown and bliss here, we neglect to have our names enrolled in the Annals of Heaven." **James Madison letter to William Bradford, November 9, 1772**

"I have sometimes thought there could not be a stronger testimony in favor of Religion or against temporal Enjoyments even the most rational and manly than for men who occupy the most honorable and gainful departments and are rising in reputation and wealth, publicly to declare their unsatisfactoriness by becoming fervent Advocates in the cause of Christ, & I wish you may give in your Evidence in this way." **James Madison letter to William Bradford, September 25, 1773**

Section 16 "That religion, or the duty which we owe to our Creator, and the manner of discharging it, can be directed only by reason and conviction, not by force or violence; and therefore all men are equally entitled to the free exercise of religion, according to the dictates of conscience; and that it is the mutual duty of all to practice Christian forbearance, love, and charity toward each other." **1776 Virginia Bill of Rights**

"It is impossible for the man of pious reflection not to perceive in it [the Constitution] a finger of that Almighty hand which has been so frequently

and signally extended to our relief in the critical stages of the revolution."
James Madison, Federalist No. 37, 1788

In 1812, President Madison signed a federal bill which economically aided the Bible Society of Philadelphia in its goal of the mass distribution of the Bible.

"An Act for the relief of the Bible Society of Philadelphia"
Approved February 2, 1813 by Congress

*"The belief in a **God** All Powerful wise and good, is so essential to the moral order of the world and to the happiness of man, that arguments which enforce it cannot be drawn from too many sources nor adapted with too much solicitude to the different characters and capacities to be impressed with it."*
James Madison letter to Rev. Frederick Beasley, November 20, 1825

James Madison was in the habit of making notes in his personal Bible.

*"Believers who are in a state of grace, have need of the **Word of God** for their edification and building up therefore implies a possibility of falling."* **Acts, Chapter 19: v. 32.**

*"Grace, it is the free gift of **God**."* **Luke. 12. 32-v.32.**

"Giver more blessed than the receiver." v. 35.

*"To neglect the means for our own preservation is to tempt **God**: and to trust to them is to neglect **Him**."* **v. 3 & Ch. 27. v. 31.**

"Humility, the better any man is, the lower thoughts he has of himself." **v. 19.**

"Ministers to take heed to themselves & their flock." **v. 28.**

*"The Apostles did greater miracles than **Christ**, in the matter, not manner, of them."* **v. 11.**

Thomas McKean

Delegate to the Continental Congress, Co-Author, "Commentaries on the Constitution", Chief Justice of Pennsylvania, Governor of Pennsylvania

"You will probably have but a short time to live. Before you launch into eternity, it behooves you to improve the time that may be allowed you in this world."

*"It behooves you most seriously to reflect upon your conduct, to repent of your evil deeds, to be incessant in prayers to the great and merciful **God** to forgive your manifold transgressions and sins, to teach you to rely upon the merit and passion of a dear **Redeemer** and thereby to avoid those regions of sorrow, those doleful shades where peace and rest can never dwell, where even hope cannot enter."*

"It behooves you to seek the fellowship, advice and prayers of pious and good men, to be persistent at the throne of grace and to learn the way that leadeth to happiness."

*"May you reflecting upon these things and pursuing the will of the great **Father of Light and Life**, be received into the company and society of angels and archangels and the spirits of just men made perfect and may you be qualified to enter into the joys of heaven, joys unspeakable and full of glory."*
RESPUBLICA v. ROBERTS, 1 U.S. 39 September, 1778

James Monroe

Fifth US President

"An institution which endeavors to rear American youth in pure love of truth and duty, and while it enlightens their minds by ingenious and liberal studies, endeavors to awaken a love of country, to soften local prejudices, and to inoculate Christian faith and charity, cannot but acquire, as it deserves, the confidence of the wise and good. " **Commenting on Harvard University in "A Narrative of a Tour of Observation," 1818**

Thomas Paine

Author, Common Sense

"As to religion, I hold it to be the indispensable duty of every government, to protect all conscientious professors thereof, and I know of no other business which government hath to do therewith."

"Let a man throw aside that narrowness of soul, that selfishness of principle, which the niggards of all professions are so unwilling to part with; and he will be at once delivered of his fears on that head. Suspicion is the companion of mean souls, and the bane of all good society."

"For myself, I fully and conscientiously believe, that it is the will of the **Almighty***, that there should be a diversity of religious opinions among us: it affords a larger field for our* **Christian** *kindness."*

"Were we all of one way of thinking, our religious dispositions would want matter for probation; and on this liberal principle, I look on the various denominations among us, to be like children of the same family, differing only, in what is called, their **Christian** *names."* **Common Sense, 1776**

Benjamin Rush

Surgeon General of the Continental Army, Signer of the Declaration of Independence, Founder of the Philadelphia Bible Society, Founder of the Society for the Abolition of Slavery

"The early respect I was taught to entertain for your character, and the agreeable connection we once had together, are the only apologies I shall offer for opening a correspondence with you upon the subject of a college at Carlisle."

"I am no stranger to the opposition that has been excited against the scheme in your county by some gentlemen in this city, nor am I unacquainted with the very illiberal reflections that have been thrown upon me for favoring the design by two of those gentlemen. I have nothing to say against them by way of retaliation. The only design of this letter is to explain more fully to you the advantages to be derived to the state at large and the Presbyterian society in particular from a nursery of religion and learning on the west side of the river Susquehanna."

"The manner in which the Presbyterians seized their present share of power in the University of Philadelphia has given such general offense that there is little doubt of an attempt being made in the course of a few years to restore it to its original owners. The old trustees say that the present charter is contrary to the Constitution of the state and to every principle of justice, and I find a great many of the most respectable members of the Assembly are of the same opinion, among whom is the Reverend Mr. Joseph Montgomery."

"But supposing the present trustees held the University by the most equitable and constitutional tenure, it cannot be viewed as a nursery for the Presbyterian Church. Only 11 out of 24 of the present trustees are Presbyterians. Dr. Ewing was elected by a majority of a single vote. He will probably be the last Presbyterian clergyman that ever will be placed at the head of that institution, should it even continue upon its present footing. From its extreme Catholicism, I am sorry to say that, as no one religion

*prevails, so no religious principles are inculcated in it. The fault here is only in the charter, for all the teachers I believe are friends to **Christianity** and men of pious and moral characters."*

"Religion is best supported under the patronage of particular societies. Instead of encouraging bigotry, I believe it prevents it by removing young men from those opportunities of controversy which a variety of sects mixed together are apt to create and which are the certain fuel of bigotry."

"Religion is necessary to correct the effects of learning. Without religion I believe learning does real mischief to the morals and principles of mankind; a mode of worship is necessary to support religion; and education is the surest way of producing a preference and constant attachment to a mode of worship."

*"Religion could not long be maintained in the world without forms and the distinctions of sects. The weaknesses of human nature require them. The distinction of sects is as necessary in the **Christian** Church towards the perfection and government of the whole as regiments and brigades are in an army. Some people talk loudly of the increase of liberality of sentiment upon religious subjects since the war, but I suspect that this boasted Catholicism arises chiefly from an indifference acquired since the war to religion itself."*

*"We only change the names of our vices and follies in different periods of time. Religious bigotry has yielded to political intolerance. The man who used to hate his neighbor for being a Churchman or a Quaker now hates him with equal cordiality for being a Tory. Colleges are the best schools for [divinity. But divinity] cannot be taught without a system, and this system must partake of the doctrines of someone sect of **Christians**--hence the necessity of the College being in the hands of someone religious society. The universities of England, Scotland, and Ireland, and I believe of every other kingdom in Europe are in the hands of particular societies, and it is from this circumstance they have become the bulwarks of the **Christian** religion throughout the world."*

"*The expense of an education in Philadelphia alone, exclusive of the influence of a large city upon the morals of youth, is sufficient to deter the farmers from sending their sons to the University of Philadelphia. The distance of the College of New Jersey from the western counties of this state makes the difference of one fifth of the expense in the education of a young man in traveling twice a year backwards and forwards to and from his father's house.*"

"*It has long been a subject of complaint among us that the principal part of the emigrants from Pennsylvania into new countries were Presbyterians. This has greatly reduced our numbers and influence in government. It is I believe pretty certain that we do not now compose more than one fourth or fifth part of the inhabitants of the state. A college at Carlisle, by diffusing the light of science and religion more generally through our society, may check this spirit of emigration among them. It may teach them to prefer civil, social, and religious advantages, with a small farm and old land, to the loss of them all with extensive tracts of woods and a more fertile soil.*" **Benjamin Rush letter to John Armstrong, March 19, 1783**

On March 28, 1787, Benjamin Rush wrote an open letter *"To the citizens of Philadelphia: A Plan for Free Schools"*.

"*Let the children...be carefully instructed in the principles and obligations of the **Christian** religion. This is the most essential part of education. The great enemy of the salvation of man, in my opinion, never invented a more effectual means of extirpating **Christianity** from the world than by persuading mankind that it was improper to read the Bible at schools.*"

Mr. Rush continued in the same letter:

"*The only foundation for a useful education in a republic is to be laid in religion. Without this there can be no virtue, and without virtue there can be no liberty.*"

Quotes by Benjamin Rush

"The Gospel of *Jesus Christ* prescribes the wisest rules for just conduct in every situation of life. Happy they who are enabled to obey them in all situations! . . . My only hope of salvation is in the infinite transcendent love of *God* manifested to the world by the death of *His Son* upon the Cross. Nothing but His blood will wash away my sins." **Acts 22:16**

"I rely exclusively upon it. Come, *Lord Jesus!* Come quickly!" **Revelation 22:20**

"I do not believe that the Constitution was the offspring of inspiration, but I am as satisfied that it is as much the work of a *Divine Providence* as any of the miracles recorded in the Old and New Testament."

Benjamin Rush letter to Elias Boudinot on July 9, 1788

"By renouncing the Bible, philosophers swing from their moorings upon all moral subjects... It is the only correct map of the human heart that ever has been published."

"The greatest discoveries in science have been made by *Christian* philosophers and . . . there is the most knowledge in those countries where there is the most *Christianity*."

"The only means of establishing and perpetuating our republican forms of government is the universal education of our youth in the principles of *Christianity* by means of the Bible."

"The great enemy of the salvation of man, in my opinion, never invented a more effective means of limiting *Christianity* from the world than by persuading mankind that it was improper to read the Bible at schools."

"*Christianity* is the only true and perfect religion; and... in proportion as mankind adopt its principles and obey its precepts, they will be wise and happy."

"The Bible contains more knowledge necessary to man in his present state than any other book in the world."

The present fashionable practice of rejecting the Bible from our schools, I suspect has originated with the deists. They discover great ingenuity in this new mode of attacking **Christianity**.

If they proceed in it, they will do more in half a century, in extirpating our religion, than Bolingbroke or Voltaire could have effected in a thousand years.

Benjamin Rush, A Defence of the Use of the Bible in Schools, 1791

"The Bible, when not read in schools, is seldom read in any subsequent period of life… The Bible… should be read in our schools in preference to all other books because it contains the greatest portion of that kind of knowledge which is calculated to produce private and public happiness." **Benjamin Rush, 1791**

Roger Sherman

Signer of the Articles of Association, Declaration of Independence, Articles of Confederation, United States Constitution

*"I believe that there is one only living and true **God**, existing in three persons, the Father, the Son, and the Holy Ghost, the same in substance, equal in power and glory."*

*"That the Scriptures of the Old and New Testaments are a revelation from **God**, and a complete rule to direct us how we may glorify and enjoy **Him**. . . . That **He** made man at first perfectly holy; that the first man sinned, and as he was the public head of his posterity, they all became sinners in consequence of his first transgression, are wholly indisposed to that which is good and inclined to evil, and on account of sin are liable to all the miseries of this life, to death, and to the pains of hell forever. I believe that **God** . . . did send **His own Son** to become man, die in the room and stead of sinners, and thus to lay a foundation for the offer of pardon and salvation to all mankind, so as all may be saved who are willing to accept the Gospel offer. . . . I believe a visible church to be a congregation of those who make a credible profession of their faith in **Christ**, and obedience to **Him**, joined by the bond of the covenant. . . . I believe that the sacraments of the New Testament are baptism and the **Lord's Supper**. . . . I believe that the souls of believers are at their death made perfectly holy, and immediately taken to glory: that at the end of this world there will be a resurrection of the dead, and a final judgment of all mankind, when the righteous shall be publicly acquitted by **Christ the Judge** and admitted to everlasting life and glory, and the wicked be sentenced to everlasting punishment."* **Theological creed, adopted by his church**

Richard Stockton

Signer of the Declaration of Independence

"I, Richard Stockton, being sick and weak in body but sound of memory, do make and ordain this my last Will and Testament in manner and forme following:

"First, I bequeath my soul into the hands of **Almighty God** *and my body to be buried at the discretion of my executors hereby named, in hopes through the merits of* **Jesus Christ** *to obtain a joyful resurrection."*

"As my children will have frequent occasion of perusing this instrument, and may probably be particularly impressed with the last words of their father, I think it proper here not only to subscribe to the entire belief of the great and leading doctrines of the **Christian** *religion, such as the being of* **God***; the universal defection and depravity of human nature; the* **Divinity** *of the person and the completeness of the redemption purchased by the blessed* **Savior***; the necessity of the operations of the* **Divine Spirit***; of* **Divine faith** *accompanied with an habitual virtuous life; and the universality of the* **Divine Providence***: but also, in the bowels of a father's affection, to exhort and charge my children that the fear of* **God** *is the beginning of wisdom, that the way of life held up in the* **Christian** *system is calculated for the most complete happiness that can be enjoyed in this mortal state, and that all occasions of vice and immorality is injurious either immediately or consequentially – even in this life."* **Last Will & Testament**

Joseph Warren

Physician, Member of the Militia, Revolutionary War General, Patriot

*"May we ever be a people favoured of **God**."*

May our land be a land of liberty, the seat of virtue, the asylum of the oppressed, a name and praise in the whole earth, until the last shock of time shall bury the empires of the world in one common undistinguished ruin!"
Boston Massacre Oration, March 5, 1772

Noah Webster

Father of American Education, Revolutionary soldier, judge, legislator, American Founder, and the creator of Webster's Dictionary

*"Almost all the civil liberty now enjoyed in the world owes its origin to the principles of the **Christian** religion...."*

"The moral principles and precepts contained in the Scripture ought to form the basis of all our civil constitutions and laws."

*"It is the sincere desire of the writer that our citizens should early understand that the genuine source of correct republican principles is the Bible, particularly the New Testament or the **Christian** religion...."*

"Every civil government is based upon some religion or philosophy of life. Education in a nation will propagate the religion of that nation."

*"**In America, the foundational religion was Christianity**. And it was sown in the hearts of Americans through the home and private and public schools for centuries. Our liberty, growth, and prosperity was the result of a Biblical philosophy of life. Our continued freedom and success is dependent on our educating the youth of America in the principles of **Christianity**."*

*"The religion which has introduced civil liberty is the religion of **Christ and His apostles**, which enjoins humility, piety, and benevolence; which acknowledges in every person a brother, or a sister, and a citizen with equal rights. This is genuine **Christianity**, and to this we owe our free Constitutions of Government..."*

"A pure democracy is generally a very bad government, It is often the most tyrannical government on earth; for a multitude is often rash, and will not hear reason."

"Every child in America should be acquainted with his own country. He should read books that furnish him with ideas that will be useful to him in life

and practice. As soon as he opens his lips, he should rehearse the history of his own country."

"The Bible is the chief moral cause of all that is good and the best corrector of all that is evil in human society; the best book for regulating the temporal [secular] concerns of men."

The Bible must be considered as the great source of all the truth by which men are to be guided in government as well as in all social transactions."

"He only can be esteemed really and permanently happy, who enjoys peace of mind in the favor of **God**."

"No truth is more evident to my mind than that the **Christian** religion must be the basis of any government intended to secure the rights and privileges of a free people... When I speak of the **Christian** religion as the basis of government... I mean the primitive **Christianity** in its simplicity as taught by **Christ and His apostles**, consisting of a belief in the being, perfections, and **government of God**; in the revelation of **His** will to men, as their supreme rule of action; in man's... accountability to **God** for his conduct in this life; and in the indispensable obligation of all men to yield entire obedience to **God's** commands in the moral law and the Gospel."

"The foundation of all free government and all social order must be laid in families and in the discipline of youth. Young persons must not only be furnished with knowledge, but they must be accustomed to subordination and subjected to the authority and influence of good principles. It will avail little that youths are made to understand truth and correct principles, unless they are accustomed to submit to be governed by them... And any system of education... which limits instruction to the arts and sciences, and rejects the aids of religion in forming the character of citizens, is essentially defective."

"If the citizens neglect their Duty and place unprincipled men in office, the government will soon be corrupted; laws will be made, not for the public good so much as for selfish or local purposes; corrupt or incompetent men will be appointed to execute the Laws; the public revenues will be squandered on unworthy men; and the rights of the citizen will be violated or disregarded."

"The moral principles and precepts contained in the Scriptures ought to form the basis of all of our civil constitutions and laws…. All the miseries and evils which men suffer from vice, crime, ambition, injustice, oppression, slavery and war, proceed from their despising or neglecting the precepts contained in the Bible."

"They choose men, not because they are just men, men of religion and integrity, but solely for the sake of supporting a party. This is a fruitful source of public evils."

"But as surely as there is a **God** in heaven, who exercises a moral government over the affairs of this world, so certainly will the neglect of the divine command, in the choice of rulers, be followed by bad laws and as bad administration; by laws unjust or partial, by corruption, tyranny, impunity of crimes, waste of public money, and a thousand other evils. Men may desire and adopt a new form of government; they may amend old forms, repair breaches and punish violators of the constitution; but there is, there can be no effectual remedy, but obedience to the divine law." "This general disposition to subject the slight and fleeting influence of human example and opinions, for the controlling authority of divine commands, is among the most gloomy presages of the present times."

"Without a great change of public taste … the progress of depravity will be as rapid, as the ultimate loss of morals, of religion, and of civil liberty, is certain. **God** has provided but one way, by which nations can secure their rights and privileges … by obedience to his laws. Without this, a nation may be great in population, great in wealth, and great in military strength; but it must be corrupt in morals, degraded in character, and distracted with factions. This is the order of **God's** moral government, as firm as his throne, and unchangeable as his purpose; and nations, disregarding this order, are doomed to incessant internal evils, and ultimately to ruin." **Instructive and Entertaining Lessons for Youth, 1835**

"An attempt to conduct the affairs of a free government with wisdom and impartiality, and to preserve the just rights of all classes of citizens, without the guidance of **Divine** precepts, will certainly end in disappointment. **God** is the supreme moral Governor of the world He has made, and as He Himself governs with perfect rectitude, He requires His rational creatures to govern themselves in like manner. If men will not submit to be controlled by His laws, He will punish them by the evils resulting from their own disobedience..."

"Any system of education, therefore, which limits instruction to the arts and sciences, and rejects the aids of religion in forming the characters of citizens, is essentially defective..."

"In my view, the **Christian** religion is the most important and one of the first things in which all children, under a free government ought to be instructed.... No truth is more evident to my mind than that the **Christian** religion must be the basis of any government intended to secure the rights and privileges of a free people." **Noah Webster letter to David McClure, 25 October 1836**

"Principles, Sir, are becoming corrupt, deeply corrupt; & unless the progress of corruption, & perversion of truth can be arrested, neither liberty nor property, will long be secure in this country. And a great evil is, that men of the first distinction seem, to a great extent, to be ignorant of the real, original causes of our public distresses." **Noah Webster letter to Charles Chauncey, 17 October 1837**

John Witherspoon

Signer of the Declaration of Independence; Ratifier of the US Constitution; President of Princeton

"There is not a single instance in history in which civil liberty was lost, and religious liberty preserved entire. If therefore we yield up our temporal property, we at the same time deliver the conscience into bondage..."

"Nothing is more certain than that a general profligacy and corruption of manners make a people ripe for destruction. A good form of government may hold the rotten materials together for some time, but beyond a certain pitch, even the best constitution will be ineffectual, and slavery must ensue. On the other hand, when the manners of a nation are pure, when true religion and internal principles maintain their vigour, the attempts of the most powerful enemies to oppress them are commonly baffled and disappointed..."

*"That he is the best friend to American liberty, who is most sincere and active in promoting true and undefiled religion, and who sets himself with the greatest firmness to bear down profanity and immorality of every kind. Whoever is an avowed enemy of **God**, I scruple not to call him an enemy of his country..."*

*"It is in the man of piety and inward principle, that we may expect to find the uncorrupted patriot, the useful citizen, and the invincible soldier. **God** grant that in America true religion and civil liberty may be inseparable and that the unjust attempts to destroy the one, may in the issue tend to the support and establishment of both."* **The Dominion of Providence over the Passions of Men, May 17, 1776**

Part Ten

The Preamble and Posterity

The definition of the word Preamble

What is posterity and what role does it play in the daily life of the people of the United States?

The Preamble

The definition of the word preamble: *"A statement attached to the beginning of the Constitution by the Constitutional Convention, declaring the purpose of the document."*

The Preamble to our US Constitution reads: *"We, the people of the United States, in order to form a more perfect union, establish justice, insure domestic tranquility, provide for the common defense, promote the general welfare, and secure the blessings of liberty to ourselves and our posterity, do ordain and establish this Constitution for the United States of America."*

This is from Joseph Story's Commentary on the US Constitution, 1833.

§ 457. *Having disposed of these preliminary inquiries, we are now arrived at that part of our labours, which involves a commentary upon the actual provisions of the constitution of the United States. It is proposed to take up the successive clauses in the order in which they stand in the instrument itself, so that the exposition may naturally flow from the terms of the text.*

§ 458. *We begin then with the preamble of the constitution. It is in the following words:*

"We, the people of the United States, in order to form a more perfect union, establish justice, insure "domestic tranquility, provide for the common defence, promote the general welfare, and secure the blessings of liberty to

ourselves and our posterity, do ordain and "establish this constitution for the United States of America."

§ 459. *The importance of examining the preamble, for the purpose of expounding the language of a statute, has been long felt, and universally conceded in all juridical discussions. It is an admitted maxim in the ordinary course of the administration of justice, that the preamble of a statute is a key to open the mind of the makers, as to the mischiefs, which are to be remedied, and the objects, which are to be accomplished by the provisions of the statute. We find it laid down in some of our earliest authorities in the common law; and civilians are accustomed to a similar expression, cessante legis praemio, cessat et ipsa lex. Probably it has a foundation in the exposition of every code of written law, from the universal principle of interpretation, that the will and intention of the legislature is to be regarded and followed. It is properly resorted to, where doubts or ambiguities arise upon the words of the enacting part; for if they are clear and unambiguous, there seems little room for interpretation, except in cases leading to an obvious absurdity, or to a direct overthrow of the intention expressed in the preamble.*

In section 459, the word MAXIM is used to describe the Preamble.

Maxim (n) is defined in the dictionary as "a succinct formulation of a fundamental principle, general truth, or rule of conduct."

In this same section (459), Story further talks about the Preamble, "*Probably it has a foundation in the exposition of every code of written law, from the universal principle of interpretation, that the will and intention of the legislature is to be regarded and followed. It is properly resorted to, where doubts or ambiguities arise upon the words of the enacting part; for if they are clear and unambiguous, there seems little room for interpretation, except in cases leading to an obvious absurdity, or to a direct overthrow of the intention expressed in the preamble.*"

§ 460. *There does not seem any reason why, in a fundamental law or constitution of government an equal attention should not be given to the intention of the framers, as stated in the preamble. And accordingly we find* that it has been constantly referred to by statesmen and jurists to aid them in the exposition of its provisions.

§ 461. The language of the preamble of the constitution was probably in a good measure drawn from that of the third article of the confederation, which declared, that "The said states hereby severally enter into a firm league of friendship with each other, for their common defence, the security of their liberties, and their mutual and general welfare. And we accordingly find, that the first resolution proposed, in the convention which framed the constitution, was, that the articles of the confederation ought to be so corrected and enlarged, as to accomplish the objects proposed by their institution, namely, common defence, security of liberty, and general welfare.

§ 463. We have already had occasion, in considering the nature of the constitution, to dwell upon the terms, in which the preamble is conceived, and the proper conclusion deducible from it. It is an act of the people, and not of the states in their political capacities. It is an ordinance or establishment of government and not a compact, though originating in consent; and it binds as a fundamental law promulgated by the sovereign authority, and not as a compact or treaty entered into and in fieri, between each and all the citizens of the United States, as distinct parties. The language is, "We, the people of the United States," not, We, the states, "do ordain and establish;" not, do contract and enter into a treaty with each other; "this constitution for the United States of America," not this treaty between the several states. And it is, therefore, an unwarrantable assumption, not to call it a most extravagant stretch of interpretation, wholly at variance with the language, to substitute other words and other senses for the words and senses incorporated, in this solemn manner, into the substance of the instrument itself. We have the strongest assurances, that this preamble was not adopted as a mere formulary; but as a solemn promulgation of a fundamental fact, vital to the character and operations of the government. The obvious object was to substitute a government of the people, for a confederacy of states; a constitution for a compact. The difficulties arising from this source were not slight; for a notion commonly enough, however incorrectly, prevailed, that, as it was ratified by the states only, the states respectively, at their pleasure, might repeal it; and *this, of itself, proved the necessity of laying the foundations of a national government deeper than in the mere sanction of delegated power. The convention determined that the fabric of American empire ought to rest and should rest on the solid basis of the consent of the people. The streams of national power ought to flow and should Dow immediately from the highest original fountain of all legitimate authority. And, accordingly, the advocates of the constitution so treated it in their reasoning in favour of its adoption. "The constitution," said the Federalist, "is to be founded on the assent and ratification of the people of America, given by deputies elected for that purpose; but this assent and ratification is to be given by the people, not as individuals composing a whole nation, but as composing the distinct and independent states, to which they belong." And the uniform doctrine of the highest judicial authority has accordingly been, that it was the act of the people, and not of the states; and that it bound the latter, as subordinate to the people. "Let us turn," said Mr. Chief Justice Jay, "to the constitution. The people therein declare, that their design in establishing it comprehended six objects: (1.) To form a more perfect union; (2.) to establish justice; (3.) to insure domestic tranquility; (4.) to provide for the common defence; (5.) to promote the general welfare; (6.) to secure the blessings of liberty to themselves and their posterity. It would," he added, "be pleasing and useful to consider and trace the relations, which each of these objects bears to the others; and to show, that, collectively, they comprise everything requisite, with the blessing of Divine Providence, to render a people prosperous and happy." In Hunter v. Martin, (1 Wheat. R. 305, 324,) the Supreme Court say, (as we have seen,) "the constitution of the United States was ordained and established, not by the states in their sovereign capacities, but emphatically, as the preamble of the constitution declares, by the people of the United States;" and language still more expressive will be found used on other solemn occasions.*

In section 463, Story says this about the Preamble, "*We have the strongest assurances, that this preamble was not adopted as a mere formulary; but as a solemn promulgation of a fundamental fact, vital to the character and operations of the government.*"

According to the dictionary, *promulgation (v) is defined as "To make known (a decree, for example) by public declaration; announce officially. To put (a law) into effect by formal public announcement. The official announcement of a new law or ordinance whereby the law or ordinance is put into effect."*

In my research, I am glad that I finally took the time to look into Joseph Story a little deeper than I did before.

You can see, but you will ignore the fact that Story does not disregard the Preamble and its importance.

Alone, the Preamble is not law but when placed at the beginning of the US Constitution the Preamble is most certainly as important and relevant as the entire Constitution; just as I said before I ever read these commentaries written by Justice Story.

The Preamble is a part of the entire Constitution making it part of a legal document concerning the governing laws and structure of the US government.

Posterity

In order to understand the meaning of the word posterity we must first look at its definition.

Posterity: *noun. 1. Future generations. 2. All of a person's descendants. 3. All succeeding generations.*

Byron White, SCOTUS Justice, *"I find nothing in the language or history of the Constitution to support the Court's judgment. The Court simply fashions and announces a new constitutional right for pregnant mothers [410 U.S. 222] and, with scarcely any reason or authority for its action, invests that right with sufficient substance to override most existing state abortion statutes."*

"Some nations have given parents the power of life and death over their children. But here in America, we have denied the power of life and death to parents."

John Witherspoon, Founding Father

James Wilson wrote an essay titled *"Of the Natural Rights of Individuals"*. In it he said this about the sanctity of life:

"With consistency, beautiful and undeviating, human life, from its commencement to its close, is protected by the common law. In the contemplation of law, life begins when the infant is first able to stir in the womb. By the law, life is protected not only from immediate destruction, but from every degree of actual violence, and, in some cases, from every degree of danger."

William Blackstone supported the words of James Wilson decades earlier:

"The immediate Gift of God-a right inherent by Nature in every Individual; and it begins in contemplation of law as soon as an infant is able to STIR IN THE MOTHER'S WOMB."

"For if a woman is quick with child, and by a potion or otherwise kills it in the WOMB; for if anyone beat her whereby the child dies in her body and she is delivered of a dead child, THIS … WAS BY THE ANCIENT LAW HOMICIDE OR MANSLAUGHTER."

William Blackstone, Commentaries on the Laws of England, 1771

Webster's Dictionary dated 2003. Under the word *"STIR"* the definitions include *"to mix and to make or be active."*

This is literally what happens at the moment of conception. Active male sperm joins with the fertile female egg and together they STIR in the womb...they mix and make active.

So according to James Wilson, a legal scholar, a Supreme Court Justice, a member of Congress, a signer of the Declaration of Independence and the US Constitution; abortion is unconstitutional. It is murder and a crime because abortion denies a human being the right to life.

The Oxford Dictionary defines a **HUMAN BEING** as a member of the **HOMO SAPIENS** specie.

A human fetus contains human DNA.

So, in scientific fact a **HUMAN FETUS** is a **HUMAN BEING** because it is a member of the **HOMO SAPIENS** specie.

Another big hole in the argument in favor of abortion lies with the issue that the Founders did not believe that people or governments grant rights to themselves or others.

"We hold these truths to be self-evident: That all men are created equal; that they are endowed by their Creator with certain unalienable rights; that among these are life, liberty, and the pursuit of happiness;"

The Declaration of Independence, 1776

The government cannot give a person their rights to anything because as surely as they grant a right they can and will take any of our rights away.

Our form of government was designed to prevent the government from infringing on our God-given rights.

What effect does abortion have on our posterity?

The answer is obvious.

Abortion kills our posterity. Abortion denies the unborn their God-given right to life and liberty.

The courts cannot make laws only the House can make a law for the President to sign. Congress never legalized abortion and no President ever signed a bill to legalize abortion.

Any proposed law to legalize abortion would have to be ruled unconstitutional by the SCOTUS because the US Constitution includes a single word that protects the unborn, **POSTERITY**.

A human fetus can only be human, it is impossible that a human fetus would evolve into a dog, a cat, monkey or any other living animal.

A human fetus contains human DNA, which is also how we know that a woman who is pregnant will give birth to a human being. It is willful blindness by abortionists to argue that a human fetus is anything other than a human being.

Abortionists believe in denying life to those they view as "unwanted and unnecessary" which is what Hitler, Stalin, Mao and other evil dictators did throughout history; yet they will never see the relationship they share with evil.

Abortion is indeed a violation of not only the US Constitution, the document which protects human rights, abortion violates human rights.

The right to life and the right to pursue happiness and prosperity is a basic human right.

The Founding Fathers stated that these rights are given to us by God the Creator.

Abortion is Murder

Many supporters of abortion try to support their defense of abortion by falsely claiming that ending a pregnancy is not ending a life, therefore abortion is legal and not murder.

Simple research of a legal dictionary proves their claim to be incorrect and an outright lie.

The Legal Definition of Murder

Modern statutes state murder comes in four varieties:

(1) Intentional murder

(2) A killing that resulted from the intent to do serious bodily injury

(3) A killing that resulted from a depraved heart or extreme recklessness

(4) Murder committed by an Accomplice during the commission of, attempt of, or flight from certain felonies

Is an abortion intentional?

Abortion is the act of taking a life.

Simple research of a dictionary provides us with the wholly accepted definition of what an abortion is.

Oxford Dictionary

Abortion: (noun)

"The deliberate termination of a human pregnancy, most often performed during the first 28 weeks of pregnancy."

The deliberate ending of a human life is murder.

Abortion is the very definition of murder.

The 3rd & 4th Amendments

Another false narrative presented by supporters of abortion is to try to use the Third and the Fourth Amendments as justification for abortion.

These same arguments were used in the case of Roe v. Wade to prove that the US Constitution permitted and actually protected the right for a woman to kill her child in the womb.

Amendment III

(Privacy of the Home)

"No Soldier shall, in time of peace be quartered in any house, without the consent of the Owner, nor in time of war, but in a manner to be prescribed by law."

Since when is a person killing their child a right to privacy?

How can killing a child in the womb be a right to privacy but killing a child outside of the womb an act of murder?

And what does having an abortion have to do with quartering soldiers without the permission of the homeowner?

This type of rationale is insanity in the least.

Amendment IV

(Privacy of the Person and Possessions)

"The right of the people to be secure in their persons, houses, papers, and effects, against unreasonable searches and seizures, shall not be violated, and no Warrants shall issue, but upon probable cause, supported by Oath or affirmation, and particularly describing the place to be searched, and the persons or things to be seized."

Is aborting a child somehow the definition of securing their person(s), their house, their papers and effects against unreasonable searches & seizures?

Is having an abortion a matter of having probable cause and necessary of a legitimately obtained warrant supported by a sworn oath or affirmation?

Whenever I question abortion supporters who use these amendments in a ridiculous manner and by using a completely false reading of these amendments, they are completely void of explanation.

None of these people can intelligently and articulately explain how these amendments authorize abortion.

The Truth about the 3rd & the 4th Amendments

Any of us who remember our grade school education concerning US Government (US Civics) will remember the American Revolution and why the Founding Fathers included protections against the intrusiveness of government into the homes of colonists in the American colonies.

I will preface the 3rd & the 4th Amendments by explaining the reason and the need for these Amendments to the US Constitution by quoting the 2nd Amendment.

The 2nd Amendment was written to protect our natural right of self-defense.

The 2ndAmendment

"A well-regulated militia, being necessary to the security of a free state, the right of the people to keep and bear arms, shall not be infringed."

Due to the intrusions of the British Crown (King George III) into the businesses, taxation of the colonists and into the homes of the colonists, the Founding Fathers included the protection of the right to self-defense because someday the day might come again where the citizen would have to protect their home, their family and even their business from the over-reach of government.

In short, the 2nd Amendment was written to prevent the government from over-powering the citizen.

Just as with the 2nd Amendment, the 3rd & the 4th Amendment were included to also protect the citizen from the government.

In the case of the 3rd Amendment, the government cannot force a homeowner to house soldiers unless a law is passed making such a requirement legal.

Nowhere in the 3rd Amendment does it even hint that a woman killing her unborn is a right to privacy.

The 4th Amendment was written to protect a citizen from the government making false accusations, illegal search & seizure, making an arrest and incarcerating a citizen without a legitimate warrant issued; sworn to or affirmed before a judge as to the reason why the warrant should be issued and the citizen detained without legal cause.

Just as with the 3rd Amendment, not a single breath of a hint that a woman has the right to kill her unborn child.

The culture in the modern-day United States of America is very lacking in the knowledge of our founding principles and why those principles are so important to the citizens of the US.

These leftist-progressive-Marxist groups and their followers preach the need for reason but they reject facts.

It is incomprehensible as what they consider reason because they are the antithesis of reason.

Their methods of argument defy the definitions of the words that they use to describe their approach to comprehension.

The 14th Amendment

Amendment XIV

Section 1

"All persons born or naturalized in the United States, and subject to the jurisdiction thereof, are citizens of the United States and of the state wherein they reside. No state shall make or enforce any law which shall abridge the privileges or immunities of citizens of the United States; nor shall any state deprive any person of life, liberty, or property, without due process of law; nor deny to any person within its jurisdiction the equal protection of the laws."

Section 2

"Representatives shall be apportioned among the several states according to their respective numbers, counting the whole number of persons in each state, excluding Indians not taxed. But when the right to vote at any election for the choice of electors for President and Vice President of the United States, Representatives in Congress, the executive and judicial officers of a state, or the members of the legislature thereof, is denied to any of the male inhabitants of such state, being twenty-one years of age, and citizens of the United States, or in any way abridged, except for participation in rebellion, or other crime, the basis of representation therein shall be reduced in the proportion which the number of such male citizens shall bear to the whole number of male citizens twenty-one years of age in such state."

Section 3

"No person shall be a Senator or Representative in Congress, or elector of President and Vice President, or hold any office, civil or military, under the United States, or under any state, who, having previously taken an oath, as a member of Congress, or as an officer of the United States, or as a member of any state legislature, or as an executive or judicial officer of any state, to support the Constitution of the United States, shall have engaged in insurrection or rebellion against the same, or given aid or comfort to the

enemies thereof. But Congress may by a vote of two-thirds of each House, remove such disability."

Section 4

"The validity of the public debt of the United States, authorized by law, including debts incurred for payment of pensions and bounties for services in suppressing insurrection or rebellion, shall not be questioned. But neither the United States nor any state shall assume or pay any debt or obligation incurred in aid of insurrection or rebellion against the United States, or any claim for the loss or emancipation of any slave; but all such debts, obligations and claims shall be held illegal and void."

Section 5

"The Congress shall have power to enforce, by appropriate legislation, the provisions of this article."

Pro-choice supporters, more correctly identified as Pro-abortionists try to use the 14th Amendment, Section 1 as support for abortion. This argument is preposterous because the 14th Amendment actually re-affirms the right to life.

This defense of the innocent is found in the wording of Section 1 of the 14th Amendment.

"No state shall make or enforce any law which shall abridge the privileges or immunities of citizens of the United States; nor shall any state deprive any person of life, liberty, or property, without due process of law; nor deny to any person within its jurisdiction the equal protection of the laws."

Section 5 seals this protection of the right to life in Section 5 of the 14th Amendment.

Section 5

"The Congress shall have power to enforce, by appropriate legislation, the provisions of this article."

Read Article 1 of the US Constitution, the power to create new laws lies SOLELY with the Legislative branch of government.

Abortionists claim that the courts have the power to create and pass laws into effect and that is not true.

NO COURT in the United States of America has the Constitutionally-legal power and authority to establish any law in the UNITED STATES OF AMERICA.

Roe v. Wade was not an actual law passed by the US Congress, sent to the US Senate and then signed into law by the President.

The courts cannot write laws, they cannot vote on laws and they cannot make laws.

Roe v. Wade did not amend the US Constitution and certainly was not passed and ratified by the majority of the States.

There is no legality to Roe v. Wade, none whatsoever.

Section 5 clearly states that *"The Congress shall have power to enforce, by appropriate legislation, the provisions of this article."*

There has not been any act of due process by which would amend the US Constitution to remove the protections previously established and then to legally pass a law by ACT of CONGRESS to legalize abortion.

This power lies solely with the US Congress not with the courts and not with activists.

The Authority of the Supreme Court Challenged

Many people are quick to accept the word of "scholars", the internet and other various sources claiming to be the "end all" when anything pertaining to the function and the authority of US courts.

I have experienced many times during discussions with people on social media, claiming that the Supreme Court has ultimate authority in deciding all matters pertaining to subjects such as abortion, but they are wrong.

I have challenged each and every one of them to prove their assertion by using Article 3 of the US Constitution and to this very day not a single one of them can prove their assertion that the courts have ultimate authority and power.

Earlier in this book, Article 3 of the US Constitution was presented which lays out the Founders' design for the Judicial Branch of government.

The 14th Amendment was mentioned earlier in this section which CLEARLY states, *""The Congress shall have power to enforce, by appropriate legislation, the provisions of this article."*

Are the courts a part of the Legislative Branch of our government? No!

The US Constitution formed our style of government in the US and the Constitution quite evidently SEPARATED the Three Branches of Government and the Judicial is not a part of the Legislative.

Federalist 78

The Federalist Papers were a series of papers written by a handful of the Founding Fathers, namely Alexander Hamilton, James Madison, and John Jay in an effort to garner public support to ratify the US Constitution.

Between October 1787 and August 1788 what is now called The Federalist Papers was originally released as a series of articles in newspapers and was published in the form of a pamphlet in 1788 entitled, **The Federalist: A Collection of Essays, Written in Favour of**

The Federalist Papers were written to explain how the US Constitution is designed to function.

Included in this part of the book concerning the unconstitutionality of abortion is Federalist 78 in which Alexander Hamilton wrote about the function of the Judicial Branch, its powers, scope and limitations.

"*The legislature not only commands the purse, but prescribes the rules by which the duties and rights of every citizen are to be regulated.*"

"*It proves incontestably, that the judiciary is beyond comparison the weakest of the three departments of power,*"

"*If it be said that the legislative body are themselves the constitutional judges of their own powers, and that the construction they put upon them is conclusive upon the other departments, it may be answered, that this cannot be the natural presumption, where it is not to be collected from any particular provisions in the Constitution. It is not otherwise to be supposed, that the Constitution could intend to enable the representatives of the people to substitute their WILL to that of their constituents. It is far more rational to suppose, that the courts were designed to be an intermediate body between the people and the legislature, in order, among other things, to keep the latter within the limits assigned to their authority.*"

"*The interpretation of the laws is the proper and peculiar province of the courts.*"

"*A constitution is, in fact, and must be regarded by the judges, as a fundamental law.*"

"*It therefore belongs to them to ascertain its meaning, as well as the meaning of any particular act proceeding from the legislative body.*"

"*If there should happen to be an irreconcilable variance between the two, that which has the superior obligation and validity ought, of course, to be preferred; or, in other words, the Constitution ought to be preferred to the statute, the intention of the people to the intention of their agents."*

"Nor does this conclusion by any means suppose a superiority of the judicial to the legislative power."

"It only supposes that the power of the people is superior to both; and that where the will of the legislature, declared in its statutes, stands in opposition to that of the people, declared in the Constitution, the judges ought to be governed by the latter rather than the former."

"They ought to regulate their decisions by the fundamental laws, rather than by those which are not fundamental."

"This simple view of the matter suggests several important consequences."

"It proves incontestably, that the judiciary is beyond comparison the weakest of the three departments of power [1]; that it can never attack with success either of the other two; and that all possible care is requisite to enable it to defend itself against their attacks. It equally proves, that though individual oppression may now and then proceed from the courts of justice, the general liberty of the people can never be endangered from that quarter; I mean so long as the judiciary remains truly distinct from both the legislature and the Executive. For I agree, that "there is no liberty, if the power of judging be not separated from the legislative and executive powers." [2] And it proves, in the last place, that as liberty can have nothing to fear from the judiciary alone, but would have everything to fear from its union with either of the other departments; that as all the effects of such a union must ensue from a dependence of the former on the latter, notwithstanding a nominal and apparent separation; that as, from the natural feebleness of the judiciary, it is in continual jeopardy of being overpowered, awed, or influenced by its co-ordinate branches; and that as nothing can contribute so much to its firmness and independence as permanency in office, this quality may therefore be justly regarded as an indispensable ingredient in its constitution, and, in a great measure, as the citadel of the public justice and the public security."

The Judicial can NEVER endanger the General Liberty of the people.

"It equally proves, that though individual oppression may now and then proceed from the courts of justice, the general liberty of the people can never be endangered from that quarter;"

"Whoever attentively considers the different departments of power must perceive, that, in a government in which they are separated from each other, the judiciary, from the nature of its functions, will always be the least dangerous to the political rights of the Constitution; because it will be least in a capacity to annoy or injure them."

"The legislature not only commands the purse, but prescribes the rules by which the duties and rights of every citizen are to be regulated."

"The judiciary, on the contrary, has no influence over either the sword or the purse; no direction either of the strength or of the wealth of the society; and can take no active resolution whatever.

"It may truly be said to have neither FORCE nor WILL, but merely judgment; and must ultimately depend upon the aid of the executive arm even for the efficacy of its judgments."

Federalist Paper 78 is very forthright as to the function, not the function and the limitations of the courts.

Notice...*"The legislature not only commands the purse, but prescribes the rules by which the duties and rights of every citizen are to be regulated."*

The SCOTUS was INTENTIONALLY designed to be the weakest branch of government because the Founders knew that if the courts had ultimate power, they could become an entity out of control.

The US Congress controls the courts.

Roe v. Wade was a social-political statement not based on the US Constitution. Roe v. Wade happened in order to galvanize a political & social movement which guaranteed a political cause to be protected by politicians looking for power and longevity in government.

The justices who gave their OPINION in support of abortion guaranteed their longevity in government by being protected by powerful activist-politicians who sided with activist groups-all of which grew rich & powerful by supporting abortion.

If abortion is to be made legal in the US then the US Constitution MUST BE AMENDED and the US Congress has to be the branch of government to establish the law creating the legalization of abortion and the laws governing the dispensation of abortion in the US.

"The legislature not only commands the purse, but prescribes the rules by which the duties and rights of every citizen are to be regulated."

The Legislative branch creates laws not the Judicial branch.

The Judicial can NEVER endanger the general liberty of the people.

Final Thoughts...

The reason for this book is to inform not to cause division among the citizens of the United States of America.

The internet is a great tool but the problem with the internet is that some websites and some bloggers have deluged the internet with misinformation, opinions and outright lies.

As US citizens our job is to know our history as a nation, both good and bad history. We should have concrete knowledge of civics-how our government functions.

Many people view history as boring; filled with names, dates and places that are too difficult to remember so sometimes people pay little heed to the information they are given.

When we were in school those same people just wanted to remember the information long enough to pass a history quiz or test because they did not want to waste more of their time on the boring subject of history.

This is where and why we lost our knowledge of history, knowledge is powerful and no one should ever turn their back on gaining knowledge.

Because of this attitude toward history, these same people fall victim to distortion of facts and to outright lies.

At the beginning of this book a letter from Thomas Jefferson to Hugh P. Taylor was quoted, *"It is the duty of every good citizen to use all the opportunities which occur to him for preserving documents relating to the history of our country."*

This book preserves many of those documents and letters of which most people will never in their lives read.

In researching this book I have learned the names and the biographies of men from our Founding era, including men that I had never heard of before. I am sure that the readers of this book will realize that we do not know very much about the founding of the United States of America and we know so little about the men and women involved in the creation of this nation.

Revisionist history is REAL and it is happening NOW.

There is a clear and present reality that these revisionists are actively working to spread lies throughout the internet, facts are being replaced with their lies.

Lies have a way of becoming truth.

The purpose of this book is to turn those lies away and replace those lies with historical facts supported by the appropriate documentation.

This book is not the entirety of the facts that exist which prove that the United States of America was founded on God's principles. Christian principles are not founded on any church or denomination of religious belief.

Our Founders wished that each generation of the American people stay united and continue as a nation to rely on God for our safety, guidance and that we continue to receive His blessings.

This book is a starting point for all of those who are curious enough to continue their search for the truth.

I hope that this book has done that for you.

The Founding Fathers: What Did They Really Say?

Bibliography

Part 1

Our Founding Documents

Declaration of Independence, first draft-Library of Congress

Declaration of Independence, adopted version-National Archives

The Articles of Confederation, National Archives

The US Constitution, National Archives

The Definitive Treaty of Peace, National Archives

The Northwest Ordinance, The National Archives

John Adams letter to Timothy Pickering, The Papers of John Adams

Patrick Henry letter to Archibald Blair on January 8, 1799, Library of Virginia

Thomas Jefferson, "A Bill for Establishing Religious Freedom", Section 1, June 18, 1779, National Archives

"A Summary View of the Rights of British America", Library of Congress

Notes on the State of Virginia, Query XVIII, University of Virginia

John Adams letter to Thomas Jefferson, June 28, 1813, National Archives

Benjamin Franklin letter to David Hartley, December 4, 1789, National Archives

Part 2

God & Country

Thomas Jefferson letter to James Fishback, September 27, 1809, National Archives

First Prayer of the Continental Congress, 1774, *Office of the US Chaplain, US House of Representatives*

Marsh v. Chambers, 463 U.S. 783, 787, 792 (1983), *The United States Supreme Court*

National & State Proclamations, *National Archives & Library of Congress*

The American Presidency Project

Thanksgiving Proclamation by Connecticut Governor Samuel Huntington, Yale University Library-The Jonathan Edwards Collection

Deism, *Webster's Dictionary*

Christian Deist website

John Adams Fast Day Proclamation (1798), *National Archives & Library of Congress*

Benjamin Franklin's speech to the 1787 Constitutional Convention, The Avalon Project, Yale Law School-Lillian Goldman Law Library

Washington's Prayer (George Washington) 1783, National Archives

Panel Three, Jefferson Memorial

"A Summary View of the Rights of British America", Thomas Jefferson

Dr. Franklin's Motion for Prayers in the Convention, The Franklin Papers

The Aitken Bible, Library of Congress

Congressional Resolution, September 10, 1782, Library of Congress

Part 3

The Barbary Pirate Treaties

The Avalon Project, Yale Law School-Lillian Goldman Law Library

Thomas Jefferson letter to Horatio Gates Paris Dec. 13, 1784, Library of Congress

Joel Barlow biography, The Barlow family

Part 4

Early American Education

1828 Webster's Dictionary

A Defense of the Use of the Bible in Schools, 1830 written by Dr. Benjamin Rush

The New England Primer, 1687

The American Spelling Book aka The Blue-Back Speller, 1787

Part 5

Separation of Church & State

The Papers of Thomas Jefferson, Princeton University Library

Library of Congress

Part 6

US State Constitutions

State government websites

Jubilee of the Constitution: A Discourse, 1839

Declaration of Independence, 1776

The Continental Congress, 1777

George Washington

George Washington's Inaugural Address, 1789

George Washington, Wednesday Morning Prayer recorded in the Prayer Journal, dated April 21-23, 1752

George Washington, letter to Benedict Arnold, September 14, 1775

George Washington, Cambridge, 14 September 1775

George Washington, General Orders, May 5, 1778, Head-Quarters V. Forge Tuesday May 5th 1778

George Washington's speech to Delaware tribal leaders on May 12, 1779

George Washington's letter to the Hebrew Congregation of Newport, Rhode Island

August 18, 1790

George Washington letter to John Armstrong, Philadelphia, March 11, 1792

George Washington, letter to the Residents of Boston, October 27, 1789

George Washington, Circular Letter Addressed to the Governors of all the States on the Disbanding of the Army, Head Quarters, Newburgh, June 8, 1783

John Adams

John Adams, Dissertation on the Canon and Feudal Law, 1765

John Adams letter to his wife Abigail, July 3, 1776

John Adams, Thoughts on Government, 1776

John Adams' diary, 1778

John Adams' diary, July, 26 1796

John Adams, Special Message to the Senate and the House, May 16 1797

John Adams to the Massachusetts Militia, October 11, 1798

John Adams letter to Thomas Jefferson, June 28, 1813

Samuel Adams

The Rights of the Colonists, 1772

Samuel Adams letter to William Checkley, 1772

Samuel Adams letter to James Warren, 1775

Samuel Adams letter to John Pitts, 1776

Samuel Adams, Speech at the State House, Philadelphia, 1776

Samuel Adams letter to James Warren, 1776

Samuel Adams letter to John Trumbull, 1778

Samuel Adams letter to Thomas Wells, 1780

Samuel Adams, Boston Gazette, 1781

Samuel Adams letter to the Legislature of Massachusetts, 1794

A Proclamation For a Day of PUBLIC FASTING, HUMILIATION and PRAYER, 1795

John Quincy Adams

An Oration Delivered Before the Inhabitants of the Town of Newburyport at their Request on the Sixty-First Anniversary of the Declaration of Independence, July 4, 1837

John Quincy Adams, letters to his son

Elias Boudinot

Speech in the First Provincial Congress of New Jersey

Elias Boudinot letter to his daughter Susan, October 30, 1782

Elias Boudinot, The Age of Revelation, or the Age of Reason Shewn to be An Age of Infidelity, 1801

Jacob Broom

Jacob Broom letter to his son James, February 24, 1794

Charles Carroll

Charles Carroll letter to John McHenry on November 4, 1800

John Dickinson

Reply to a Committee in Barbados, 1766

Political Writings, 1774

Declaration of taking up arms, Resolutions of the Second Continental Congress, John Dickinson and Thomas Jefferson July 6, 1775.

John Dickinson, The Political Writings of John Dickinson, 1801

Last Will & Testament of John Dickinson, attested March 25, 1808

Benjamin Franklin

Poor Richard's Almanack, 1751

Benjamin Franklin letter to Joseph Huey, 1753

Benjamin Franklin letter to Richard Price, October 9, 1780

Benjamin Franklin, Motion for Prayers in the Convention, June 28, 1787

Benjamin Franklin's speech to the Constitutional Convention, 1787

Benjamin Franklin letter to Ezra Stiles, March 9, 1790

Alexander Hamilton

Alexander Hamilton's address to the Constitutional Convention, 1787

The Christian Constitutional Society, 1802

Alexander Hamilton letter to James Bayard, 1802

Alexander Hamilton, July 12, 1804

John Hancock

A PROCLAMATION For a Day of Public FASTING, HUMILIATION, AND PRAYER, 1793

John Joseph Henry

Personal journal, 1811

Patrick Henry

Quotes from Patrick Henry's Give Me Liberty Or Give Me Death Speech, before the Virginia House of Burgesses at St. John's Church on March 23, 1775

Patrick Henry in conversation with a neighbor

Patrick Henry letter to his daughter, August 20, 1796

Spoken on his deathbed

Last Will and Testament, November 20, 1798

John Jay

John Jay, December 1776

John Jay letter to Peter Augustus Jay, April 8, 1784

John Jay letter to his wife Sally April 1794

John Jay Letter to Reverend Uzal Ogden, 1796

John Jay letter to Jedidiah Morse, 1797

John Jay letter to John Bristed, 1811

Prayer found among John Jay's papers and in his handwriting.

John Jay letter to John Murray, April 15, 1818

John Jay, Address at the Annual Meeting of the American Bible Society, May 13, 1824

John Jay to the Committee of the Corporation of the City of New York on June 29, 1826

Last Will and Testament

Thomas Jefferson

Proclamations, National Archives

Thomas Jefferson letter to Thomas Law, 13 June 1814

Thomas Jefferson letter to Benjamin Rush, April 21, 1803

Thomas Jefferson letter to Richard Rush May 31, 1813

Thomas Jefferson letter to Miles King, September 26, 1814

Thomas Jefferson letter to Charles Thomson, January 9, 1816

Thomas Jefferson letter to Timothy Pickering, February 27, 1821

Thomas Jefferson letter to John Adams April 11, 1823

Thomas Jefferson letter to Dr. Benjamin Rush, September 23, 1800

Rufus King

Rufus King letter to C. Gore on February 17, 1820

Abraham Lincoln

The Gettysburg Address, 1863

Thanksgiving Proclamation, The National Archives

James Madison

James Madison letter to William Bradford, November 9, 1772

James Madison letter to William Bradford, September 25, 1773

1776 Virginia Bill of Rights

Memorial and Remonstrance Against Religious Assessments, 1785

Federalist No. 37, 1788

"An Act for the relief of the Bible Society of Philadelphia"

James Madison letter to Rev. Frederick Beasley, November 20, 1825

James Madison, notes in his personal Bible

Thomas McKean

RESPUBLICA v. ROBERTS, 1 U.S. 39 September, 1778

James Monroe

A Narrative of a Tour of Observation, 1818

Thomas Paine

Common Sense, 1776

Benjamin Rush

Benjamin Rush letter to John Armstrong, March 19, 1783

Benjamin Rush, To the citizens of Philadelphia: A Plan for Free Schools

Benjamin Rush, personal quotes

Benjamin Rush letter to Elias Boudinot on July 9, 1788

Benjamin Rush, A Defence of the Use of the Bible in Schools, 1791

Roger Sherman

Theological creed, adopted by his church

Richard Stockton

Last Will & Testament

Joseph Warren

Boston Massacre Oration, March 5, 1772

Noah Webster

History of the United States, 1832

Value of the Bible (unpublished manuscript), 1834

Instructive and Entertaining Lessons for Youth, 1835